Christmas '92

To Jim Morris_
  Mick Jagg_
  Peter Sute_
David.
Have a lovely Christmas.
  Love
    Debbie
    xx

THE COMPLETE
VEGETARIAN
COOKBOOK

THE COMPLETE
VEGETARIAN
COOKBOOK

edited by Susie Ward

TIGER BOOKS INTERNATIONAL
LONDON

A QUINTET BOOK

This edition first published in 1991 by Tiger Books International plc, London

Copyright © 1991 Quintet Publishing Limited

ISBN 1-85501-182-4

This book was designed and produced by
Quintet Publishing Limited, 6 Blundell Street, London N7 9BH

Designer: Melanie Williams
Project Editors: Laura Sandelson, Damian Thompson
Editor: Susie Ward

Typeset in Great Britain by En to En Typesetters, Kent
Manufactured in Singapore by Chroma Graphics (Overseas) Pte. Ltd.
Printed in Hong Kong by Leefung-Asco Printers Limited

The material in this publication previously appeared in
*The Almost Vegetarian Cookbook, The Bread Book, Chinese Vegetarian Cooking, Cooking
with Yogurt, Indian Vegetarian Cooking, Meal Planner/Healthy Cooking, Microwave Cooking
for Vegetarians, Microwave Library/Cooking with Vegetables, The Pasta and Pizza Cookbook,
Sensational Salads, Tapas, The Wholefood Cookbook.*

CONTENTS

INTRODUCTION

Vegetarian food is different, delicious, nourishing and fresh. It can turn cooking, as well as eating, into a daily pleasure. The simple goodness of fresh ingredients in a loaf of home-made bread and a bowl of soup often give more satisfaction than the most complicated concoction smothered in butter-rich sauce. Learning to cook without meat and even most fish is something of a challenge, so used are we all to having one or the other as the main dish of the meal.

Vegetarianism and wholefood cookery are enjoying a new surge of popularity in the developed world as a reaction to the high-fat, high-sugar, high-starch junk foods that have so dominated our diets for the past 30 years.

The first pleasure of wholefood cookery is the goodness it brings to your table. The freshness and flavour of natural foods, unrefined and free from additives, offers a range of ingredients that is infinitely rich and subtle. But wholefood eating doesn't only satisfy the palate, it brings long-term health benefits too.

Our Western diet tends to be soft, sweet and high in animal fats. Over-refined and processed foods contain fewer vitamins and minerals, and chemical additives can cause unpleasant side effects. The foods closest to nature - fresh fruit and vegetables, unrefined grains, nuts and pulses - are high in vitamins and minerals, high in fibre and low in fat. They provide cheaper protein and satisfy at moderate calorie levels.

So vegetarianism also makes economic and ecological sense. A field of soya beans will yield 30 times as much protein as the same field given over to the rearing of beef cattle. Surprisingly though, it is still the case that agricultural land is devoted to feeding animals, far more than to growing crops. A further cruel reality is that economic pressures tend to encourage under-developed countries to export their grain as cattle feed for richer countries.

For many people, it is the slaughter of animals for food which has made them turn to a vegetarian life, as has the practice of keeping battery hens in tiny cages for the duration of their short lives. In addition, though modern food production methods have effectively made meat much cheaper than ever before, inevitably the taste of mass-produced meat, from animals reared on chemically treated feed and injected with hormones, suffers from a uniform blandness. A true free

range chicken is practically impossible to buy in the Western world – in America 98 per cent of chickens are battery reared. Considerations such as this have given many a less ideological but as valid a reason to prefer a largely wholefood and vegetarian lifestyle.

Other healthy products - for instance yoghurt, complement much vegetarian fare. It is perhaps the best known of all cultured milk products and has had an amazing rise from relative obscurity as an indigenous Middle Eastern food to a world-wide popularity - all within the last 20 or so years. It has been credited with extraordinary properties, particularly since scientists about 100 years ago became fascinated by the microbiological processes which take place in milk during fermentation. At that time a Russian scientist, Ilya Mechnikov, isolated the bacteria found in yoghurt. It is recorded that ancient physicians used to prescribe sour milk for dysentery, tuberculosis, liver problems and various other illnesses. It was found that an acid milk is more easily digested than ordinary milk, and modern medical practitioners have used it to counteract the effect of some antibiotics which destroy beneficial intestinal flora. Today aficionados of yoghurt are able to enjoy a wide selection of the product and the truly devoted sleuth may be able to track down some very unusual varieties.

So you see, you don't have to be vegetarian to enjoy this book, but you might adopt a new attitude to eating. For instance, you could break away from the traditional three-course meal and serve several complementary dishes at once, as in Eastern countries, or you could serve one large salad as a main course and offer home-made bread and an assortment of dressings. The best thing about vegetarianism is that it is an adventure and opens new possibilities to the diner, and to the cook.

GLOSSARY OF EUROPEAN/AMERICAN TERMS

aubergine — *eggplant*

bean curd — *tofu*

beetroot — *beet*

bicarbonate of soda — *baking soda*

bilberries — *blueberries*

biscuits (savoury) — *crackers*

biscuits (sweet) — *cookies*

broad beans — *lima beans*

castor sugar — *granulated sugar*

chickpea — *garbanzo bean*

chicory — *Belgian endive*

courgette — *zucchini*

coriander — *cilantro*

cornflour — *cornstarch*

curd cheese — *farmer's cheese or large-curd cottage cheese*

double cream — *heavy cream*

endive — *frisee chicory*

essence (as in vanilla or almond) — *extract*

French beans — *thin small green beans*

fructose — *fruit sugar*

ginger root — *root ginger*

gluten flour — *high gluten flour*

green pepper — *green bell pepper*

icing sugar — *confectioner's sugar*

mange-tout — *snow peas*

marmite — *yeast extract spread*

marrow — *large squash*

plain flour — *all-purpose flour*

red pepper — *red bell pepper*

rind — *zest*

rolled oats — *fine oatmeal*

rose cocoa beans — *pinto beans*

runner beans — *large green beans*

self-raising flour — *self-rising flour*

single cream — *half-and-half*

soured cream — *sour cream*

spring onions — *green onion or scallions*

string beans — *green beans*

stones (as in fruit) — *pits*

sultanas — *golden raisins*

swede — *rutabaga*

tahini paste — *sesame paste*

tomato puree — *tomato paste*

turnip — *swede*

wood ears — *Chinese black tree fungus*

TECHNICAL TERMS

baking tray — *cookie sheet*

cling film — *plastic wrap*

greaseproof paper — *waxed paper*

palette knife — *spatula*

plait — *braid*

Swiss roll tin — *jelly roll pan*

tin — *pan*

top-and-tail — *trim*

SOUPS

The goodness of soup has always appealed to those who appreciate real home cooking. Hearty and wholesome, soups preserve all the vitamins and nutrients of their cooked ingredients, but contain relatively few calories. And the country French say that you can always tell a true cook by her soup!

Cold tomato soup

Waste-nothing Vegetable Stock

INGREDIENTS *serves 4-6*
1-2 tbsp/15-30ml oil
2 large onions, chopped
1 clove garlic, chopped
2 carrots, sliced
2 sticks celery, sliced
juice of half a lemon
1 large potato, peeled and diced
½ cup/100g/4oz lentils, presoaked
cabbage or cauliflower stalks
outer leaves of cabbage, lettuce etc.
any vegetables past their prime, such as
    soft tomatoes or mushrooms
chopped fresh herbs
8¾ cups/2l/3½pts water, including any
    leftover from cooking vegetables,
    tomato juice drained from cans etc.
salt and freshly ground black pepper
2-3 tbsp/30-45ml soy sauce

METHOD
Heat oil in a large saucepan and stir-fry onion and garlic until transparent.

Add carrots, celery and lemon juice. Turn the heat to low, cover the pan and sweat, stirring occasionally, for 5-10 minutes.

Add remaining vegetables and herbs and pour over the water. Season well and simmer, covered, for about 40 minutes, until vegetables are mushy.

Blend the stock in a food processor or blender and add soy sauce to taste. Keep in the fridge to use within a couple of days or freeze in ice cube trays.

Bean Soup

INGREDIENTS *serves 4-6*
1 cup/250g/8oz field beans
1-2 tbsp/15-30ml oil
1 onion, chopped
1 clove garlic, chopped
2 carrots, chopped
2 stalks celery, sliced
¾ cup/200g/7oz tomatoes, peeled (or a
    small can)
1 slice lemon
soy sauce
salt and freshly ground black pepper
parsley

METHOD
Soak the beans overnight. Bring to the boil in a large pan of water (about 5 cups/1½pts) and simmer until tender.

Meanwhile, heat oil in a frying pan and cook onion and garlic until soft. Add carrots, celery and tomatoes, in that order, stirring all the while.

Tip vegetables into the pan with the cooked beans. Add the slice of lemon and soy sauce. Taste and adjust seasoning. Heat through and serve sprinkled with chopped parsley. The soup may be partly blended if you like.

Beetroot and Cabbage Borsch

INGREDIENTS *serves 6-8*

butter or margarine
2 strips bacon, chopped
4 cups/450g/1lb cooked beets, peeled and diced
2 tbsp/15g flour
2 tbsp/30ml vinegar
9 cups/700g/1½lbs red cabbage, finely shredded
1 bay leaf
1 clove garlic, crushed
1 tbsp/15ml sugar
8¾ cups/2l/3½pts vegetable stock
salt and freshly ground black pepper
⅔ cup/150ml/¼ pint soured cream

METHOD

Heat the butter and fry the bacon. Add the beetroot and toss it for 1 minute. Add the flour and stir well off the heat. Return to the heat and add the vinegar, mixing it in well.

Add the cabbage, bay leaf, garlic, sugar, stock, salt and pepper. Bring to the boil and then simmer, covered, for 1 hour, adding a little more stock if necessary. Serve hot with a generous spoonful of sour cream in each bowl.

◀ Waste-nothing vegetable stock
▶ Beetroot and cabbage borsch

Harvest Soup

INGREDIENTS *serves 4-6*

1-2 tsp/5-10ml oil
1 onion, chopped
2¼ cups/350g/12oz pumpkin, peeled
and diced
2 cups/250g/8oz carrots, sliced
2 potatoes
juice of half a lemon
5 cups/1.1l/2pts stock
salt and freshly ground black pepper
1 courgette, sliced (optional)
⅓ cup/50g/2oz runner beans, sliced
(optional)
basil leaves to garnish

METHOD
Heat oil in a large saucepan and fry onion until translucent.

Add pumpkin, carrots and potatoes and pour over lemon juice. Sweat, covered, for 5 minutes.

Add stock and seasoning and simmer until potatoes are cooked. Blend or part-blend the soup.

If liked, add courgettes and beans and simmer for a further 4 minutes. Check seasoning.

Serve garnished with basil leaves. This soup can also be served sprinkled with Parmesan cheese.

► Cream of cauliflower soup
► ▼ Garlic soup
▼ Harvest soup

Cream of Cauliflower Soup

INGREDIENTS *serves 4*
1 small cauliflower
salt and freshly ground black pepper
4 tbsp/50g/2oz butter
¼ cup/25g/1oz plain untreated flour
6 tbsp/120ml/4fl oz single cream
1-2 egg yolks
1 tbsp/15ml chopped chives

METHOD
Trim the outer leaves off the cauliflower and steam it whole in boiling salted water in a pan with the lid on until tender. Allow the cauliflower to cool and reserve the water.

Melt the butter in a saucepan and stir in the flour. Gradually stir in the cauliflower water, made up to 3¾ cups/900ml/1½pts with fresh water.

Reserve some of the cauliflower florets for garnishing. Discard the tougher stalks and purée the rest in a blender. Add to the saucepan.

Beat the cream and egg yolks together in a bowl. Beat in some of the soup, then return to the pan. Add reserved cauliflower florets. Heat through but do not boil. Season and add chopped chives. Serve with triangles of hot toast.

Garlic Soup

INGREDIENTS *serves 4-6*
5 cups/1.1l/2pts vegetable stock
4 garlic cloves, crushed
3 level tsp/15ml paprika
3 level tsp/15ml cumin
salt and pepper
2 pieces bread, toasted
oil
6 eggs (optional)

METHOD
Pour chicken stock into a pan, add the garlic, paprika and cumin, and bring to the boil. Season.

Break the toast into cubes and put into hot soup bowls.

Place a pan on the heat, lightly oil and fry the eggs until the white forms. Tip out 1 egg into each soup bowl and pour over the boiling soup.

Cheese and Onion Soup

INGREDIENTS *serves 4-6*

1-2 tbsp/15-30ml oil
2 medium onions, sliced
5 cups/1.1l/2pts stock
250g/8oz potatoes
1½ cups/175g/6oz grated
　cheddar cheese
salt
soy sauce

METHOD

Heat oil in a large saucepan and stir-fry onions until lightly browned. Add stock and bring to the boil.

Meanwhile, peel the potatoes and grate them into the saucepan. Turn down the heat and simmer until potatoes have cooked and soup has thickened.

Add the grated cheese, stirring to melt. Season to taste with salt and soy sauce. Serve with wholewheat bread and a crisp green salad.

Butterbean and Mushroom Chowder

INGREDIENTS *serves 4-6*

1 cup/100g/4oz butter beans soaked
　overnight in cold water
1 tsp/5ml olive oil
2 onions, chopped
2 stalks celery, sliced
8oz/225g potatoes, peeled and diced
4oz/100g button mushrooms, sliced
½ cup/50g/2oz sweetcorn kernels
1¼ cups/300ml/½pt skimmed milk
salt and freshly ground black pepper
2 tbsp/30ml chopped parsley

METHOD

Drain the beans and place in a large saucepan covered with fresh water. Boil fast for 10 minutes, then simmer for a further 35-40 minutes, or until soft.

Drain the beans and reserve 2 cups/450ml/¾pt of the stock.

Heat the oil in a large saucepan and gently fry the onion. Add the celery and potato and cook for 2-3 minutes, stirring from time to time. Add the reserved stock and mushrooms, bring to the boil, cover and simmer for 10 minutes.

Add the beans, sweetcorn and milk, bring to the boil and simmer for 2-3 minutes. Season to taste.

Serve in individual soup bowls sprinkled with parsley. Serve slices of wholewheat bread separately.

Curried Marrow or Squash Soup

INGREDIENTS *serves 4*
oil
1 large onion, chopped
2 tbsp/30ml curry powder
1 small squash (about 1½lb/700g), peeled and chopped
4¼ cups/1l/1¾pts vegetable stock
⅔ cup/150ml/¼pt yoghurt
2 tbsp/30ml mango chutney

METHOD
Heat the oil, add the onion and cook until it has just softened but not browned. Stir in the curry powder and cook it for 1 minute. Add the squash and stir well.

Pour in the stock. Bring to the boil and then simmer until the squash is soft.

Blend the soup in a food processor or blender and return it to the pan.

Keep the soup warm while you mix the yoghurt and chutney together. Stir into the soup and serve immediately.

NOTE
If you prefer to make this in advance, don't add the yoghurt mixture until you reheat it. You could serve a little desiccated coconut with this and additional chutney if desired.

◄ ▲ Cheese and onion soup
◄ Butterbean and mushroom chowder
► Curried marrow soup

Bean Sprout Soup

INGREDIENTS *serves 4*
8oz/225g fresh bean sprouts
1 small red pepper, cored and seeded
2 tbsp/30ml oil
2 tsp/10g salt
2½ cups/600ml/1pt water
1 spring onion, finely chopped

METHOD
Wash the bean sprouts in cold water, discarding the husks and other bits and pieces that float to the surface. It is not necessary to top and tail (trim) each sprout.

Thinly shred the red pepper.

Heat a wok or large pot, add the oil and wait for it to smoke. Add the bean sprouts and red pepper and stir a few times. Add the salt and water.

When the soup starts to boil, garnish with finely chopped spring onion and serve hot.

Tomato and Egg Flower Soup

INGREDIENTS *serves 6*
9oz/250g tomatoes, skinned
1 egg
2 spring onions, finely chopped
1 tbsp/15ml oil
4¼ cups/1l/1¾pt water
2 tbsp/30ml light soy sauce
1 tsp/5ml cornflour mixed with 2 tsp/ 10ml water

METHOD
Skin the tomatoes by dipping them in boiling water for a minute or so and then peel them. Cut into large slices.

Beat the egg. Finely chop the spring onions.

Heat a wok or pan over a high heat. Add the oil and wait for it to smoke. Add the spring onions to flavour the oil and then pour in the water.

Drop in the tomatoes and bring to a boil.

Stir in the soy sauce and very slowly pour in the beaten egg. Add the cornflour and water mixture. Stir for a few minutes and serve.

◀ Bean sprout soup
▶ Tomato and egg flower soup

Chinese Cabbage Soup

INGREDIENTS *serves 4-6*
9oz/250g Chinese cabbage
3-4 dried Chinese mushrooms, soaked in warm water for 30 minutes
2 tbsp/30ml oil
2 tsp/10g salt
1 tbsp/15ml rice wine or dry sherry
3¾ cups/900ml/1½pts water
1 tsp/5ml sesame seed oil

METHOD
Wash the cabbage and cut it into thin slices. Squeeze dry the soaked mushrooms. Discard the hard stalks and cut the mushrooms into small pieces. (Reserve the water in which the mushrooms have been soaked for use later.)

Heat a wok or large pot until hot, add the oil and wait for it to smoke. Add the cabbage and mushrooms and stir.

Add the salt, wine, water and the mushroom soaking water. Bring to the boil.

Stir in the sesame seed oil and serve.

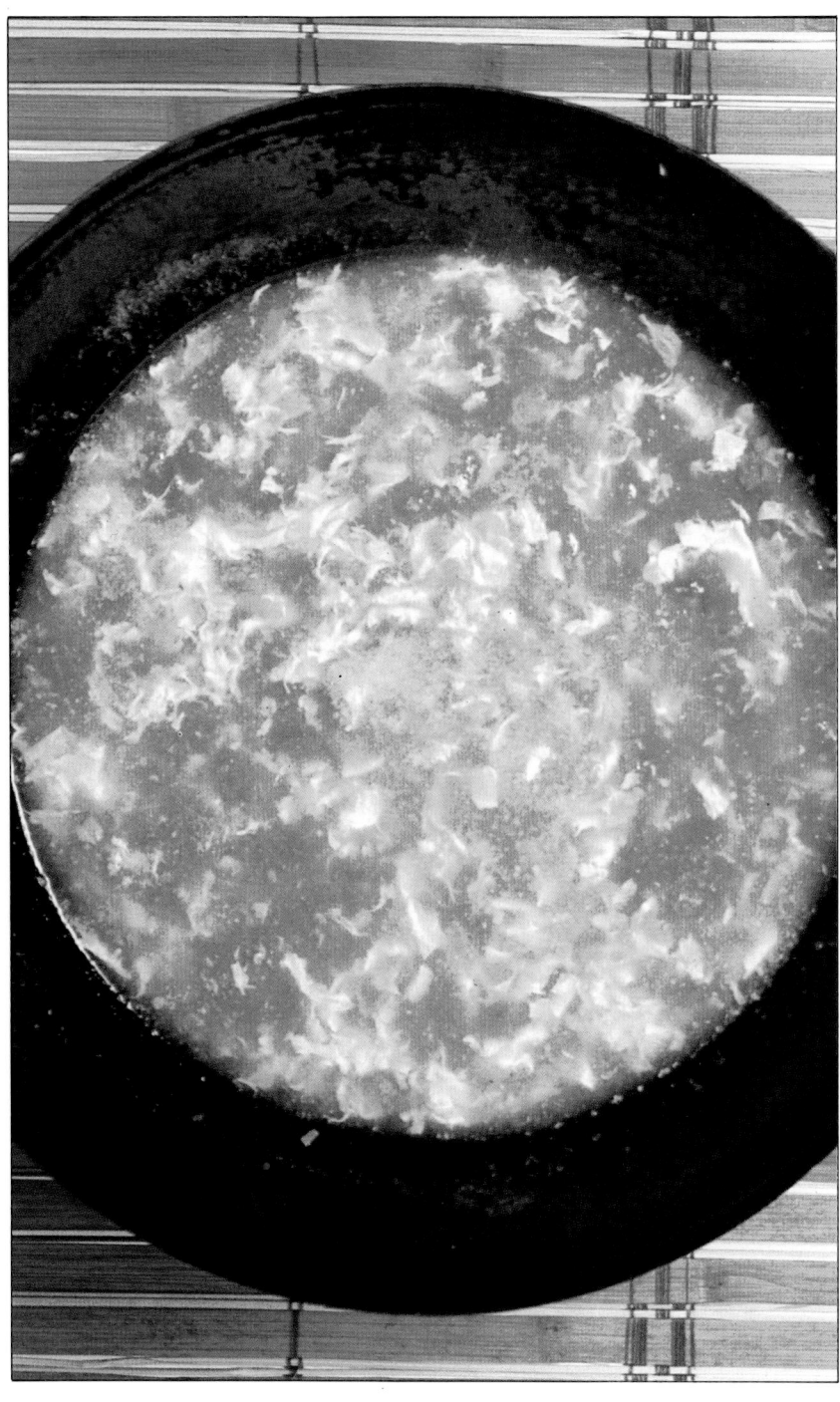

Cantonese Hot and Sour Soup

INGREDIENTS *serves 6*

3 dried Chinese mushrooms, soaked in warm water for 30 minutes

2 cakes bean curd

¹/₂ cup/50g/2oz Sichuan preserved vegetables (available from Oriental shops)

¹/₂ cup/50g/2oz/Chinese pickled vegetables, such as cucumber, cabbage or string beans (available from Oriental shops, or page 136)

2 spring onions, finely chopped

2 slices ginger root, thinly shredded

3³/₄ cups/900ml/1¹/₂pts water

1 tsp/5g salt

2 tbsp/30ml rice wine or sherry

1 tbsp/15ml soy sauce

freshly ground pepper to taste

1 tsp/5ml sesame seed oil

1 tsp/3g cornflour with 2 tsp/10ml water

METHOD

Squeeze dry the mushrooms after soaking. Discard the hard stalks and cut mushrooms into thin shreds. Reserve the water for use later.

Thinly shred the bean curd, Sichuan preserved vegetables, pickled vegetables and ginger. Finely chop the spring onions.

In a wok or large pot, bring the water to the boil. Add all the ingredients and seasonings and simmer for 2 minutes.

Add the sesame seed oil and thicken the soup by stirring in the cornflour and water mixture. Serve hot!

NOTE

A little vinegar can be added to the soup if you find that the pickled vegetables do not give a sour enough taste.

Chinese Mushroom Soup

INGREDIENTS *serves 4*
6 dried Chinese mushrooms
2 tsp/6ml cornflour
1 tbsp/15ml cold water
3 egg whites
2 tsp/10ml salt
2½ cups/600ml/1pt water
1 spring onion, finely chopped

METHOD

Soak the dried mushrooms in warm water for 25-30 minutes. Squeeze them dry, discard the hard stalks and cut each mushroom into thin slices. Reserve the mushroom soaking water for use later.

Mix the cornflour with the water to make a smooth paste. Comb the egg whites with your fingers to loosen them.

Mix the water and the mushroom soaking water in a pan and bring to the boil. Add the mushrooms and cook for about 1 minute. Now add the cornflour and water mixture, stir and add the salt.

Pour the egg whites very slowly into the soup, stirring constantly.

Garnish with the finely chopped spring onions and serve hot.

Sweetcorn and Asparagus Soup

INGREDIENTS *serves 4*
6oz/175g white asparagus
1 egg white
1 tbsp/8ml cornflour
2 tbsp/30ml water
2½ cups/600ml/1pt water
1 tsp/5g salt
1 cup/100g/4oz sweetcorn
1 spring onion finely chopped, to garnish

METHOD

Cut the asparagus spears into small cubes.

Beat the egg white lightly. Mix the cornflour with the water to make a smooth paste.

Bring the water to a rolling boil. Add the salt, sweetcorn and asparagus. When the water starts to boil again, add the cornflour and water mixture, stirring constantly.

Add the egg white very slowly and stir. Serve hot, garnished with finely chopped spring onions.

◄◄ Cantonese hot and sour soup
◄ Chinese mushroom soup

Red-Hot Lentil Soup

INGREDIENTS *serves 6*
3 tbsp/40g/1½oz butter
1 large onion, chopped
1 clove garlic, chopped
1 slice fresh ginger root, unpeeled
1 slice lemon
1⅛ cups/225g/8oz red lentils
7 cups/1.5l/2¾pts water
salt
pinch of paprika
1 green chilli, deseeded and chopped

METHOD
Heat 2 tbsp/25g/1oz butter in a pan and add the onion, garlic, ginger and lemon. Sweat with the lid on over a low heat for 5 minutes.

Add the lentils and the water (small red lentils do not need to be presoaked) and season with salt and paprika. Cook for about 40 minutes until lentils have thickened the soup.

Heat the remaining butter in a pan and quickly fry the chilli. Serve the soup with chilli topping.

Mushroom Soup

INGREDIENTS *serves 6*
butter or oil
1 large onion, sliced
6 cups/350g/12oz sliced mushrooms
grated nutmeg
1 tbsp/15ml flour
2 cups/450ml/¾pt vegetable stock
1¼ cups/300ml/½pt yoghurt
2 tbsp/30ml sherry (optional)

METHOD
Heat the butter and cook the onion until it has just softened but not browned. Add the mushrooms, stir and leave them to cook for 2 minutes. Add more butter if necessary.

Add the nutmeg and flour and stir well. Slowly add the stock, stirring until the mixture is smooth.

Bring the soup to the boil sand then simmer for 5 minutes. Stir in the yoghurt and just warm it through. Add the sherry. Serve hot.

Cream of Nettle Soup

INGREDIENTS *serves 6*
2lb/900g young nettles
2 tbsp/25g/1oz butter
1 small onion, chopped
¼ cup/25g/1oz flour
3¾ cups/900ml/30fl oz milk
salt and freshly ground black pepper
2 egg yolks
1 tbsp/15ml single cream
cream and croûtons to serve

METHOD
Pick the young nettle leaves before the plants flower. Discard the stalks, wash the leaves and press them into a pan with only the water that is clinging to them. Cover the pan and cook until soft (5-8 minutes). Purée in a blender.

Heat the butter in a pan and cook the onion until soft. Stir in the flour. Stir in a little milk and cook until thick. Stir in enough of the remaining milk to make a very thin sauce. Add the milk and the sauce to the nettles. Season well.

Beat the egg yolks with the cream. Stir in a little of the soup, then return to the pan. Heat through and check seasoning.

To serve, add a swirl of cream and some croûtons to each individual bowl.

▲ ▲ Red-hot lentil soup
▲ Cream of nettle soup

Spinach Soup

INGREDIENTS *serves 4-6*
oil
1 large onion, sliced
3 cups/750g/1½lbs spinach, washed and
    picked over
1 clove garlic, crushed
4¼ cups/1l/1¾pts chicken stock
1¼ cups/300ml/½pt yoghurt
salt and freshly ground black pepper

METHOD
Heat the oil, add the onion and cook until it
has just softened but not browned. Add the
spinach and garlic and stir.

   Add the stock, bring to the boil and then
simmer, covered, for 15 minutes.

   Liquidize the soup, adding the yoghurt
slowly. Adjust the seasoning. Serve hot or
cold.

NOTE
Use frozen spinach if you prefer, about 2
cups/450g/1lb would do.

▶ Spinach soup

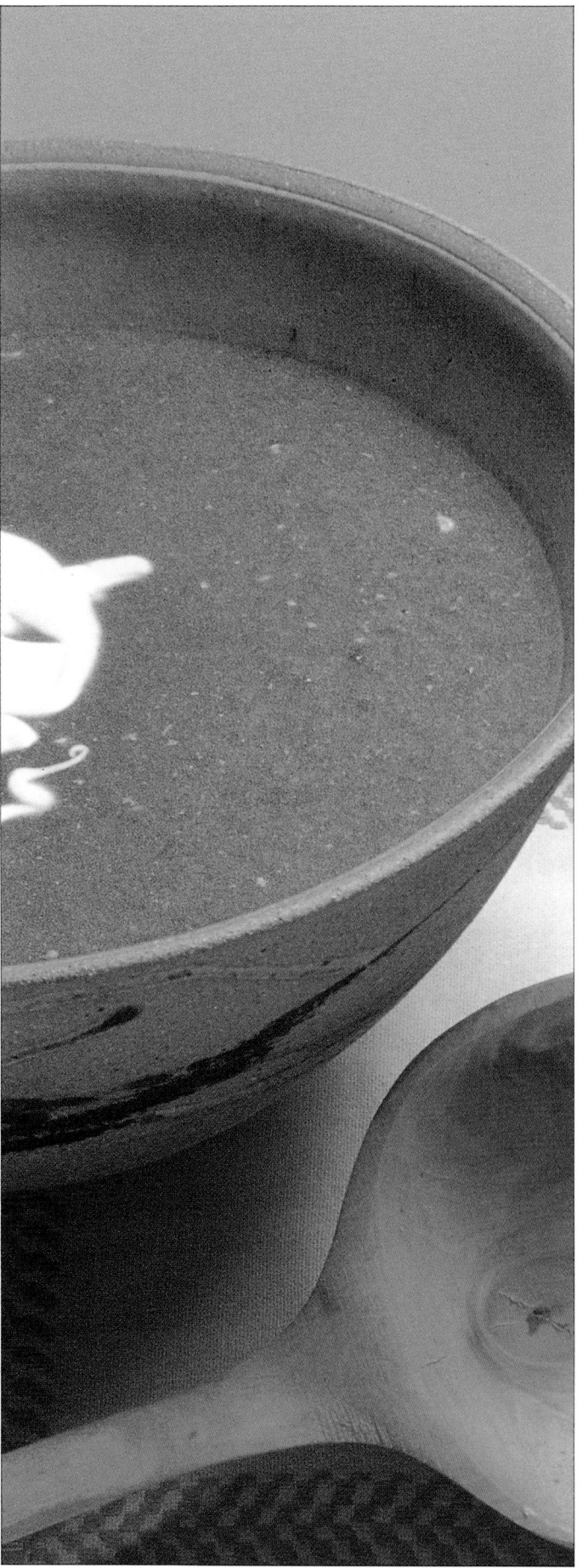

Pumpkin Soup

INGREDIENTS *serves 4-6*
1 tbsp/15ml sunflower oil
1 onion, chopped
12oz/350g pumpkin or squash, peeled,
    pips removed and diced
8oz/225g carrots, diced
2 potatoes, diced
2¹/₂ cups/600ml/1pt vegetable stock
2 small courgettes, thinly sliced
freshly ground black pepper
chopped parsley

METHOD

Place the oil and onion in a saucepan and cook for 2-3 minutes, to soften.

Add the pumpkin or squash, carrots, potatoes and stock. Bring to the boil, cover and simmer for 15 minutes, or until the vegetables are nearly tender.

Add the courgettes and cook for 5 minutes more.

Purée half the soup, blend with the remaining soup and season with pepper, to taste.

Reheat if necessary and serve in individual bowls. Make sure some of the courgettes float on the top to decorate.

Sprinkle with parsley to serve. The golden colour of this soup, and its ingredients, make it an appropriately autumnal choice.

Watercress and Potato Soup

INGREDIENTS *serves 4-6*
butter or margarine
1 medium onion, chopped
3 cups/450g/1lb peeled and sliced
    potatoes
2 bunches watercress
2¹/₂ cups/600ml/1pt vegetable stock
2 cups/450ml/³/₄pt yoghurt
1 egg
salt and freshly ground black pepper

METHOD

Heat the butter, add the onion and cook until it has just softened but not browned.

Add the potatoes and watercress and stir and leave on a low heat for 3 minutes. Pour in the stock and simmer for 20 minutes.

Mix the yoghurt with the egg. When the potatoes are soft, liquidize the soup, adding the yoghurt mixture slowly, as the machine is running. If you wish to serve warm, return to the saucepan, and stir over low heat to avoid curdling.

If you prefer the soup cold, chill for about 1 hour, then serve garnished with thinly sliced radish.

Cold Apple Soup

INGREDIENTS *serves 6*
3 medium/450g/1lb cooking apples,
    peeled and cored
²/₃ cup/150ml/¹/₄pt water
¹/₃ cup/75g/3oz sugar
juice of ¹/₂ lemon
1 tbsp/15g ground cinnamon
2 cloves
salt
1 tbsp/15ml white wine
scant 2 cups/450ml/³/₄pt yoghurt
²/₃ cup/150ml/¹/₄pt soured cream
    (optional)

METHOD

Cube the apples and cook them with the water, sugar, lemon juice, cinnamon, cloves and salt to taste until they are soft. Remove the cloves and mash the apples and leave them to cool.

Add the wine and yoghurt to the apples and mix together well. Serve, well chilled, with the soured cream if desired.

VARIATION

This Hungarian soup can be made with plums, pears, peaches or cherries. Reserve a little of the chosen fruit to garnish the soup.

These fruit "soups" – really purées – are traditionally served before meals of duck or goose, favourite Hungarian main courses. The sweet acid of the fruit complements the flavour of the birds and helps to cut their fatty richness.

◄ Pumpkin soup
► Cold apple soup

Watercress Soup

INGREDIENTS *serves 4*
butter
1 large onion, chopped
8oz/225g potatoes, peeled
5 cups/1.1l/2pts stock
salt and freshly ground black pepper
3 bunches watercress
cream

METHOD
Melt the butter in a large saucepan, add the onion and cook, stirring, until transparent.

Add the potatoes, stock and seasoning. bring to the boil, then simmer until potatoes can be mashed with a fork.

Wash the watercress and discard tough stalks and yellow leaves. Reserve a few sprigs for garnish, roughly chop the rest and add to the soup. Continue cooking for 2 minutes.

Allow the soup to cool slightly, then blend in a liquidizer. Allow to cool completely. Taste and adjust seasoning. Chill and serve with sprigs of watercress to garnish and a swirl of cream.

◀ Watercress soup
▶ Gazpacho soup

Carrot and Coriander Soup

INGREDIENTS *serves 6-8*
oil or butter
1 medium onion, sliced
9 cups/700g/1½lbs carrots, sliced
1 tsp/5ml ground coriander
3¾ cups/900ml/1½pts vegetable stock
⅔ cup/150ml/¼pt soured cream
salt and freshly ground black pepper
parsley to garnish

METHOD
Heat the oil, add the onion and cook until it has just softened but not browned. Add the carrots and coriander and stir well. Leave the carrots to cook gently for 3 minutes.

Pour in the stock and bring the mixture to the boil, then simmer, covered, for 25 minutes.

Liquidize the soup, adding the soured cream. Adjust the seasoning. Serve very cold, garnished with parsley.

Gazpacho

INGREDIENTS *serves 4-6*
1lb/450g large ripe tomatoes
1 large onion
2 cloves garlic
1 green pepper
1 red pepper
½ cucumber
2 slices wholewheat bread
3 tbsp/45ml olive oil
3 tbsp/45ml wine vinegar
1¼ cups/300ml/½pt tomato juice
1¼ cups/300ml/½pt water
salt and freshly ground black pepper

METHOD
Skin tomatoes, discard seeds and juice and chop the flesh. Peel and finely chop the onion and garlic. Remove pith and seeds from peppers and dice. Peel and dice the cucumber. Cut the crusts from the bread and dice.

Put vegetables and bread in a large bowl, pour over the remaining ingredients, stir and season. Chill well - overnight is best for a good tasty soup.

You can partly blend the soup if you wish, or blend all of it, in which case offer small bowls of chopped onions, tomatoes, peppers, cucumber and croûtons as a garnish.

Broccoli and Orange Soup

INGREDIENTS *serves 6*
1 medium onion, chopped
1 tbsp/15ml oil
1lb/450g broccoli, chopped
juice of 2 oranges
2½ cups/600ml/1pt vegetable stock
1¼ cups/300ml/½pt yoghurt
1 tbsp/15ml cornstarch
2 tbsp/30ml water
salt and freshly ground black pepper

METHOD
(Reserve some small pieces of broccoli for garnish, together with a little grated orange rind.) Heat the oil and cook the onion until it has just softened but not browned. Add the broccoli and stir round. Cook, covered, for a few minutes and then add the organge juice and stock. Bring to the boil, cover and simmer for about 20 minutes, until the broccoli is soft. Purée the soup in a blender. Mix the cornstarch and water to a smooth paste and stir into the soup with salt and pepper to taste. Return the soup to the heat and cook for a further five minutes. Serve, garnished with the reserved broccoli and the orange rind.

Use frozen broccoli if fresh is not available. Serve cold if preferred.

Persian Cucumber Soup

INGREDIENTS *serves 6*
1 large cucumber, finely grated
2½ cups/600ml/1pt yoghurt
2 tbsp tarragon vinegar
dill
2 tbsp/25g raisins soaked in 2 tbsp/
    30ml brandy for a few hours
2 hard-boiled eggs, finely chopped
1 large clove garlic, crushed
1 tsp/5ml sugar
⅔ cup/150ml/¼pt cream
salt and freshly ground black pepper

METHOD
Combine all the ingredients and stir
thoroughly. Refrigerate for a minimum of 3
hours and serve very cold.

VARIATION
John Tovey of the Miller Howe Hotel in the
English Lake District has his own special
twists to this classic Persian soup. He
suggests adding or subtracting ingredients
as you like. You may prefer mint or tarragon
to dill, and chopped apples, celery, fennel,
radishes can all be tried.

Avocado Soup

INGREDIENTS *serves 4*
2 large ripe avocados
2½ cups/600ml/1pt yoghurt
1 clove garlic, crushed
juice 1 lemon
salt and freshly ground black pepper

METHOD
Halve the avocados, remove the stones and
peel them. Blend all the ingredients
together. Serve very well chilled, garnished
with chives if desired.

NOTE
The thickness of the soup will depend as
much on the size of the avocados as the
thickness of the yoghurt used. You can thin
it down with a little milk or cream if you
need to.

Cold Tomato Soup

INGREDIENTS *serves 6-8*
2½ cups/600ml/1pt tomato juice
2½ cups/600ml/1pt yoghurt
3 spring onions, chopped
1 green pepper, chopped
1 large tomato, skinned and chopped
salt and freshly ground black pepper

METHOD
Blend the juice and yoghurt and pour the
mixture into a large bowl. Add the onions,
pepper and tomato and season to taste.
Serve well chilled, with some ice cubes
floating in the soup.

VARIATION
You can add or subtract ingredients to this
according to what you have handy. Try
sliced avocados; shrimps (prawns); fresh
basil; chopped olives; cucumber cut into
fine dice; raw sliced mushrooms; chopped
fennel; fried croutons.

▼ Persian cucumber soup

HORS D'ŒUVRES AND APPETIZERS

International cuisine offers a wide selection of vegetarian and wholefood appetizers and first courses. Vegetable pastes and pates take a variety of forms, from Greek hummus and Egyptian broad bean pate to Mexican avocado guacamole and Italian-inspired courgette moulds. Stuffed vegetables – like aubergines and artichokes – and deep-fried mouthfuls, including Indian samosas, Chinese spring rolls and Bulgarian eggs, tempt from the four corners of the world.

Samosas

Hummus

INGREDIENTS *serves 4*
1¼ cups/225g/8oz dried chick peas,
    soaked overnight
1 bouquet garni
1 small onion, sliced
2 cloves garlic, crushed
juice of 2 lemons
4 tbsp/60ml/2oz tahini paste
3 tbsp/45ml olive oil
salt and freshly ground black pepper
1 tomato, sliced
sprig of parsley

METHOD
Drain the chick peas and place in a large saucepan with plenty of water, the bouquet garni and onion. Bring to the boil then simmer gently for 1¼-2 hours, or until tender.

Drain, reserving a little of the cooking liquid. Discard the onion and bouquet garni.

Place the garlic, lemon juice, tahini, olive oil and seasoning in a food processor or blender. Add the cooked chick peas and process to a smooth paste.

Add a little of the reserved cooking liquid if the paste is too thick, and stir rapidly.

Arrange the hummus in a dish, edge with halved tomato slices and garnish with parsley. Serve with warmed pitta bread.

Guacamole

INGREDIENTS *serves 2-4*
2 large ripe avocados
2 large ripe tomatoes
1 bunch spring onions
1-2 tbsp/15-30ml olive oil
1-2 tbsp/15-30ml lemon juice
salt and freshly ground black pepper
2 green chillies

METHOD
Remove the flesh from the avocados and mash. Skin the tomatoes, remove the seeds and chop finely. Chop the spring onions.

Mix vegetables together with olive oil and lemon juice and season to taste. Garnish with chopped green chillies and serve, chilled, as a dip or with hot pitta bread (see page 151).

Israeli Avocado Cream

INGREDIENTS *serves 4*
1 large avocado
½ cup/75g/3oz cream cheese
½ small onion, finely chopped
dash Tabasco
2 tbsp/30ml lemon juice
salt and freshly ground black pepper

METHOD
Mash the flesh of the avocado. Add the remaining ingredients, mixing them in very well. Spoon the mixture into a serving dish and cover it well. Refrigerate until required. Do not make this too long before you intend to serve it, as avocado discolours easily.

NOTE
Serve with raw vegetables or crackers as a dip or spread.

Yoghurt and Tahini Dip

INGREDIENTS *serves 4-6*
2 cloves garlic, crushed
⅔ cup/150ml/¼pt tahini paste
⅔ cup/150ml/¼pt yoghurt
juice of 2 lemons
salt and freshly ground black pepper
chopped parsley

METHOD
Blend everything together except the parsley until smooth. Taste and add more lemon juice and seasoning if necessary. Turn into a bowl and garnish with the chopped parsley.

NOTE
Serve as a dip, with pita or crackers, or as an accompaniment to vegetables, salads or meat or fish dishes.

◄▲ Hummus
◄ Guacamole
► Israeli avocado cream

Blue Cheese Pâté

INGREDIENTS *serves 4*
1¼ cups/300ml/½pt yoghurt
1 cup/100g/4oz crumbled blue cheese
2-4 tbsp/30-60ml cream

METHOD
Drain the yoghurt for about 5 hours. Remove the resulting cheese from the cloth carefully.

Liquidize the drained yoghurt with the blue cheese and just enough cream to reach the required consistency. Refrigerate the mixture until required. It will firm up considerably.

NOTE
This mixture is useful as a filling for fruit (especially good with pears) or choux pastry, for stuffed tomatoes or celery, or as a salad dressing, in which case add more cream or creamy milk. Use ⅔ cup/100g/4oz quark or curd cheese instead of the drained yoghurt.

▶ Blue cheese pâté

Celery Mousse

INGREDIENTS *serves 4-6*
1 tbsp/15ml gelatine
2 tbsp/30ml boiling water
1 medium head of celery with leaves,
    roughly chopped
$^7/_8$ cup/200ml/7fl oz yoghurt
squeeze lemon juice
1 small onion
parsley
$^3/_4$ cup/150g/5oz curd cheese
salt and freshly ground black pepper

METHOD
Dissolve the gelatine in the boiling water.
Blend all the remaining ingredients, except
the curd cheese, feeding them into a
liquidizer or food processor a little at a time.

Add the dissolved gelatine and curd
cheese and blend it into the mixture. Turn
into a moistened mould (a small ring mould
looks nice). Refrigerate until set. Unmould
and serve as a part of a cold buffet, an
accompaniment to cold meat or chicken or
fish.

NOTE
For a richer version, substitute mayonnaise
for the yoghurt.

Broad Bean Pâté

INGREDIENTS *serves 4*
1½ cup/350g/12oz shelled broad beans
about 1 cup/175g/6oz cream cheese
salt and freshly ground black pepper
mint sprigs

METHOD
If the beans are old, remove the skins before
or after cooking. Boil lightly in salted water
until tender.

Mash or put through a vegetable mill
with enough cream cheese to make a thick
paste. Season with salt and pepper. Press
into individual dishes and garnish each with
a sprig of mint. Serve with triangles of
wholewheat toast.

▲ ▶ Celery mousse
▶ Broad bean pâté

Tarama Salad

INGREDIENTS *serves 6-8*
3 large potatoes
3 tbsp/45ml milk
4oz/100g red caviar or red lumpfish roe
6 tbsp/90ml water
4 tbsp/60ml fresh lemon juice
1 small onion, finely chopped
¾ cup/175ml/6fl oz pure olive oil

METHOD
Peel the potatoes. Cook them in boiling water until very soft, about 20 minutes. Drain the potatoes and put them in a mixing bowl. By hand or with an electric beater, mash the potatoes, slowly adding the milk, until smooth. Add the caviar and water to the potatoes. Mix well.

Stir the lemon juice and onion into the mixture and mix briefly. Slowly beat in the olive oil. Continue to beat until a smooth paste is formed.

Transfer to a serving bowl. Arrange the *crudités* around the dip and serve.

Stuffed Peppers

INGREDIENTS *serves 4*
2 large green peppers (or 1 red and 1 green)
1½ cups/225g/8oz ricotta cheese
1 small pickled cucumber, finely chopped
1 tbsp/15ml chopped parsley
1 tbsp/15ml chopped dill (or half or dried)
salt and freshly ground black pepper
crisp lettuce to serve

METHOD
Remove the stalk end of the peppers and discard the seeds. Mix the ricotta with the pickled cucumber, parsley, dill and salt and pepper.

Stuff the mixture into the peppers and refrigerate for several hours.

With a very sharp knife, cut the peppers into slices about 1cm/½in thick. Serve the pepper slices on a bed of crisp lettuce.

NOTE
Use curd or cottage cheese if you prefer instead of the ricotta, or a mixture of low-fat soft cheeses.

▼ Tarama salad

Stuffed Tomatoes

INGREDIENTS *serves 4*
8 English (small) tomatoes, or 3 beef
   (large) tomatoes
4 hard-boiled eggs, cooled and peeled
6 tbsp/90ml mayonnaise
1 tsp/5ml garlic paste
salt and freshly ground black pepper
1 tbsp/15ml parsley, chopped
1 tbsp/15ml white breadcrumbs for the
   beef (large) tomatoes

METHOD
Skin the tomatoes, first by cutting out the core with a sharp knife and making a '+' incision on the other end of the tomato. Then place in a pan of boiling water for 10 seconds, remove and plunge into a bowl of iced or very cold water (this latter step is to stop the tomatoes from cooking and going mushy).

Slice the tops off the tomatoes, and just enough of their bases to remove the rounded ends so that the tomatoes will sit squarely on the plate. Keep the tops if using small tomatoes, but not for the large tomatoes.

Remove the seeds and inside, either with a teaspoon or small, sharp knife. Mash the eggs with the mayonnaise, garlic paste, salt, pepper and parsley.

Fill the tomatoes, firmly pressing the filling down. With small tomatoes, replace the lids at a jaunty angle. If keeping to serve later, brush them with olive oil and black pepper to prevent from drying out. Cover with plastic film and keep.

NOTE
For large tomatoes, the filling must be very firm, so it can be sliced. If you make your own mayonnaise, thicken it by using more egg yolks. If you use shop-bought mayonnaise, add enough white breadcrumbs until the mixture is the consistency of mashed potatoes. Season well, to taste. Fill the tomatoes, pressing down firmly until level. Refrigerate for 1 hour, then slice with a sharp carving knife into rings. Sprinkle with chopped parsley.

▲ ◄ Stuffed tomatoes

◄ Tonno e fagioli

Tonno e Fagioli

INGREDIENTS *serves 4*
1½ cups/400g/15oz can red kidney
   beans, drained
1 onion chopped
7oz/200g can tuna fish
handful chopped parsley
dash lemon juice
freshly ground black pepper

METHOD
Mix the beans with the onion. Drain the tuna fish, reserving the oil. Flake and add to the salad.

Add the parsley, a dash of lemon juice and plenty of black pepper. Toss and add some of the reserved fish oil and more lemon and pepper to taste.

Courgette Moulds

INGREDIENTS *serves 4*
1lb/450g courgettes, sliced
1 onion, chopped
2 tbsp/30ml lemon juice
2 tsp/10ml fresh coriander leaves,
  chopped
4oz/100g fromage blanc
salt and freshly ground black pepper
1 sachet gelatine
²/₃ cup/150ml/¹/₄pt natural low fat
  yoghurt
5 tbsp/75ml/3fl oz skimmed milk
1 egg yolk
1 tsp/5ml curry paste

METHOD
Place the courgettes and onions in a saucepan with 2×15ml sp/2 tbsp water and the lemon juice. Cover and cook over a gentle heat for 8-10 minutes, or until softened.

Cool slightly and purée in a food processor or blender. Add the coriander leaves, cheese and seasoning and purée until smooth. Leave until lukewarm.

Sprinkle the gelatine over 2 tbsp/30ml water in a cup. Stand in a saucepan of hot water and stir to dissolve. Add to the purée and pour into four ²/₃ cup/150ml/¹/₄pt ramekin dishes. Chill for 1-1¹/₂ hours until set.

Meanwhile mix the yoghurt, milk, egg yolk and curry paste together and heat gently until slightly thickened. Do not boil. Leave to cool.

Pour the sauce across the base of a serving dish, loosen the moulds and turn out on to the dish. Garnish the tops of the moulds with chervil and serve.

Mozzarella and Avocado Bees

INGREDIENTS *serves 2*
1 ripe avocado
4oz/100g Mozzarella cheese
1 tbsp/15ml olive oil
1 tbsp/15ml tarragon vinegar
salt and freshly ground black pepper

METHOD
Cut the avocado in half and remove the stone. With a palette knife carefully remove the skin from each half of the avocado. Lay the avocado halves flat-side downwards and cut horizontally into ¹/₄in/1cm slices.

Cut semi-circular slices from the Mozzarella, with 4 extra semi-circles for wings.

Arrange the cheese slices between the avocado slices to form the striped body of the bee, and arrange the wings at the sides.

Mix the oil and vinegar together and season well. Pour over the bees and serve.

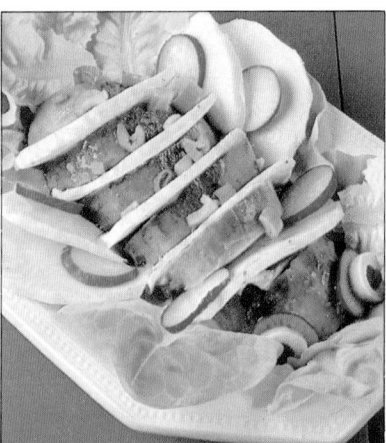

Vegetables in Aspic

INGREDIENTS *serves 4*
2¹/₂ cups/600ml/20fl oz aspic or
  equivalent
1 cup/100g/4oz peeled and diced carrot
1 cup/100g/4oz trimmed and sliced
  green beans
1 tbsp/15ml walnut oil
1 cup/100g/4oz sliced button
  mushrooms
1 tbsp/15ml stuffed olives, sliced
²/₃ cup/150ml/¹/₄ pt thick mayonnaise

METHOD
Prepare the aspic or equivalent and allow it to cool. Chill a mould. Wet the mould and when the aspic is almost set, line the mould with it. Place in the fridge to set.

Meanwhile cook the carrot and green beans in salted water until tender. Refresh in cold water. Heat the walnut oil in a pan and gently sauté the mushrooms. Allow to cool.

Mix the vegetables together with the olives, mayonnaise and the remaining aspic and fill the mould. Chill until set.

Dip the mould into hot water and turn out onto a plate. Cut into wedges and serve each wedge with a crisp lettuce leaf and a triange of wholemeal toast.

▶ Vegetables in aspic
◀ Mozzarella and avocado bees
▼ Courgette moulds

Summer Posy Mousse

INGREDIENTS *serves 4-6*
12g/¹/₂oz (2 envelopes) powdered
   gelatine
2 tbsp/30ml warm water
2 eggs, separated, plus 1 egg white
²/₃ cup/150ml/¹/₄pt double cream
1 cup/100g/4oz Roquefort cheese,
   crumbled
3 tbsp/45ml soured cream
salt and freshly ground white pepper
few drops Tabasco sauce

THE POSY
nasturtium flowers and leaves
borage flowers and leaves
summer savoury
sprigs of mint, fennel and dill

METHOD
Put the gelatine and water into a small bowl
and stand it in a pan of simmering water. Stir
well until the gelatine has dissolved.

Beat the egg yolks with half the double
cream, the soured cream and the gelatine.
Mash in the cheese. Whip the remaining

▲ Melon and Ugli fruit with lemon sauce

double cream, fold into the mixture, season
and add Tabasco sauce. Chill.

Whip the egg whites until soft peaks
form. Fold them into the mixture. Oil a ring
mould, pour in the mousse and chill until
set.

Dip the mould into hot water, invert a
plate over it and turn the mousse out. Fill the
centre with a posy of edible flowers and
delicate leafy herbs. This dish can form the
centrepiece of a summer lunch in the
garden. Serve with brown bread.

Melon and Ugli Fruit with Lemon Sauce

INGREDIENTS *serves 4*
2 Charentais melons
2 ugli fruit, pith removed and
   segmented
2 tsp/10ml light brown muscovado
   sugar
juice 2 lemons
grated rind ¹/₂ lemon
twists lemon peel

METHOD
Halve the melons, remove the seeds and
scoop out balls of flesh using a vegetable
baller.

Cut the ugli fruit segments in half, if large,
and mix with the melon balls.

Scoop out the remaining melon flesh
from the skins and place in a food processor
or blender. Add the sugar, lemon juice and
rind and blend.

Pour over the fruit and chill until
required. To serve, divide the fruit between
four tall individual glass dishes. Decorate
the glass sides with twists of lemon peel.

Date and Cream Cheese Spread

INGREDIENTS *makes 1 cup/
250ml/8fl oz*
⅓ cup/50g/2oz cream cheese
2 tbsp/30ml milk
1½ cups/225g/8oz finely chopped fresh
   dates
1 tbsp/15ml finely grated lemon rind.

METHOD
Mix the cheese with the milk to a smooth cream. Add the dates and lemon rind and mix together well.

NOTE
Fresh dates are so different from the more widely known semi-dried variety, familiar to us at Christmas time. They are not as sweet as the boxed ones and lend themselves to interesting combinations. This spread can be used on bread (try granary) or as a cocktail appetizer on small crackers.

VARIATION
Another delicious way to use fresh dates is to make a stuffing of cream cheese, with chopped raisins, chopped ginger or chopped nuts and fill the dates, which are left whole but with the stone removed.

Tomato and Mozzarella Salad

INGREDIENTS *serves 4*
2 to 3 large tomatoes, thinly sliced
4oz/100g fresh Mozzarella cheese, thinly
   sliced
2 tbsp/10ml fresh basil
6 tbsp/90ml extra virgin olive oil
salt and freshly ground black pepper

METHOD
Arrange the tomatoes and Mozzarella in alternating layers in a serving dish.
   Garnish the salad with the basil.
   Sprinkle the salad with the olive oil and with the salt and pepper. Serve.

◄ Summer posy mousse
► Date and cream cheese spread

Crudites with hot Anchovy Dip

INGREDIENTS *serves 6-8*
a selection of crisp raw vegetables, cut
    into manageable pieces
carrots
celery
green, red and yellow peppers
cucumber
cauliflower florets
radishes
mushrooms

DIP
8 tbsp/100g/4oz butter
2 cloves garlic, crushed
8 anchovy fillets
1¼ cups/300ml/½pt thick cream

METHOD
Prepare the vegetables and arrange them on
a serving platter. Keep cold.

Prepare the dip. Heat the butter in a pan
and add the garlic. Drain the anchovy fillets
and pat dry with kitchen paper. When the
garlic has softened, pound the anchovies
into the pan until you have a smooth paste.

Beat in the cream and bring back to the
boil. Cook, stirring until the dip has
thickened. Serve hot. If you use a small
copper pan or a fondue pan, you can serve
the dip in the pan you cooked it in.

▲ ▶ Garlic mushrooms
◀ Crudites with hot anchovy dip

Garlic Mushrooms

INGREDIENTS *serves 4-6*
6 tbsp/75g/3oz butter
750g/1½lb mushrooms, button or cap
few drops lemon juice
salt and freshly ground black pepper
2 cloves garlic, crushed
1 tbsp/5g chopped coriander or parsley

METHOD
Heat the butter in a large pan. Add the mushrooms and sweat gently, covered, for 5 minutes, shaking occasionally.

Add the lemon juice, salt and pepper. Increase the heat, tossing the mushrooms well. Add the garlic, toss and cook for 2 minutes.

Add the coriander or parsley and cook for 1 minute. Remove from the heat and serve.

Stuffed Garlic Mushrooms

INGREDIENTS *serves 4*
16 open mushrooms, about 1½in/3cm across
2 slices wholewheat bread, crumbled
⅔ cup/150ml/¼pt warm milk
4 cloves garlic
1 cup/50g/2oz fresh mixed herbs, chopped
oil
salt and freshly ground black pepper
few sprigs watercress

METHOD
Preheat the oven to 350°F/180°C/Gas 4.

Wipe the mushroom caps clean. Remove, chop and reserve stalks. Soak the breadcrumbs in milk until soft, then squeeze out excess milk.

In a mortar, pound the garlic with herbs and enough oil to make a paste. Pound in the stalks. Mix together with the breadcrumbs and season well with salt and pepper.

Spoon the filling into the mushroom caps and arrange them in a lightly oiled ovenproof dish. Bake for about 15 minutes until mushrooms are soft and juicy and filling has crisped a little on the top. Serve hot with sprigs of watercress. Serves 4 as a starter.

39

Vegetarian Spring Rolls

INGREDIENTS *serves 4*
1 pack of 20 frozen spring roll skins
8oz/225g fresh bean sprouts
8oz/225g young tender leeks or spring
   onions
4oz/100g carrots
4oz/100g white mushrooms
oil for deep-frying
1½ tsp/8ml salt
1 tsp/5ml sugar
1 tbsp/15ml light soy sauce

METHOD
Take the spring roll skins out of the packet
and leave them to defrost thoroughly under
a damp cloth.

Wash and rinse the bean sprouts in a bowl
of cold water and discard the husks and
other bits and pieces that float to the
surface. Drain.

Cut the leeks or spring onions, carrots
and mushrooms into thin shreds.

Heat 3-4 tbsp/45-60ml of oil in a
preheated wok or frying pan and stir-fry all
the vegetables for a few seconds. Add the
salt, sugar and soy sauce and continue
stirring for about 1-1½ minutes. Remove
and leave to cool a little.

Cut each spring roll in half diagonally.
Place about 2 tsp/10ml of the filling on the
skin about a third of the way down, with the
triangle pointing away from you. Lift the
lower flap over the filling and roll once, then
fold in both ends and roll once more.

Brush the upper edge with a little flour
and water paste and roll into a neat package.
Repeat until all filling is used up.

Heat about 6⅓ cups/1.5l/2½pts oil in a
wok or deep-fryer until it smokes. Reduce
the heat or even turn it off for a few minutes
to cool the oil a little before adding the
spring rolls. Deep-fry 6-8 at a time for 3-4
minutes or until golden and crispy. Increase
the heat to high again before frying each
batch. As each batch is cooked, remove and
drain it on absorbent paper. Serve hot with a
dip sauce such as soy sauce, vinegar, chilli
sauce or mustard.

NOTE
These spring rolls are ideal for a buffet-style
meal or as cocktail snacks. (They can also be
frozen for up to 3 months.)

Sichuan-Style Cucumber

INGREDIENTS *serves 4*
1 cucumber
1 tsp/5ml salt
2 tbsp/30ml sugar
2 tbsp/30ml vinegar
1 tbsp/15ml chilli oil

METHOD
Split the cucumber in two lengthways and
then cut each piece into strips rather like
potato chips (French fries). Sprinkle with
the salt and leave for about 10 minutes to
extract the bitter juices.

Remove each cucumber strip. Place it on
a firm surface and soften it by gently tapping
it with the blade of a cleaver or knife.

Place the cucumber strips on a plate.
Sprinkle the sugar evenly over them and
then add the vinegar and chilli oil just before
serving.

▶ Crispy seaweed
▼ Vegetarian Spring Rolls

Crispy Seaweed

INGREDIENTS *serves 4*
1½/1¾lb/ 750g spring greens
2½ cups/600ml/1pt oil for deep-frying
1 tsp/5ml salt
1 tsp/5ml sugar

METHOD
Wash and dry the spring green leaves and
shred them with a sharp knife into the
thinnest possible shavings. Spread them out
on absorbent paper or put in a large
colander to dry thoroughly.

Heat the oil in a wok or deep-fryer. Before
the oil gets too hot, turn off the heat for 30
seconds. Add the spring green shavings in
several batches and turn the heat up to
medium high. Stir with a pair of cooking
chopsticks.

When the shavings start to float to the
surface, scoop them out gently with a
slotted spoon and drain on absorbent paper
to remove as much of the oil as possible.
Sprinkle the salt and sugar evenly on top
and mix gently. Serve cold.

VARIATION
Deep-fry ½ cup/50g/2oz split almonds until
crisp and add to the 'seaweed' as a garnish,
to give the dish a new dimension.

Devilled Eggs

INGREDIENTS *serves 4*
4 hard-boiled eggs, cut in half,
    lengthwise
1½ tbsp/23g onions, finely chopped
2 green chillis, finely chopped
1 tbsp/5ml coriander leaves, chopped
½ tsp/2.5ml salt
2 tbsp/30g mashed potatoes
oil for deep frying
1 tbsp/15ml plain flour
2fl oz/60ml/¼ cup water

METHOD
Remove the yolks and mix with the onions, chillis, coriander leaves, salt and mashed potatoes. Put the mixture back into the egg whites. Chill for 30 minutes.

Heat the oil in a karai over high heat. While the oil is heating up make a batter with the flour and water. Be careful not to allow the oil to catch fire.

Dip the eggs into the batter and slip into the hot oil. Fry until golden, turning once.

Stuffed Aubergines

INGREDIENTS *serves 4-8*
4 aubergines
olive oil
1 large onion, chopped
2-3 cloves garlic, crushed
4 large tomatoes, skinned and chopped
2 tbsp/10g fresh herbs, chopped
salt and freshly ground black pepper
4oz/100g Mozzarella cheese
4 tbsp/60ml brown breadcrumbs
a little butter

METHOD
Preheat the oven to 400°F/200°C/Gas 6. Wash the aubergines. Cut in half lengthwise and score the cut surface deeply with a knife. Sprinkle with salt and leave, cut surface down, for 30 minutes.

Meanwhile heat 1-2 tbsp/15-30ml oil in a pan and fry the onion and garlic until translucent. Transfer to a bowl and mix in the tomatoes and chopped herbs.

Add more oil to the pan. Rinse the aubergines and pat dry. Place them cut surface down in the pan and cook gently for about 15 minutes. They absorb a lot of oil,

▼ Stuffed aubergines   ▲ Devilled eggs

so you will need to keep adding a little more.

Scoop some of the flesh out of the aubergines, mash and mix it with the rest of the filling. Season well. Pile the filling onto the aubergines and top with thinly sliced Mozzarella. Sprinkle with breadcrumbs and dot with butter. Place aubergines in a greased ovenproof dish and bake for 20 minutes until the cheese has melted and the breadcrumbs are crispy.

Bulgarian Eggs

INGREDIENTS *serves 4*
1¼ cups/300ml/½pt yoghurt
1 small clove garlic, crushed
salt and freshly ground black pepper
2 tbsp/25g/1oz butter, melted
½ tsp/2.5ml paprika

METHOD
Softly poach the eggs. Mix the yoghurt with the garlic, salt and pepper and warm it through gently but don't let it boil. Spoon it into four shallow dishes. Place one egg, well drained, into each dish. Add the paprika to the melted butter and drizzle it onto the eggs. Serve immediately, with hot French bread or pita.

▼ Artichokes with Tomato Sauce

NOTE
This amount makes a good appetizer or very light supper dish. Double the quantity for a more substantial meal.

Artichokes with Tomato Sauce

INGREDIENTS *serves 4*
4 large artichokes
1-2 tbsp/15-30ml oil
1 large onion, chopped
2 cloves garlic, chopped
1½ cups/400g/15oz can tomatoes, mashed
1 tbsp/15ml tomato purée
2 tsp/10ml fresh oregano, chopped
lemon juice
salt and freshly ground black pepper

METHOD
Rinse the artichokes thoroughly under the cold tap and leave them upside down to drain. Bring a very large pan of salted water to the boil, put the artichokes in and boil fast for 30-50 minutes, depending on the size. When an outer leaf comes away at a gentle tug, the artichokes are ready.

Meanwhile, make the sauce. Heat the oil in a pan and fry the onion and garlic until transparent. Add the tomatoes, tomato purée and oregano and reduce until the sauce is of pouring consistency but not sloppy. Season with salt and pepper and a dash of lemon juice to taste.

Drain the artichokes. When cool, pull out the tiny inner leaves together with the hairy inedible choke. Spoon in some tomato sauce. Stand each artichoke in a pool of sauce on an individual dish and serve.

Pakoras

INGREDIENTS *makes enough for 1lb/ 450g vegetables*
4 tbsp/60g chick pea flour
2 tsp/10ml oil
1 tsp/5ml baking powder
½ tsp/2.5ml salt
6 tbsp/75ml/3fl oz water
Any of the following vegetables can be used
aubergines, cut into very thin rounds
onions, cut into ⅛in/0.25cm rings
potatoes, cut into very thin rounds
cauliflower, cut into ¾in/1.5cm florets
chilli, left whole
pumpkin, cut into thin slices
green pepper, cut into thin strips
oil for deep frying

METHOD
Mix all the batter ingredients together and beat until smooth. Wash the slices of vegetables and pat dry.

Heat the oil in a karai till very hot. Dip a slice of the vegetable in the batter and put into the hot oil. Place as many slices as you can in the oil. Fry till crisp and golden. Drain and serve with mint or coriander chutney (page 134).

Samosas

INGREDIENTS *serves 4-6*
3 tbsp/45ml oil
¼ tsp/1.5ml whole cumin seeds
4 cups/450g/1lb potatoes, diced into ½in/1.2cm cubes
1 green chilli, finely chopped
pinch turmeric
½ tsp/2.5ml salt
3oz/75g/scant ½ cup peas
1 tsp/5ml ground roasted cumin (oven-roasted for 5 minutes)

DOUGH
2¼ cups/225g/8oz plain flour
1 tsp/5ml salt
3 tbsp/45ml oil
scant ½ cup/90ml/3½fl oz oil for deep frying

METHOD
Heat the oil in a karai over medium high heat and add the cumin seeds. Let them sizzle for a few seconds.

Add the potatoes and green chilli and fry for 2-3 minutes. Add the turmeric and salt and, stirring occasionally, cook for 5 minutes.

Add the peas and the ground roasted cumin. Stir to mix. Cover, lower heat and cook a further 10 minutes until the potatoes are tender. Cool.

Meanwhile, sieve together the flour and salt. Rub in the oil. Add enough water to form a stiff dough. Knead for 10 minutes until smooth.

Divide into 12 balls. Roll each ball into a round of about 6in/15cm across. Cut in half. Pick up one half, flatten it slightly and form a cone, sealing the overlapping edge with a little water. Fill the cone with 1½ tsp of the filling and seal the top with a little water. In a similar way make all the samosas.

Heat oil in a karai over medium heat. Put in as many samosas as you can into the hot oil and fry until crisp and golden. Drain. Serve with a chutney.

◀ Pakoras

44

SALADS

Salads today have come far beyond the tossed green version. All kinds of vegetables – and fruit – homely and exotic, have joined the cast list in the modern salad repertoire. The influence of Californian and nouvelle cuisines vie with that of the East to make your choice as interesting as possible.

Pear salad

Tomato Salad with Modern Vinaigrette

INGREDIENTS *serves 4*
3 beef (large) tomatoes
1/2 onion, finely sliced
few black olives
1¼ cups/300ml/½pt Modern Vinaigrette
(see page 128)

METHOD
Slice the tomatoes horizontally. Arrange either in a large bowl with onion in between layers, or on a large plate. Sprinkle with black olives.

Dredge the tomatoes with the dressing and serve.

NOTE
If keeping to serve later, add the dressing 20 minutes before required.

▲ Tomato Salad with Modern Vinaigrette

Swedish Tomato Salad

INGREDIENTS *serves 6*
6 large tomatoes, seeded and halved
¾ cup/175ml/6fl oz walnut oil
6 tbsp/90ml white wine vinegar
2 garlic cloves, crushed
¾ tsp/4ml dried dill
¼ tsp/1.5ml sugar
¼ tsp/1.5ml honey
½ tsp/2.5ml Dijon-style mustard
2 tbsp/10ml chopped fresh chives
½ tsp/2.5ml salt
¼ tsp/1.5ml freshly ground black pepper
6 to 8 lettuce leaves
6 fresh parsley sprigs

METHOD
Put the tomatoes, cut-side down, in a shallow dish.

Put the walnut oil, vinegar, garlic, dill, sugar, honey, mustard, chives, salt and pepper in a jar with a tightly fitting lid. Cover tightly and shake vigorously until all the ingredients are blended.

Pour the dressing over the tomatoes. Chill the salad for 2½ hours. Every 30 minutes spoon the dressing over the tomatoes.

Line a serving dish with lettuce leaves. Remove the tomatoes from the dish and place them on the lettuce leaves. Pour the dressing over the tomatoes. Garnish with the parsley sprigs and serve.

Italian Fontina Cheese Salad

INGREDIENTS *serves 6*
2 large sweet yellow peppers, seeded and halved
2 large sweet red peppers, seeded and halved
8oz/225g Fontina cheese, diced
2oz/50g pitted green olives, thinly sliced
6 tbsp/90ml pure olive oil
1½ tsp/8ml Dijon-style mustard
3 tbsp/45ml single cream
1 tbsp/15ml chopped spring onion
¾ tsp/4ml salt
1 tsp/5ml freshly ground black pepper
1 tbsp/15ml chopped fresh parsley

METHOD
Preheat the grill. Place the yellow and red peppers on a baking tray and grill until the skins are blistered and slightly blackened, about 10 to 15 minutes. Remove the peppers from the heat.

When the peppers are cool enough to handle, remove the blistered skin. Cut the peppers into strips about ⅛in/9mm wide. Put the pepper strips, Fontina cheese and olives in a serving bowl.

Put the olive oil, mustard, cream, spring onion, salt and pepper in a jar with a tightly fitting lid. Cover tightly and shake until well blended.

Pour the dressing over the salad and toss. Chill the salad for 1 to 2 hours. Garnish with the chopped parsley and toss again lightly before serving.

Japanese Cucumber Salad

INGREDIENTS *serves 4*
2 medium-sized cucumbers, thinly sliced
1 tsp/5ml salt
4 tbsp/60ml rice wine vinegar
2 tbsp/30ml soy sauce
1 tsp/5ml sugar
2 tsp/10ml white sesame seeds

▲ Japanese cucumber salad

METHOD
Put the cucumber slices in a colander. Sprinkle with the salt. Let the cucumber slices drain for 30 minutes.

Remove the cucumber slices from the colander. Put the slices between two layers of paper towels and pat them dry.

Into a jar with a tightly fitting lid, put the vinegar, soy sauce and sugar. Cover tightly and shake well until the sugar dissolves.

Put the cucumber slices in a salad bowl. Add the dressing and toss lightly.

Toast the sesame seeds in a dry frying pan over a high heat, shaking the pan frequently. When the seeds begin to jump, remove them from the pan and crush them with a pestle. Sprinkle the crushed sesame seeds on the salad and serve.

Pine Nuts and Watercress

INGREDIENTS *serves 4*
2 tbsp/30g pine nuts
2 large bunches watercress
4oz/100g fresh parsley, finely chopped
3½oz/90ml fresh chives, finely chopped
¾ cup/175ml/6fl oz Lemon Dressing (see page 131)

METHOD
Preheat the oven to 350°F/180°C/Gas 4. Put the pine nuts on a baking tray and toast them in the oven until browned, about 8 to 10 minutes.

Put the watercress, parsley and chives in a salad bowl. Add the Lemon Dressing and toss. Add the pine nuts and toss again.

Orange and Walnut Salad

INGREDIENTS *serves 4*
3 plump heads chicory
2 large sweet oranges, peel and pith
  removed, segmented
3oz/75g walnuts, chopped

MUSTARD DRESSING
2 tbsp/30ml walnut oil
pinch mustard powder
1 tbsp/15ml orange juice
1 tbsp/15ml lemon juice

METHOD
Mix the chicory slices, oranges and half the
walnuts together and place in a serving dish.
  Sprinkle over the remaining walnuts.
  Whisk the walnut oil and mustard
powder together, then gradually whisk in
the orange and lemon juices.
  Pour the dressing over the salad and serve
immediately.

Mixed Greens and Mushrooms with Raspberry Vinaigrette

INGREDIENTS *serves 4*
4 tbsp/60g pine nuts
2 heads cabbage lettuce or other soft
lettuce
2 heads chicory
1 small head radicchio
8oz/225g stemmed small mushrooms

RASPBERRY VINAIGRETTE
4 tbsp/60ml olive oil
2 tbsp/30ml raspberry vinegar
1 finely chopped shallot
1 tsp/5ml Dijon-style mustard
2 tsp/10ml single cream
salt and freshly ground black pepper to
  taste

METHOD
Pre-heat the oven to 350°F/180°C/Gas 4.
Place the pine nuts in a shallow baking dish
and toast them in the oven until lightly
browned, about 5 minutes. Remove from
oven and set aside.
  Wash and gently dry the cabbage lettuce,
chicory and radicchio. Tear the lettuce and
radicchio into bite-sized pieces. Cut the
chicory into thin slices. Put the greens into a
large salad bowl. Add the mushrooms and
toasted pine nuts.
  In a mixing bowl combine the olive oil,
vinegar, shallot, mustard, cream, salt and
pepper. Whisk until the vinaigrette is
smooth and well blended.
  Pour the vinaigrette over the greens and
toss well. Serve at once.

▲ ◄ Orange and walnut salad
◄ Mixed greens and mushroom salad

Orange and Mixed Green Salad

INGREDIENTS *serves 4*

1/2 head cabbage lettuce or mignonette
  lettuce
2 large navel oranges
8oz/225g carrots, cut in strips
1/3 cup/50g/2oz sultanas or currants
3/4 cup/175ml/6fl oz Cheese Herb
  Dressing (see page 130)

METHOD

Tear the lettuce into bite-sized pieces.
Arrange them in a salad bowl. Peel the
oranges and divide them into segments. Cut
each segment into halves or thirds. Add the
pieces to the salad bowl. Add the carrots
and sultanas to the salad bowl and toss.
Pour on the Cheese Herb Dressing and toss.

Garden Mixed Green Salad

INGREDIENTS *serves 6-8*

1 head cabbage lettuce or garden
  lettuce
1 medium-sized head cos lettuce
3 heads chicory
stalk celery, chopped
3 hard-boiled eggs, sliced
4oz/100g watercress, thick stems
  removed, coarsely chopped
1/2 medium-sized onion, sliced into rings
2 large tomatoes, peeled and cut in
  wedges
4oz/100g pickled beetroot, cut in strips
2 tbsp/30ml fresh parsley, chopped
1 1/4 cups/300ml/1/2pt Rich French
  Dressing (see page 129)

METHOD

Line the salad bowl with some leaves of the
cabbage or garden lettuce.

Tear the remaining cabbage lettuce and
the cos lettuce into bite-sized pieces. Add
them to the salad bowl.

Cut the chicory into bite-sized pieces.
Add them to the salad bowl.

Add the celery, eggs, watercress, onion
rings and tomatoes to the salad bowl. Toss
gently. Refrigerate until ready to serve.

Before serving, add the beetroot, parsley
and Rich French dressing. Toss and serve.

▼ Orange and mixed green salad

Curly Endive and Alfalfa Salad

INGREDIENTS *serves 4-6*
½ small curly endive, torn into pieces
40oz/100g alfalfa sprouts
2oz/50g small button mushrooms, thinly
    sliced
½ red pepper, sliced

DRESSING
juice 1 lemon
2tsp/10ml olive oil
1 small onion, grated
¼tsp/1.5g Chinese five spice powder

METHOD
Arrange the curly endive on a large serving
plate or 4 individual plates.

Mix the alfalfa, mushrooms and pepper
together in a bowl.

Mix the dressing ingredients together
and add to the bowl of vegetables. Toss well
and arrange on top of the lettuce.

California Waldorf Salad

INGREDIENTS *serves 6*
3½oz/90g mung bean sprouts or alfalfa
    sprouts
3 tart apples, cored and diced but not
    peeled
1lb/450g celery, chopped
½ cup/50g/2oz slivered almonds
3 large mushrooms, coarsely chopped
8fl oz/250ml Yoghurt Mayonnaise (see
    page 131)
10 lettuce leaves
3½oz/90g seedless grapes, halved

METHOD
Blanch the bean sprouts in a pan of boiling
water for 45 seconds. Drain and rinse in
cold water. Drain well again. Coarsely chop
the bean sprouts.

Put the apple, celery, almonds and
mushrooms in a large mixing bowl. Mix
well with a wooden spoon.

Add the Yoghurt Mayonnaise and mix
thoroughly.

Line a serving platter with the lettuce
leaves. Mound the bean sprouts in the
centre. Transfer the mixed ingredients to the
platter and garnish with the halved grapes.

Classic Waldorf Salad

INGREDIENTS *serves 2 - 4*
8 stalks crisp celery
2 rosy-skinned dessert apples
lemon juice
½ cup/50g/2oz walnuts
6 tbsp/90ml good mayonnaise
salt and freshly ground black pepper

METHOD
If the celery is not crisp, immerse it in ice-
cold water. It will soon freshen up. Pat dry
and slice.

Core the apples but do not peel - the pink
skin will give colour contrast to the salad.
Slice and sprinkle with lemon juice to
prevent discolouring. Toss all the
ingredients in the mayonnaise and season
well.

VARIATION
This salad also tastes good with blue cheese
dressing. Blend the mayonnaise with 1 tbsp
blue cheese before adding to the salad.

▲▲ Curly endive and alfalfa salad
▲ California Waldorf salad
▶ Waldorf salad

Greek Salad

INGREDIENTS *serves 4*
1 head crunchy lettuce, shredded
2 Mediterranean tomatoes, sliced
$\frac{1}{2}$ cucumber, thinly sliced
1 onion, coarsely chopped
handful black olives
1$\frac{1}{2}$ cup/175g/6oz feta cheese, cubed
olive oil
salt and freshly ground black pepper

METHOD
Combine the vegetables and cheese in a
large bowl. Pour over enough olive oil to just
coat the salad. Season well and toss.

Chill for an hour. Toss again, check
seasoning and serve.

Strawberry and Avocado Salad

INGREDIENTS *serves 2*
1 ripe avocado
6oz/175g strawberries
1 tbsp/15ml strawberry vinegar
1 tbsp/15ml olive oil
freshly ground black pepper

METHOD
Cut avocado in half lengthways and remove
the stone. Carefully remove the flesh from
the shell in one piece, using a metal spoon or
pallet knife. Cut each half into slices and
arrange around the edge of the serving
plate.

Hull and slice the strawberries. Pile in the
middle of the plate.

Mix together the strawberry vinegar and
olive oil and pour over salad. Season with
lots of black pepper.

▶ Greek salad

Avocado and Grapefruit Salad

INGREDIENTS *serves 6*
1 ripe avocado
2 tbsp/30ml fresh lemon juice
1 head cos lettuce
3½ cups/1½lb/700g seeded grapefruit
   segments
1 red onion, thinly sliced
1 cup/8fl oz/250ml Rich French Dressing
   (see page 128)

METHOD
Peel the avocado and cut it into slices. Put the slices in a bowl and sprinkle with the lemon juice.

Tear the lettuce into bite-sized pieces. Put the lettuce in a salad bowl. Add the grapefruit, avocado and onion to the salad bowl. Pour over the French dressing. Refrigerate for 30 minutes before serving.

Russian Radish and Cucumber Zakusky

INGREDIENTS *serves 4-6*
2 hard-boiled eggs
1 cup/8fl oz/250ml soured cream
¾ tsp/4g salt
1 tsp/5g freshly ground black pepper
3 tbsp/15g chopped fresh dill
8oz/225g radishes, thinly sliced
1 large cucumber, peeled, seeded and thinly sliced

METHOD
Remove the yolks from the eggs. Put them in a small mixing bowl and mash well with a fork. Chop the whites and set them aside.

Add the soured cream, salt, pepper and 2 tbsp of the dill to the mixing bowl. Stir until well blended.

Arrange the radishes and cucumber slices on a serving platter. Add the egg yolk and soured cream mixture. Garnish with the remaining dill and the chopped egg whites, and serve with black bread and small glasses of vodka in the Russian manner.

▼ Avocado and grapefruit salad

53

Cauliflower, Blue Cheese and Yoghurt Salad

INGREDIENTS *serves 4*
1 head cauliflower
4 tbsp/60ml yoghurt
2 tbsp/30ml blue cheese, softened
4 tbsp/20g parsley, chopped
salt and freshly ground black pepper

METHOD
Cut the cauliflower into tiny florets - reserve the stalks for use in a soup.

Cream the yoghurt and blue cheese together. Toss cauliflower and parsley in the dressing and season well.

Summer Macaroni Salad

INGREDIENTS *serves 6 - 8*
¾ cup/75ml/6fl oz mayonnaise
2 tsp/10ml Dijon-style mustard
1 tbsp/15ml white wine vinegar
¼ tsp/1.5g celery seeds
1lb/450g macaroni, cooked
3½oz/90g celery, chopped
3oz/75g raw carrots, chopped
2oz/50g radishes, sliced
3 tbsp/45g chopped pimento-stuffed
  green olives
3 tbsp/45g chopped sweet red pepper
5 tbsp/75g chopped spring onion
2 tbsp/10g chopped fresh parsley
¾ tsp/4g salt
¼ tsp/1.5g freshly ground black pepper

METHOD
Put the mayonnaise, mustard, vinegar and celery seeds in a small mixing bowl. Beat with a fork or electric beater until well blended.

Put the macaroni in a large serving bowl and add the mayonnaise mixture. Toss until the macaroni is well coated. Add the celery, carrots, radishes, olives, red peppers, spring onions and parsley. Toss well. Add the salt and pepper. Toss lightly.

Cover the bowl and chill for 1½ hours. Remove from the refrigerator and serve.

▲ ◄ Cauliflower, blue cheese and yoghurt salad
◄ Summer macaroni salad

Double Gloucester Salad

INGREDIENTS *serves 2*
4oz/100g Double Gloucester cheese
1 bunch watercress
2 handfuls young spinach leaves
2 large Mediterranean tomatoes
2oz/50g mushrooms
6-8 spring onions
2 tbsp/30ml olive oil
1 tbsp/15ml wine vinegar
1-2 tsp/5-10ml mustard powder
salt and freshly ground black pepper

METHOD
Cube the cheese. Wash the spinach and watercress, discarding stalks and any tough or yellow leaves. Immerse the tomatoes in boiling water until their skins split, then refresh with cold water, peel and roughly chop. Slice the mushrooms. Trim the spring onions; make several lengthwise cuts around each into the onion and splay out the layers in a decorative fashion.

Make the dressing by combining the oil, vinegar, mustard and seasoning.

Combine the watercress, spinach, tomatoes and mushrooms in a salad bowl, add the dressing and toss. Top with the cheese and onions.

Coleslaw

INGREDIENTS *serves 6*
1 small crisp head white cabbage
1 cup/225g/8oz carrots
2 tbsp/30ml chives, chopped
$1/3$ cup/50g/2oz sultanas
1 tbsp/15g sesame seeds
Mayonnaise (see page 128)

METHOD
Shred the cabbage finely, discarding the stalk. Grate the carrots.

Toss all the ingredients together in the Mayonnaise and mix well. Taste and adjust seasoning. Chill overnight in the fridge. Mix well again before serving.

▶ ▲ Double Gloucester salad

Middle Eastern Coleslaw

INGREDIENTS *serves 4-6*
$1^1/_2$lb/700g cabbage, coarsely shredded
2 - 3 tbsp/30-45ml salt
1 cup/250ml/8fl oz fresh orange juice
3 tbsp/45ml fresh lemon juice
$1/_4$ tsp/1.5ml sugar
$1/_2$ tsp/2.5ml honey
1 tsp/5ml hot red pepper flakes
2 tsp/10ml white wine vinegar
$1/_2$ tsp/2.5ml salt

METHOD
Put the shredded cabbage in a colander. Sprinkle the 2 to 3 tbsp of salt over the cabbage and let stand for 1 hour.

Rinse the salt from the cabbage. Drain. Wrap the cabbage in a kitchen towel and squeeze as much liquid from it as possible.

Put the orange juice, lemon juice, sugar, honey, hot red pepper flakes, vinegar and salt in a salad bowl. Stir until mixed. Add the cabbage to the salad bowl and toss well.

Potato Salad with Horseradish

INGREDIENTS *serves 4*
1½lb/700g new potatoes
⅔ cup/150ml/¼pt soured cream
3 tbsp/45ml finely grated horseradish
pinch paprika
½ tsp/2.5ml honey
salt and freshly ground black pepper
bunch spring onions or chives
handful chopped parsley

METHOD
Wash the potatoes, but do not peel. Boil in salted water until tender.

Meanwhile, make the dressing. Combine the soured cream with the horseradish, paprika and honey. Mix well and season with salt and pepper.

Trim the spring onions and slit down the stalks so that they curl outwards. Chop the chives.

When the potatoes are done, slice them while still hot and mix into the dressing with the parsley. Toss in the onions or chives. Serve immediately, or chill and serve cold.

Traditional Potato Salad

INGREDIENTS *serves 4-6*
7 medium-sized potatoes, peeled, cooked and diced
1 medium-sized onion, finely chopped
2 tbsp/30ml finely chopped pimento-stuffed green olives
8oz/225g celery, sliced
2 hard-boiled eggs, chopped
⅔ cup/175ml/6fl oz mayonnaise
2 tbsp/30ml wine vinegar
½ tsp/2.5ml salt
1 tsp/5g finely ground black pepper
2 tbsp/30ml chopped fresh parsley

METHOD
In a salad bowl, put the potatoes, onion, olives, celery and eggs. Mix lightly.

Add the mayonnaise, vinegar, salt and pepper. Toss to coat all the ingredients. Garnish with parsley and serve.

Italian Courgette Salad

INGREDIENTS *serves 4*
2 medium-sized courgettes
8 tbsp/120ml pure olive oil
3 tbsp/45ml red wine vinegar
1 spring onion, white part only, finely chopped
½ tsp/2.5ml dried basil
⅛ tsp/large pinch dried oregano
⅛ tsp/large pinch dried marjoram
1 garlic clove, crushed
¼ tsp/15g salt
2 tbsp/30ml chopped fresh parsley
½ tsp/2.5ml freshly ground black pepper

METHOD
Cook the courgettes in a pot of salted boiling water for 7 to 8 minutes. Drain well and rinse in very cold water for 5 minutes. Drain again. Slice the courgettes thinly.

Put the olive oil, vinegar, spring onion, basil, oregano, marjoram, garlic and salt in a jar with a tightly fitting lid. Cover tightly and shake until well blended.

Put the courgettes and the dressing in a salad bowl. Toss very gently. Let stand for 15 to 20 minutes. Sprinkle with parsley and pepper and serve.

German Potato Salad

INGREDIENTS *serves 6*

6 large potatoes or 2lb/900g small
 potatoes
4 whole spring onions, finely chopped
1 garlic clove, finely chopped
1 tsp/5ml drained capers
2 tbsp/30ml chopped fresh dill
2 tbsp/30ml chopped fresh parsley
1 tsp/5ml salt
1 tsp/5ml freshly ground black pepper
4 tbsp/75ml/2½fl oz pure olive oil
3 tbsp/45ml wine vinegar
1 tbsp/15ml vegetable stock (optional)
½ tsp/2.5ml sugar

METHOD

Cook the potatoes, in their skins, in a large pot of lightly salted boiling water. Drain well, peel while warm and dice. (Leave small potatoes whole and unpeeled, if you prefer.)

Put the potatoes in a salad bowl and add the spring onions, garlic, capers, dill and parsley. Toss lightly.

Into a jar with a tightly fitting lid, put the salt, pepper, olive oil, vinegar, vegetable stock and sugar. Cover and shake until blended.

Pour the dressing over the potato salad and toss lightly. Let stand at room temperature for 1½ hours before serving.

▲ ◄ Potato salad with horseradish
► German potato salad

Lentil and Feta Cheese Salad

INGREDIENTS *serves 6*
2 cups/350g/12oz brown lentils
1 bay leaf
1/2 tsp/2.5ml dried basil
2 garlic cloves, crushed
stalk celery, finely chopped
1 small onion, chopped
3 tbsp/45ml fresh chives, chopped
1 1/2 cups/175g/6oz crumbled feta cheese
6 tbsp/90ml/3fl oz virgin olive oil
3 tbsp/45ml wine vinegar
1/8 tsp/large pinch dried oregano
salt and freshly ground black pepper

METHOD

Put the lentils in a bowl. Add 3 cups/750ml/1 1/4pts cold water and soak the lentils for 2 hours. Drain.

Put the lentils in a saucepan and add enough cold water to cover them completely. Add the bay leaf, basil and 1 garlic clove. Bring to the boil and simmer, covered, for 20 minutes.

Add the celery and onion. Add enough additional water to cover the lentils. Cover the saucepan and simmer for 10 more minutes.

Drain the lentils, celery and onion and discard the bay leaf and garlic clove. Put the lentils, celery and onion in a serving bowl. Add the chives and feta cheese. Toss.

Put the olive oil, vinegar, oregano, remaining garlic clove, salt and pepper in a jar with a tightly fitting lid. Cover tightly and shake until well blended.

Pour the dressing over the lentil salad and toss. Let the salad stand for 2 hours, tossing occasionally, before serving.

Egg and Pasta Salad

INGREDIENTS *serves 4*
1 cup/225g/8oz green or wholewheat
   pasta shapes
2 tsp/10ml oil
4 eggs
1 cup/100g/4oz green beans
2 stalks celery
1 dessert apple
1/2 cup/50g/2oz walnuts
Mayonnaise (see page 128)
salt and freshly ground black pepper
1-2 tbsp/15-30ml dill
sliced chicken meat, optional

METHOD

Cook the pasta in plenty of boiling salted water, to which you have added oil, until al dente. Drain and allow to cool.

Hard boil the eggs, peel under cold running water and allow to cool. Cut into quarters.

Top and tail the beans and cut into manageable lengths. Simmer in salted water until cooked but not soft. Drain and allow to cool.

Chop the celery. Peel, core and dice the apple. Toss all the ingredients except the eggs together in the Mayonnaise. Season and garnish with eggs and dill. Meat eaters can add sliced chicken to this dish.

Haricot Bean Salad

INGREDIENTS *serves 4*
1 cup/175g/6oz dried haricot beans,
   soaked overnight
2 cloves garlic, crushed
2 tbsp/30ml wine vinegar
2 tbsp/30ml olive oil
1 tsp/5ml French mustard
salt and freshly ground black pepper
1 red pepper, seeded and thinly sliced
1 leek, thinly sliced
2 spring onions, green and white parts
   chopped separately

METHOD

Place the beans in a large saucepan and coker with fresh water. Bring to the boil and boil fast for 10 minutes, then cover and simmer for 40-50 minutes or until tender. Drain.

Combine the garlic, vinegar, olive oil, mustard and seasoning in a screw top jar, seal and shake well.

Pour over the hot beans and leave to cool. Stir in the pepper, leek and white parts of the spring onions and place in a serving dish.

Sprinkle with green chopped onions and serve.

▲ Haricot bean salad
▶ Egg and pasta salad

Ossum Salad

INGREDIENTS *serves 6*
1 cup/225g/8oz red kidney beans,
    soaked overnight
3 tbsp/45ml/Modern Vinaigrette (see
    page 128)
1 small onion, finely chopped
3 hard-boiled eggs, chopped
1 small head celery, chopped
    or 1 small cauliflower, chopped
3 tbsp/45ml brown or mustard pickle
5 anchovy fillets, chopped (optional)
²⁄₃ cup/150ml/¼pt soured cream
salt and pepper

METHOD
Bring the soaked beans to the boil in fresh
water and boil rapidly for 10 minutes, then
cook for 1 to 1½ hours, until they are tender
but not soft. Drain them and pour over the
Modern Vinaigrette and onion while they
are still warm.

When the beans are cold, add the
remaining ingredients, mixing everything
together well. Use yoghurt instead of
soured cream if preferred. Refrigerate and
serve cold.

◄ Ossum salad

Barbecue Salad

INGREDIENTS *serves 4*
3 large tomatoes, quartered
2 large sweet green peppers, seeded
    and quartered
1 sweet red pepper, seeded and
    quartered
1 large aubergine, peeled and quartered
2 large onions, halved
250ml/8fl oz Herb Dressing or Touch of
    Asia Dressing

METHOD
Thread the tomato, green pepper, red
pepper and aubergine quarters and the
onion halves on to 6 (or more) long skewers.

Lay the skewers on the barbecue grill over
white coals or place them under an oven grill
at a high heat. Cook for 12 to 15 minutes,
turning frequently.

Remove the skewers from the grill.
Remove the vegetables from the skewers.
Put the aubergine and tomato pieces in a
bowl.

While still hot, peel the skin from the
pepper pieces. Add the pieces to the salad
bowl. Coarsely chop the onions and add
them to the salad bowl. Add the dressing
and toss. Refrigerate for 30 minutes before
serving.

Kidney Bean, Chickpea (garbanzo) and Corn Salad

INGREDIENTS *serves 4*
¾ cup/175g/6oz kidney beans
¾ cup/175g/6oz chickpeas
1 cup/175g/6oz corn kernels, cooked
6 spring onions
2 very large tomatoes
Tofu Dressing (see page 128)

METHOD
Soak the kidney beans and the chickpeas
separately overnight, then simmer in water
until cooked. Drain and cool.

Chop the spring onions and slice the
tomatoes.

Toss all the ingredients in tofu dressing
and serve at room temperature with hot
pitta bread.

▲ Kidney bean, chickpea and corn salad

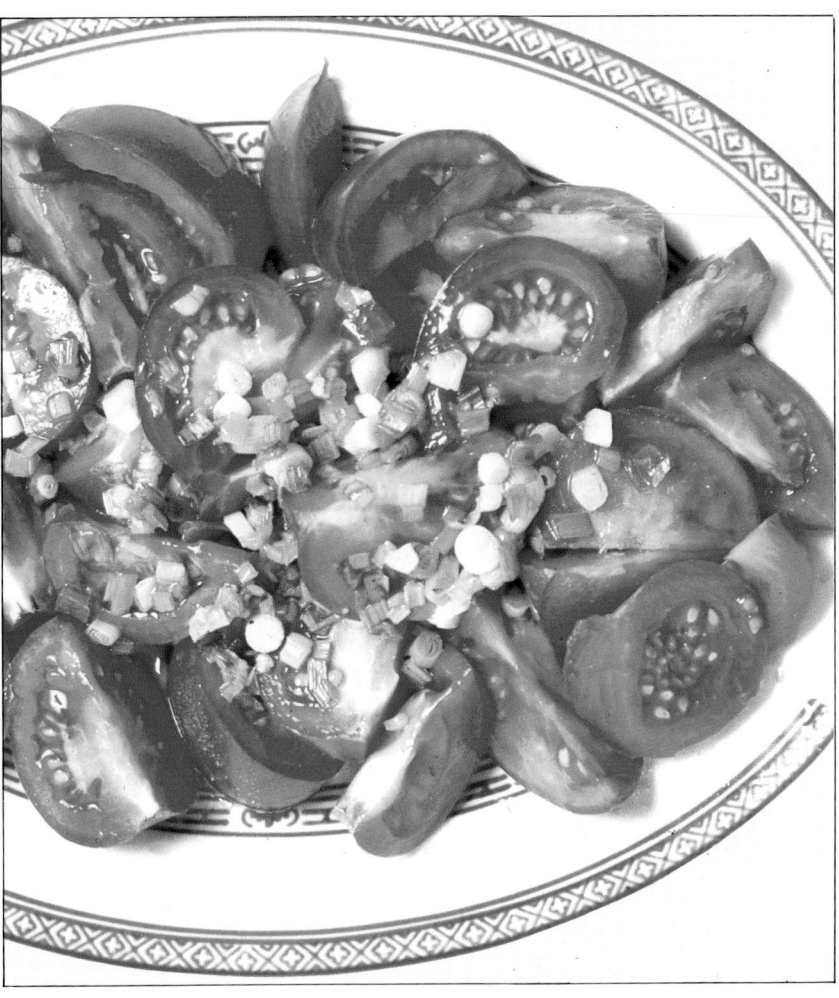

French Bean and Pepper Salad

INGREDIENTS *serves 4*
8oz/225g French beans
1 medium or 2 small red peppers, cored
and seeded
2 slices fresh ginger root, thinly
shredded
1½ tsp/8ml salt
1 tsp/5ml sugar
1 tbsp/15ml sesame seed oil

METHOD
Wash the French beans, snip off the ends
and cut into 5cm/2in lengths. Cut the red
peppers into thin shreds. Blanch them both
in boiling water and drain.

Put the French beans, red peppers and
ginger into a bowl. Add the salt, sugar and
sesame seed oil. Toss well and serve.

Tomato Salad with Spring Onion and Oil Dressing

INGREDIENTS *serves 4*
10oz/275g hard tomatoes
1 tsp/5ml salt
1 tsp/5ml sugar
3-4 spring onions, finely chopped
3 tbsp/45ml salad oil

METHOD
Wash and dry the tomatoes. Cut them into
thick slices. Sprinkle with salt and sugar.
Leave to marinate for 10-15 minutes.

Place the finely chopped spring onions in
a heat-resistant bowl. In a pan, heat the oil
until quite hot and pour over the spring
onions. Add the tomatoes, toss well and
serve.

NOTE
Other vegetables such as cucumber, celery
and green peppers can be served in the same
way.

Chinese Cabbage Salad

INGREDIENTS *serves 4*
1 small Chinese cabbage
2 tbsp/30ml light soy sauce
1 tsp/5ml salt
1 tsp/5ml sugar
1 tbsp/15ml sesame seed oil

METHOD
Wash the cabbage thoroughly, cut into thick
slices and place in a bowl.

Add the soy sauce, salt, sugar and sesame
seed oil to the cabbage. Toss well and serve.

NOTE
Green or red peppers (or both) can be added
to the cabbage.

▶ Chinese cabbage salad
◀▲ French bean and pepper salad
▲ Tomato salad with spring onion

Bean Sprout Salad

INGREDIENTS *serves 4*
1lb/450g fresh bean sprouts
1 tsp/5ml salt
10 cups/2.3l/¼pt water
2 tbsp/30ml light soy sauce
1 tbsp/15ml vinegar
2 spring onions, finely shredded

METHOD
Wash and rinse the bean sprouts in cold water, discarding the husks and other bits and pieces that float to the surface. It is not necessary to trim each sprout.

Blanch the sprouts in a pan of salted, boiling water. Pour them into a colander and rinse in cold water until cool. Drain.

Place the sprouts in a bowl or a deep dish and add the soy sauce, vinegar and sesame seed oil. Toss well and garnish with thinly shredded spring onions just before serving.

Sweet and Sour Cucumber Salad

INGREDIENTS *serves 4*
1 cucumber
2 tsp/10ml finely chopped fresh ginger root
1 tsp/5ml sesame seed oil
2 tbsp/30ml sugar
2 tbsp/30ml rice vinegar

METHOD
Select a dark green and slender cucumber; the fat pale green ones contain too much water and have far less flavour. Cut it in half lengthways, then cut each piece into slices. Marinate with the ginger and sesame seed oil for about 10-15 minutes.

Make the dressing with the sugar and vinegar in a bowl, stirring well to dissolve the sugar.

Place the cucumber slices on a plate. Just before serving, pour the sugar and vinegar dressing evenly over them and toss well.

Celery Salad

INGREDIENTS *serves 4*
1 celery
1 tsp/5ml salt
7½ cups/1.7l/⅓pt water
2 tbsp/30ml light soy sauce
1 tbsp/15ml vinegar
1 tbsp/15ml sesame seed oil
2 slices fresh ginger root, finely shredded

METHOD
Remove the leaves and outer tough stalks of the celery. Thinly slice the tender parts diagonally. Blanch them in a pan of boiling, salted water. Then pour them into a colander and rinse in cold water until cool. Drain.

Mix together the soy sauce, vinegar and sesame seed oil. Add to the celery and toss well.

Garnish the salad with finely shredded ginger root and serve.

▲ ▲ Bean sprout salad
▲ Celery Salad

► Caribbean fruit salad

Caribbean Fruit Salad

INGREDIENTS *serves 6-8*

1½ cups/225g/8oz blueberries or
   blackcurrants
2 peaches, stoned and thinly sliced
¾ cup/225g/8oz green and black
   seedless grapes, halved
1 cup/225g/8oz fresh pineapple chunks
1 cup/225g/8oz diced honeydew melon
5 tangerines, peeled, white membrane
   removed, segmented and seeded
1 cup/225g/8oz diced cantaloupe melon
1 cup/225g/8oz cubed Gruyère cheese
8oz/225g fresh dates
8fl oz/250ml Yoghurt Mayonnaise (see
   page 131)
1 tbsp/15ml honey
2 tbsp/30ml rum
2 large bananas, halved
¾ cup/90g/3½oz finely chopped
   almonds

METHOD

Arrange the blueberries, peaches, grapes, pineapple, honeydew melon, tangerines, cantaloupe melon, cheese and dates on a large platter.

In a small mixing bowl, add the honey and rum to the Yoghurt Mayonnaise and stir until well mixed. Place the dressing in a separate bowl in the centre of the platter.

Lightly roll the banana pieces in the chopped almonds and add them to the rest of the fruit. Let each guest take some fruit and dressing and toss the salad on individual plates.

South Seas Fruit Salad

INGREDIENTS *serves 6-8*

2 ripe papayas, peeled, seeded and
   cubed
2 large bananas, peeled and diced
½ cup/90ml/3½oz seedless green
   grapes, halved
1 cup/225g/8oz cubed pineapple
3 tangerines, peeled, white membrane
   removed, segmented and seeded
5 tbsp/75ml peanut oil
1 tbsp/15ml sesame oil
4 tbsp/60ml fresh lime juice
¼ tsp/1.5ml salt
2 tsp/10ml sugar

METHOD

Arrange the papaya, banana, grapes, pineapple and tangerine segments in serving bowls.

Into a blender or food processor, put the peanut oil, sesame oil, lime juice, salt and sugar. Blend until well mixed.

Pour the dressing over the salad. Cover the bowls and chill for 1 to 2 hours before serving.

Melon Salad with Ginger Sauce

INGREDIENTS *serves 6-8*
3/4 cup/175ml/6fl oz double cream
1 tsp/5ml fresh lemon juice
1 tbsp/15g/1/2oz icing sugar
1/8 tsp/large pinch cayenne pepper
3 large pieces preserved ginger, finely
    chopped
50g/2oz almonds, chopped
2 large melons of your choice, peeled,
    seeded and cubed

METHOD
Put the cream, lemon juice, sugar and
cayenne pepper in a mixing bowl. Beat or
whisk the cream until it becomes thick but
not stiff. Add the ginger and the almonds,
reserving 1 tbsp/15ml of the almonds.
Continue to beat or whisk until the cream
becomes stiff. Cover the bowl and chill until
ready to serve.

Put the melon in a serving dish and chill
until ready to serve. Just before serving, top
the melon cubes with the ginger cream.
Sprinkle the remaining almonds on top.

Persimmon Salad

INGREDIENTS *serves 4*
4 very ripe persimmons
4 crisp butter lettuce leaves
4 tbsp/60ml plain yoghurt or soured
    cream
1 tsp/5ml lemon juice
3/4 cup/100g/4oz chopped raw cashews

METHOD
Place the persimmons stem-side down on a
flat surface. Carefully cut an X into the top
surface of the skin. Gently peel the skin
away from the pulp, a little bit at a time,
about halfway down the side of the
persimmon. Keeping the skin intact, loosen
the remaining pulp from the skin with a
spoon. Place each persimmon on a lettuce
leaf.

In a small bowl combine the yoghurt and
lemon juice. Spoon equal amounts over
each persimmon and sprinkle with the
chopped nuts. Serve immediately or chill
briefly.

Pear Salad

INGREDIENTS *serves 4*
4 dessert pears
1 clove garlic, crushed
1 tsp/5ml salt
1 1/2 tsp/8ml sugar
1/2 tsp/2.5ml dried tarragon, crumbled
1/2 tsp/2.5ml dried basil, crumbled
2 1/2 tbsp/40ml red wine vinegar
2 1/2 tbsp/40ml olive oil
2 1/2 tbsp/40ml water
1 tbsp/15ml sherry
4oz/100g celery, coarsely chopped
4oz/100g green pepper, coarsely
    chopped
3 spring onions, sliced
2 large ripe tomatoes, finely chopped
4 cos lettuce leaves, chilled

METHOD
Wash the pears and refrigerate. In a bowl
mix together the garlic, salt and sugar. Add
the tarragon, basil, vinegar, oil, water and
sherry. Whisk until well blended. Transfer to
a 16oz/1/2l jar, cover, and let stand for 1 to 1 1/2
hours.

Place the celery, green pepper, spring
onions and tomatoes in a bowl. Chill for 1
hour.

Remove the vegetables and pears from
the refrigerator. Shake the dressing to mix
well. Pour half the dressing over the
vegetables and toss.

Place 1 lettuce leaf on each of 4 serving
plates. Halve and core the pears. Arrange 2
pear halves, cut-side up, on each lettuce
leaf. Top with the dressed vegetables. Spoon
the remaining dressing over the pears and
serve.

◄ Melon salad with ginger sauce

Pasta and Pancake Dishes

Tasty and filling, pasta is a much-loved favourite, from the youngest to the most sophisticated diner. Available in myriad shapes and sizes, it is exceptionally versatile and does service as first course, luncheon special, main dish or party piece. Pancakes and crepes may have had a less voluble press, but they are every bit as delectable.

Vegetarian bolognese

Asparagus Pancakes

INGREDIENTS *serves 2*

1 small clove garlic, crushed
2 tbsp/15g/½oz chopped fresh basil
    leaves
1 tbsp/25g/1oz pine kernels
3 tbsp/45ml Parmesan cheese, grated
2 tbsp/30ml olive oil
salt and freshly ground black pepper
6 tbsp/40g/1½oz plain wholewheat
    flour
2 tbsp/15g/½oz buckwheat flour
1 egg, lightly beaten
⅔ cup/150ml/¼pt skimmed milk
200g/7oz frozen asparagus spears
3 tomatoes, skinned, seeded and
    chopped

METHOD

Place the garlic, basil, pine kernels and 2 tbsp/30ml Parmesan cheese in a food processor or blender and purée. With the motor running gradually add the oil and blend to a smooth sauce. Season to taste.

Place the flours in a bowl, gradually add the egg and milk, beating well to form a smooth batter.

Heat a lightly oiled 18cm/7in heavy based frying pan. Pour in sufficient batter to thinly coat the base.

Cook for 1-2 minutes, loosen the edge, turn or toss and cook the second side. Transfer to a plate and keep hot. Repeat with the remaining batter to make 4 pancakes. Stack the pancakes with greaseproof paper between them and keep warm.

Place the asparagus in a saucepan, pour over just sufficient boiling water to cover and simmer for 6 minutes.

Divide the asparagus between the pancakes, top with sauce and fold up. Place in a shallow ovenproof dish, sprinkle with tomatoes and remaining cheese.

Place under a grill until browned.

Pancakes

INGREDIENTS *Makes 5 cups/1.1l/2 pints*

2½ cups/600ml/1pt milk
2¼ cups/225g/8oz flour
pinch salt
2 eggs
butter or oil for frying

METHOD

Mix the milk and flour together until smooth. Add the salt and eggs and beat in well.

Heat a little butter or oil in a heavy pan (preferably one used only for pancakes). Tip out excess butter.

Pour in just enough batter to coat the bottom of the pan. Fry on one side only if the pancakes are to be filled.

Mushroom Pancakes

INGREDIENTS *serves 4*

1 recipe pancakes (page 68)
2 tbsp/25g/1oz butter
1 large onion, finely chopped
4 cups/450g/1lb mushrooms, chopped
2 tbsp/25g/1oz canned red pimentos,
    finely chopped
⅔ cup/150ml/¼pt soured cream
salt and freshly ground black pepper
melted butter

METHOD

Make the pancakes and keep warm.

Melt the butter, and the onion and cook until it has softened but not browned. Add the mushrooms and cook until soft. Drain off excess liquid. Mix in the pimentos, soured cream, salt and pepper.

Put a spoonful of the mixture on to each pancake on the cooked side. Roll up the pancakes, tucking in the edges.

Place the rolled pancakes in a buttered oven dish, drizzle a little melted butter over the top. Warm through in the oven at 350°F/180°C/Gas 4 for 25 minutes.

Serve with more soured cream if desired.

▲ Asparagus pancakes
► Mushroom pancakes

Stuffed Cheese Pancakes

INGREDIENTS *serves 3-4*
⅜ cup/40g/1½oz plain untreated flour
⅜ cup/40g/1½oz wholewheat flour
pinch salt
1 egg
⅔ cup/150ml/5fl oz milk
1 tbsp/15ml melted butter

CHEESE AND HERB FILLING
2 cups/450g/1lb curd or cottage cheese
2 tbsp/30ml cream
1 fat clove garlic, crushed
2 tbsp/30ml finely chopped fresh herbs
1 tbsp/15ml chopped spring onion

METHOD
To make the pancake batter, sift the flour and salt into a bowl. Make a well in the middle of it and add the egg. Gradually beat in the milk. When half of the milk has been added, beat in the melted butter. Continue beating in the milk until you have a thin batter. Allow the batter to stand for half an hour.

Meanwhile, prepare the filling. Combine the curd cheese with the rest of the ingredients and mix well.

To make the pancakes, oil a heavy-bottomed frying pan 7in/18cm in diameter. Place it on the flame and when it is very hot, add 2 tbsp/30ml of the batter. Tilt the pan so that the batter covers the base. Cook until the pancake is beginning to brown on the underside and then turn over and cook the top. You may have to throw the first pancake away, as it will absorb the excess oil in the pan.

Continue making pancakes, keeping them warm, until all the batter is used up. Divide the filling between them, rolling the pancakes around it into a cigar shape. Arrange the stuffed pancakes in an ovenproof dish and heat in a moderate oven for about 1½ minutes.

Genoese Pasta with Pesto Sauce

INGREDIENTS *serves 4-6*
2 tbsp/25g/1oz fresh basil leaves
2 cloves garlic
pinch salt
½ cup/50g/2oz pine kernels
½ cup/50g/2oz Parmesan cheese
½ cup/100ml/4fl oz olive oil
1lb/450g spaghetti or tagletteli, cooked and drained
2 tbsp/25g/1oz butter

METHOD
Blend the basil leaves in a liquidizer. Add the crushed cloves of garlic and olive oil. Process for a few seconds.

Gradually add the pine kernels, Parmesan cheese, season remembering that Parmesan has a salty taste. The consistency should be thick and creamy.

Melt the butter in the saucepan and re-heat the cooked pasta. Remove from the heat and mix 2 tbsp/25g/1oz pesto with the pasta. Serve on individual plates with a spoonful of pesto on each helping. Parmesan can be added last.

NOTE
The pesto is never heated. It can be served at the table but make sure the pasta is hot.

Fettucini Romana

INGREDIENTS *serves 4*
1lb/450g fettucini
4 tbsp/50g/2oz butter
½ tsp/2.5ml ground nutmeg
⅔ cup/150ml/¼pt cream
salt and freshly ground black pepper
1 cup/100g/4oz Parmesan cheese

METHOD
Bring a well filled saucepan of salted water to the boil, add a few drops of oil and salt. Feed in the fettucini and cook until al dente - fresh pasta will only take about 2 minutes. Drain in a colander.

Melt the butter in the saucepan, add ground nutmeg. Pour in half the cream and stir until shiny and bubbles start to appear.

Add the fettucini and stir around in the pan. Pour in the remaining cream and cheese alternately, forking the pasta as it is mixed. Serve immediately.

NOTE
This is a real pasta-lovers' dish. To obtain best results use freshly grated Parmesan cheese rather than the commercially grated variety.

◀ Stuffed cheese pancakes
▶ Genoese pasta with pesto sauce

Aubergine and Apple Pasta

INGREDIENTS *serves 2-3*
1 large aubergine
1 large cooking apple
1 egg, beaten
seasoned untreated white flour
4 tbsp/60ml walnut oil
2 cloves garlic, crushed
1 cup/225g/8oz wholewheat or spinach
    pasta shapes
salt and freshly ground black pepper

METHOD
Slice the aubergine, sprinkle liberally with salt and leave in a colander for 30 minutes. Rinse and dry on kitchen paper and cut into strips. Peel, core and dice the apple.

Toss aubergine and apple in the beaten egg, and then in the seasoned flour to give a light coating. Heat some oil in a pan and fry aubergine, apple and garlic, stirring, until crisp.

Meanwhile, cook pasta shells in plenty of salted water at a full rolling boil, until al dente. Add a few drops of oil to the water to prevent the pasta from sticking. Drain well, season with black pepper and toss in a little walnut oil. Stir in the aubergine mixture and serve with Parmesan cheese.

Spinach Tagliatelle with Asparagus

INGREDIENTS *serves 2*
6-7 spears/225g/8oz asparagus
2 tbsp/15g/1oz butter
4 tbsp/60ml single cream
salt and freshly ground black pepper
1 cup/225g/8oz green tagliatelle
2 tsp/10ml oil
Parmesan cheese, grated

METHOD
If you are using fresh asparagus, clean it under cold running water, tie it in a bundle and stand upright in a tall saucepan containing about 3in/7cm boiling salted water. Cover with foil so that the asparagus tips cook by steaming. Alternatively, use a double boiler, inverting the inner saucepan over the bottom one. The asparagus will take 10-20 minutes to cook, depending on

its thickness. (Test by piercing half way up the stalk with a sharp knife - if you can insert the knife easily, the asparagus is done.) Drain it. Cut off and discard the woody lower pieces. Cut the asparagus into bite-sized pieces.

Melt the butter in a saucepan and toss the asparagus in it. Add half the cream, season and leave for a few minutes over a very low heat to thicken.

Meanwhile, cook the pasta until al dente in plenty of boiling salted water to which you have added 2 tsp/10ml oil.

Drain the pasta, toss in the remaining cream and pour over the asparagus sauce. Serve and offer a generous amount of Parmesan cheese.

Spinach and Ricotta Pasta

INGREDIENTS *serves 6-8*
1¼ cups/300ml/½pt Béchamel Sauce
  (page 126)
½ cup/225g/8oz (after cooking) fresh or
  frozen spinach
⅔ cup/100g/4oz ricotta cheese
½ tsp/2.5ml nutmeg
salt and freshly ground pepper
3-4 cups/500-750g/1-1½lb cooked pasta

METHOD
Make up the Béchamel sauce.

Cook the spinach for a few minutes and then drain well. Squeeze against the colander to remove the liquid.

You will need to cook approx 1½lb/750g fresh spinach to be left with the amount required by the recipe. Chop or liquidize.

Mix the ricotta with the spinach and season well, add nutmeg. Gradually stir into the Béchamel sauce and re-heat carefully over a low heat.

Serve in spoonfuls over portions of the cooked pasta.

VARIATION
This sauce is also delicious used in a vegetable or chicken lasagne.

◄▲ Aubergine and apple pasta
► Spinach and ricotta pasta

Tagliatelle with Sweet Pepper Sauce

INGREDIENTS *serves 4*
12oz/350g spinach tagliatelle noodles
2 tsp/10ml oil
½ tsp/2.5ml salt

THE SAUCE
1 small firm red pepper
1 small green pepper
1 small yellow pepper
1-2 tbsp/15-30ml olive oil
1 onion, chopped
2 cloves garlic, chopped
1½ cups/400g/15oz can tomatoes
1 tbsp/15ml tomato purée
fresh basil leaves, snipped
salt and freshly ground black pepper

METHOD
Trim and de-seed the peppers and cut into narrow strips. You can make the sauce with green peppers alone if you wish, but the red and yellow varieties are sweeter and make the dish look more colourful. Blanch the peppers for a minute in boiling salted water, refresh in cold water, then drain.

Heat the olive oil in a pan, add the garlic and onions and cook gently, stirring, until soft. Add the tomatoes, tomato purée and basil. Break up the tomatoes with a wooden spoon and simmer for about 5 minutes. Season to taste and blend the sauce in a blender. Return to the pan over a very low heat and add the peppers.

Cook the pasta in a large pan with plenty of water to which you have added a little oil and the salt. The water should be at a full rolling boil. The pasta will be ready in about 9 minutes. Drain and divide between individual warmed serving bowls.

Spoon the sauce over each helping of pasta and serve at once with Parmesan cheese.

▲ Spaghetti with Mascarpone
◀ Tagliatelle with sweet pepper sauce

Spaghetti Putanesca

INGREDIENTS *serves 4-6*
1 onion, peeled and diced
2 tbsp/30ml oil
2 cloves garlic, crushed
1 carrot, scraped and chopped
1½ cups/425g/15oz canned tomatoes
2 tomatoes, skinned and chopped
4 tbsp/60ml white wine
1 bay leaf
3-4 basil leaves or 1 tsp/15ml dried basil
salt and freshly ground pepper
1 tbsp/15ml capers, chopped
1 small can anchovies
½ cup/50g/2oz stoned black olives
3 drops Tabasco sauce
1 tbsp/15ml freshly chopped parsley
450g/1lb cooked spaghetti
grated Parmesan cheese to serve

METHOD
Put the onion into the oil in a frying saucepan over a low heat. Allow to cook gently for 4 minutes, add the crushed garlic and carrots. Turn in the oil twice more.

Add the tomatoes, the white wine, bay leaf, basil, some seasoning and 4 anchovy fillets. Bring to the boil and simmer for 30 minutes. Sieve or liquidize and return the sauce to the saucepan. Add the chopped capers, the remainder of the anchovies chopped into small pieces, chopped olives and the spicy Tabasco sauce. Re-heat and serve over the pasta, with Parmesan cheese.

Spaghetti with Mascarpone

INGREDIENTS *serves 4*
12oz/350g wholewheat spaghetti
a little oil
100g/4oz Mascarpone or cream cheese
2 egg yolks
salt and freshly ground black pepper
grated Parmesan cheese to serve

METHOD
Cook the pasta in boiling salted water, to which you have added a few drops of oil, until *al dente*.

While you are draining the spaghetti, stir the egg yolks and Mascarpone together in a large pan over a low heat.

When the sauce begins to set, toss in the spaghetti. Serve at once with plenty of black pepper and Parmesan. This dish should be accompanied by a crunchy salad.

Pasta with Mushroom Sauce

INGREDIENTS *serves 1-2*
2-4 handfuls green pasta spirals
1 tsp/15ml oil
1 cup/50g/2oz mushrooms
milk
salt and freshly ground black pepper
yolk of 1 egg
1 tbsp/15ml cream
as much parsley as you like, chopped
Parmesan cheese, grated

METHOD
Cook the pasta in plenty of boiling salted water with 1 tsp/5ml oil, until al dente.

Meanwhile, wipe and slice the mushrooms. Place in a pan with a little milk, season well and poach gently, stirring, until soft and very black and the liquid has almost gone.

Beat the egg yolk with the cream and stir in the mushrooms.

Drain the pasta and stir in the mushroom mixture with plenty of parsley. Serve at once with Parmesan and a tender lettuce salad.

Spaghetti with Fresh Tomato and Basil Sauce

INGREDIENTS *serves* 4
2 tsp/10ml olive oil
1 onion, chopped
4 stalks celery, chopped
1 green chilli, seeded and finely chopped
2 cloves garlic, crushed
2¼ cups/700g/1½lb skinned and roughly chopped tomatoes
3 tbsp/45ml tomato purée
1 tbsp/15ml basil leaves, chopped
1 tbsp/15ml marjoram, chopped
12oz/350g wholewheat spaghetti or 6oz/175g wholewheat spaghetti and 6oz/175g spaghetti verdi
⅔ cup/50g/2oz black olives, stoned
3 tbsp/25g/1oz Parmesan cheese, grated
3 tbsp/25g/1oz pine kernels
basil sprigs

METHOD
Heat the oil in a saucepan, add the onion, celery, chilli and garlic and fry until soft. Add the tomatoes and tomato purée, 4 tbsp/60ml water, half the basil and marjoram. Bring to the boil and simmer for 10 minutes.

Place the wholewheat spaghetti in a large saucepan of boiling lightly salted water and cook for 12 minutes, or until just tender. Add the spaghetti verdi, if using, 2 minutes after the wholewheat spaghetti.

Drain the pasta and divide between 4 individual warmed plates. Stir the olives and remaining basil into the sauce and place on top of the spaghetti.

Sprinkle with cheese and nuts, garnish with basil sprigs and serve.

Vegetarian Bolonese Sauce

INGREDIENTS *serves* 4-6
1¼ cups/225g/8oz brown lentils
salt and freshly ground black pepper
1 bay leaf
1-2 tbsp/15-30ml olive oil
2 cloves garlic, chopped
1 onion, chopped
1 carrot, chopped
1 stick celery, chopped
1½ cups/400g/15oz can tomatoes, mashed
1 tbsp/15ml tomato purée
½ tsp/2.5ml dried mixed herbs
2 tbsp/30ml red wine
350g/12oz wholewheat or spinach pasta

METHOD
Soak the lentils overnight and simmer in salted water with a bay leaf until they can be mashed with a fork. Drain and discard the bayleaf.

Heat the oil in a pan and fry the onions and garlic until translucent. Add the carrot and celery and cook for a further 2 minutes.

Add the tomatoes and a little juice. Add the remaining ingredients and the lentils. Simmer until the sauce is quite thick. Blend or part-blend in a blender.

Serve the sauce in healthy spoonfuls over the warmed cooked pasta.

Hot Pasta Salad

INGREDIENTS *serves* 4
2 cloves garlic
3 tbsp/45ml olive oil
handful fresh basil leaves
1 tbsp/15ml grated Parmesan cheese

THE SALAD
4oz/100g Mozzarella cheese
1lb/450g Mediterranean tomatoes
1 cup/75g/3oz black olives
salt and freshly ground black pepper

THE PASTA
12oz/350g spinach pasta twists
1 tsp/5ml olive oil

METHOD
Chop the garlic and put it in a mortar. Pour in a little of the olive oil and pound it to a pulp. Gradually add the basil leaves and cheese with the rest of the oil, pounding all the time. You should have a thick paste.

Dice the Mozzarella. Peel the tomatoes by immersing them in boiling water until their skins burst. Chop them roughly. Mix the cheese, tomatoes and olives together and season.

Cook the pasta in boiling salted water, to which you have added a little olive oil, until *al dente*. Drain. Toss the pasta in the dressing. Pile it into four warmed serving bowls and top with the salad.

▲ ◀ Spaghetti with fresh tomato and basil Sauce

MAIN COURSES

Our vegetarian main courses should appeal as much to everyday meat-eaters as to herbivore gourmets. These cosmopolitan combinations of vegetables, cheeses, herbs and spices result in dishes as full in flavour and varied in texture as any meat-, poultry- or fish-based dishes.

Potato-topped vegetable pie

Chicory Soufflé

INGREDIENTS *serves 4-6*

3 heads chicory
salt
juice 1 lemon
3 tbsp/40g/1½oz butter
⅜ cup/40g/1½oz flour
1¼ cups/300ml/10fl oz milk
½ cup/50g/2oz grated cheese
4 eggs, separated
1 tbsp/15ml dry brown breadcrumbs

METHOD

Heat the oven to 400°F/200°C/Gas 6. Trim the chicory and cook in salted water to which you have added the lemon juice. This will stop it discolouring.

When the chicory is tender, drain and set aside. When it is cool, press the water out from between the leaves with your fingers. Chop the chicory very finely.

Meanwhile, melt the butter in a heavy-bottomed pan. Stir in the flour. Remove from the heat and stir in the milk. Return from the heat and stir until the sauce has thickened. Add the cheese and cook for a further minute. Allow to cool.

When the sauce has cooled, mix in the chicory, then the egg yolks.

Whisk the whites until they form soft peaks and fold into the chicory mixture. Spoon into a greased soufflé dish and sprinkle the top with breadcrumbs.

Bake in the oven for 20-25 minutes until lightly set, well risen and golden on top. Serve this soufflé with a strongly flavoured salad, such as watercress garnished with slivers of orange.

Savoury Pumpkin Tart

INGREDIENTS *serves 4-6*
1 recipe Wholewheat Pastry (page 158)
1lb/450g pumpkin flesh
4 eggs
²⁄₃ cup/150ml/5fl oz double cream
²⁄₃ cup/150ml/5fl oz milk
2 large tomatoes, peeled and chopped
1 tbsp/15ml chopped fresh basil leaves
freshly ground black pepper

METHOD
Make the pastry as directed on page xx. Roll out and line a greased 8in/22cm quiche pan.

Pre-heat the oven to 375°F/190°C/Gas 5.

Remove rind and seeds from pumpkin and cut into slivers. Pack into a pan with very little water and cook over a low heat, covered. Check the pan occasionally to make sure the pumpkin hasn't dried out. After about 20 minutes you should be able to mash it into a purée.

Beat the eggs with the cream and milk. Mix in the pumpkin, tomato and basil and pour into the crust. Bake for 45 minutes until set and golden.

Spinach and Cheese Soufflé

INGREDIENTS *serves 4*
2 cups/450g/1lb spinach, washed and
  picked over
4 tbsp/50g/2oz butter or margarine
½ cup/50g/2oz flour
2 cups/450ml/¾pt milk
6 eggs
1⅓ cups/225g/8oz cottage cheese
grated nutmeg
salt and freshly ground black pepper
grated Parmesan (optional)

METHOD
Cook the spinach without any excess water. Drain it very well (between two plates is the most effective way).

While the spinach is cooking, melt the butter and stir in the flour off the heat. Slowly add the milk and return the pan to the heat. Stir to thicken the sauce. Remove the pan from the heat.

Separate the eggs and add the yolks, one at a time, mixing after each one. Add the cooked and drained spinach, cottage cheese, nutmeg, salt and pepper to taste. Mix everything together well.

Whisk the whites until they are very stiff. Take a scoop of the whites and fold it gently into the spinach mixture to lighten it a little and then incorporate the rest of the whites into it, mixing it in lightly. Turn the soufflé mixture into a greased soufflé dish measuring about 8¼×3½in/21×9cm. Bake at 375°F/190°C/Gas 5 for 30 minutes. Test with a clean knife to see if it is ready. If the mixture is still very runny, return the dish to the oven for a further 5 minutes or so. If you like, sprinkle some grated Parmesan on the top 10 minutes before the end of cooking.

◄▲ Chicory soufflé
► Savoury pumpkin tart

Flageolet and Sage Derby Quiche

INGREDIENTS *serves 4-6*
6oz/175g shortcrust pastry (enough for a
    single-crust pie)
4 large tomatoes
4oz/100g Sage Derby cheese
3 eggs
$^2/_3$ cup/150ml/5fl oz milk
salt and freshly ground black pepper
1 cup/175g/6oz flageolet beans, pre-
    soaked and cooked

METHOD
Pre-heat the oven to 400°F/200°C/Gas 6.
Pour boiling water over the tomatoes. After
a minute the skins will begin to split.
Refresh with cold water. Peel the tomatoes
and slice them thickly.

Line a 8in/22cm quiche pan with the
pastry and crumble the cheese into it.
Arrange the tomato slices to cover the
cheese.

Break the eggs into a bowl and lightly
beat with the milk and seasoning. Pour egg
mixture into the pie crust, gently pressing
down the tomatoes with a fork.

Bake in the centre of the oven for 15-20
minutes, until set and golden.

Onion Tart

INGREDIENTS *serves 4-6*
6oz/175g pastry (enough for a single-
    crust pie) (see page 158)
1 tbsp/15g/$^1/_2$oz butter
1 tbsp/15ml oil
$2^1/_2$ cups/550g/1lb 2oz finely chopped
    onions
2 eggs plus 1 yolk
2 cups/450ml/$^3/_4$pt single cream
1-2 heaped tbsp/15-30ml grated
    Cheddar cheese
1-2 heaped tbsp/15-30ml chopped
    parsley
salt and freshly ground black pepper
pinch of cayenne pepper

METHOD
Heat the oven to 375°F/190°C/Gas 5 and
line a 22cm/8in quiche pan with the pastry.

Heat the butter and olive oil in a pan. Stir
in the onions. Cover the pan, turn down the
heat and sweat for about 5 minutes, stirring
occasionally until soft and transparent.

Beat the eggs, cream and cheese together
and add the onions and parsley. Season with
salt, pepper and cayenne to taste, pour into
the pastry crust and bake in the middle of
the oven for 30-40 minutes until golden and
set.

VARIATION
To make an onion and blue cheese tart,
combine 1-2 tbsp crumbled blue cheese
with the cream before beating it with the
eggs. Omit the Cheddar, parsley and
cayenne pepper.

◀◀ Flageolet and Sage Derby quiche
◀ Onion tart

Leek Quiche

INGREDIENTS *serves 4-6*
pie plate 8in/20cm lined with pastry
butter
3 cups/450g/1lb leeks, trimmed and
    chopped
1 large onion, chopped
1⅓ cups/225g/8oz cottage cheese
3 eggs
salt and freshly ground pepper
a pinch of ground allspice

METHOD
Bake the pastry case for 10 minutes at
350°F/180°C/Gas 4.

Heat the butter and soften the leeks and
onion in it for 5 minutes. Mix the cottage
cheese with the remaining ingredients.

Cover the bottom of the lined pie plate
with the cooked leeks and onions. Spoon
over the cottage cheese mixture. Bake at
350°F/180°C/Gas 4 for 35 minutes. Serve
hot or at room temperature.

Green Pea Tarts with Poached Eggs

INGREDIENTS *makes 8 tarts*
8oz/250g shortcrust pastry (enough for
    a single-crust pie)
2lb/900g dried marrowfat peas, pre-
    soaked and cooked
4 tbsp/50g/2oz butter
salt and freshly ground black pepper
8 eggs

THE TOMATO SAUCE
1-2 tbsp/15-30ml olive oil
1 onion, chopped
2 cloves garlic, chopped
1¾ cups/425g/15oz can tomatoes
1 tbsp/15ml tomato purée
2 tsp/10ml dried oregano
salt and freshly ground black pepper

METHOD
Pre-heat the oven to 400°F/200°C/Gas 6.
Roll out the pastry and line eight greased
fluted tartlet pans. Prick with a fork and
bake blind for 20 minutes until golden.
Remove tart crusts from the oven and turn
the heat down to 350°F/180°C/Gas 4.

In the meantime, make the tomato sauce.
Heat the oil in a pan and add the onion and
garlic. Cook until soft. Add the tomatoes,
tomato purée, oregano and seasoning.
Simmer for 5 minutes, then blend in a
blender and keep hot.

Cook the peas until mushy, then drain
and purée them in a blender. Heat the butter
in a pan and stir in the pea purée. Season
well with salt and plenty of black pepper.
Divide the pea purée among the tart cases.

Poach the eggs until just set. Lift them
carefully into the tart crusts and return to
the oven for 2-3 minutes. Don't let the eggs
harden. Serve each tart with a spoonful of
tomato sauce.

◀ Green pea tarts with poached eggs
▶ Spinach roulade

Nut Loaf

INGREDIENTS *serves 4*
1 cup/175g/6oz mixed nuts, chopped
1 small aubergine
olive oil
1 large onion, finely chopped
2 cloves garlic, chopped
³/₄ cup/175g/6oz brown rice, cooked
³/₄ cup/200g/7oz can tomatoes, drained
   and mashed
salt and freshly ground black pepper
2 eggs, beaten

METHOD
Pre-heat the oven to 375°F/190°C/Gas 5. Put the nuts on a baking sheet and toast them at the top of the oven for 10 minutes.

Slice the aubergine, sprinkle with salt and leave for 20 minutes. Rinse off the salt, pat dry and dice.

Heat 1-2 tbsp oil in a pan. Add the onion and garlic and fry till translucent. Add the aubergine and cook, stirring occasionally, for about 10 minutes. Add more oil as necessary.

Transfer the aubergine mixture to a large bowl and stir in the nuts, brown rice and tomatoes. Mix well and season to taste. Stir in the beaten egg.

Pour into a greased small loaf pan and smooth the top. Bake in the centre of the oven for 35 minutes until firm. Turn out of the pan and cut into slices to serve.

Spinach Roulade

INGREDIENTS *serves 6-8*
3 cups/700g/1½lb fresh spinach, washed
   and picked over
1 tbsp/15g/½oz butter
4 eggs, separated
grated nutmeg
salt and freshly ground black pepper
³/₄ cup/100g/4oz curd cheese
²/₃ cup/150ml/¼pt soured cream
4 spring onions, finely chopped

METHOD
Cook the spinach without any excess water. Drain the spinach very well (press it between two plates for most effective drainage) and when all the liquid has been removed, either chop the spinach very finely or blend it just enough to chop it.

Add the butter, egg yolks, grated nutmeg and salt and pepper to taste. Mix together very well.

Whisk the egg whites until they are stiff. Fold a spoonful of the beaten whites into the spinach mixture to lighten it and then fold in the remaining whites. Mix through carefully.

Turn the mixture on to a Swiss roll tin 15×10in/38×25cm which has been lined with greased proof paper or foil. Bake at 400°F/200°C/Gas 6 for 10 minutes only.

While the spinach is cooking, mix the curd cheese with the soured cream and green onions. Season to taste. Have a clean tea towel spread on a board and when the spinach mixture is cooked, turn it upside down on to the tea towel. Carefully peel off the paper. Spread the cheese and soured cream mixture over the spinach base, taking care not to tear the surface. Using the tea towel to help you, roll the spinach up into a roll and on to a serving plate. Serve immediately.

NOTE
Although this is usually served hot, in fact it is very good cold.

Mushroom and Broccoli Nut Loaf

INGREDIENTS *serves 6*
3/4 cup/50g/2oz sliced button
 mushrooms
2 tbsp/25g/1oz polyunsaturated
 margarine
2 stalks celery, chopped
1 clove garlic, crushed
1 onion, grated
1 tbsp/15ml wholemeal flour
1 1/2 cups/400g/15oz can chopped
 tomatoes
2 cups/100g/4oz wholemeal
 breadcrumbs
1 cup/100g/4oz ground walnuts
1 egg
1 tsp/5ml fresh basil, chopped
1 tsp/5ml fresh oregano, chopped
1 tbsp/15ml parsley, chopped
salt and freshly ground black pepper
4oz/100g broccoli spears, cooked

SAUCE
1 cup/50g/2oz chopped mushrooms
3 tbsp/20g/3/4oz wholemeal flour
1/2 cup/120ml/4fl oz vegetable stock
1/2 cup/120ml/4fl oz skimmed milk
celery leaves

METHOD
Sauté the mushroom slices in a frying pan
with 1 tbsp/15g/1/2oz margarine, drain and
place in a line down the centre of a lightly
greased 2pt/1.1l loaf tin.

Cook the celery, garlic and onion in the
pan until softened.

Stir in the flour and tomatoes and stir
until thickened.

Add the breadcrumbs, nuts, egg, herbs
and seasoning. Place half in the tin. Add the
broccoli spears and top with the remaining
mixture.

Cover with foil, place in a roasting pan
filled with boiling water and cook at 350°F/
180°C/Gas 4 for 1 1/4-1 1/2 hours.

Melt the remaining margarine, add the
chopped mushrooms and cook for 2-3
minutes. Stir in the flour, and cook for 1
minute.

Add the stock, milk and seasoning and
stir until boiled.

Turn out the loaf, garnish with celery
leaves and serve with the sauce separately.

Summer Vegetable Pasties

INGREDIENTS *makes 4*
1 recipe Wholewheat Pastry (page 158)
beaten egg to glaze

FILLING
1 cup/100g/4oz potatoes, diced
4 baby carrots, sliced
1/4 cup/50g/2oz garden peas
2 baby courgettes, sliced
2 stalks celery, sliced
1/2 green pepper, diced

CHEESE SAUCE
2 tbsp/25g/1oz butter
4 tbsp/25g/1oz untreated (unbleached)
 white flour
up to 1 1/4 cups/300ml/1/2pt milk
1/2 cup/50g/2oz Cheddar cheese, grated
salt and freshly ground black pepper

METHOD
Make the pastry. Pre-heat the oven to
350°F/180°C/Gas 4.

Boil the potatoes and carrots in salted
water until just tender. In another pan, boil
the remaining vegetables for about 2
minutes. Drain.

To make the cheese sauce, melt the butter
in a heavy-bottomed pan, stir in the flour
and gradually add half the milk, stirring.
Add the cheese. Stir until melted. Add a
little more milk and season to taste. Don't
make the sauce too thin or it will pour out of
the pastry shells. Mix sauce into vegetables
to coat them generously.

Divide the pastry into 4 balls and roll out.
Share the mixture between the pastry
rounds. Crimp together to form pasties and
brush with beaten egg. Put the pasties on a
baking tray and bake in the oven for 30
minutes or until the pastry is cooked.

Lentil and Vegetable Patties or Balls

INGREDIENTS *serves 4*
1 cup/225g/8oz lentils
2½-4 cups/600-900ml/1-1½ pts stock
1-1½ tbsp/15-25ml oil
1 small onion, chopped
1 clove garlic, chopped
½ cup/50g/2oz potato
¼ cup/50g/2oz peas
½ tbsp/7.5ml fresh thyme leaves
salt and freshly ground black pepper
beaten egg for binding
wholewheat flour for coating
parsley to garnish

METHOD
Soak the lentils for 4 hours and simmer in vegetable stock, or meat stock if preferred, until they can be mashed with a fork. If you use a mild stock, add a little yeast extract to give a sharper taste. Drain the lentils.

Heat the oil and fry the onion and garlic until transparent. Boil the potatoes in salted water until cooked, adding the peas just before the end of cooking time. Drain.

Put all the vegetables through a mill or mincer. Mix in the thyme and season to taste. Stir in enough egg to make a sticky dough. Form dough into small patties or balls about 1½in/3cm in diameter.

Roll the balls in wholewheat flour and shallow fry in hot oil until crispy on all sides. Garnish with parsley and serve with Hot Tomato Sauce (see page 127) and puréed spinach or marrow in a cheese sauce.

◄▲ Mushroom and broccoli nut loaf
◄ Summer vegetable pasties
► Lentil and vegetable patties

85

Sabzi Vegetable Cutlet

INGREDIENTS *serves 4-6*
1 cup/100g/4oz beetroot, diced
1 cup/100g/4oz carrots, diced
2 cups/225g/8oz potatoes, diced
1½ cups/100g/4oz cabbage, shredded
½ tsp/2.5ml chilli powder
½ tsp/2.5ml ground roasted cumin
salt and freshly ground black pepper
Large pinch sugar
1 tbsp/15ml raisins (optional)
½ cup/50g/2oz flour
½ cup/120ml/4oz milk
breadcrumbs
oil for deep frying

METHOD
Boil the beetroot, carrots, potatoes and cabbage together until tender. Drain.

Mash the boiled vegetables with the chilli, roasted cumin, black pepper, salt, sugar and raisins. Divide into 12 balls and flatten. Chill for 1 hour.

Make a batter with the flour and milk and dip a cutlet in it. Then roll it in breadcrumbs until well coated.

Heat the oil in a large frying pan and fry the cutlets for 2-3 minutes turning once, until crisp and golden. Serve with coriander chutney (see page 134).

Azuki Bean Burgers

INGREDIENTS *serves 4*
1 cup/450g/8oz azuki beans
bay leaf
2 onions, chopped
3 cloves garlic, chopped
1-2 tbsp/15-30ml oil
4 carrots, peeled and grated
juice 1 lemon
4 tbsp/60ml parsley, chopped
salt and freshly ground black pepper
soy sauce to taste
beaten egg for binding
wholewheat flour for coating

METHOD
Soak the azuki beans overnight. Drain, then cook until tender in fresh water with a bay leaf added. Drain, reserving the liquid.

Fry the onion and garlic in oil until transparent. Add the carrot and lemon juice and sweat, covered, until soft.

Add the beans, mix well and purée in a blender, adding a little of the bean liquor if necessary to form a malleable consistency. Stir in the parsley, season and add soy sauce to taste. Stir in enough beaten egg to bind.

Form into balls or burgers, coat with flour and shallow fry until brown and crispy on the outside. Serve with homemade Marinara Sauce (page 127).

▶ Azuki bean burgers
▼ Sabzi vegetable cutlets

Spinach Ring

INGREDIENTS *serves 4*
2lb/900g spinach
6 tbsp/45g/3oz butter
$\frac{1}{2}$ cup/50g/2oz untreated plain flour
1$\frac{1}{4}$ cups/300ml/$\frac{1}{2}$pt milk
$\frac{1}{3}$ cup/50g/2oz Parmesan cheese
salt and freshly ground black pepper
3 eggs

TOMATO SAUCE
1-2 tbsp/15-30ml oil
1 onion, finely chopped
2 cloves garlic, crushed
1$\frac{1}{4}$ cups/425g/15oz can tomatoes,
    mashed
1 tbsp/15ml tomato purée
salt and freshly ground black pepper

METHOD
Pre-heat the oven to 375°F/190°C/Gas 5.
Grease a 7$\frac{1}{2}$ cups/1.7l/3pt ring mould.

Wash the spinach and discard tough
stalks. Pack spinach into a large pan with 2
tbsp/15g/1oz butter and seasoning and
cover tightly. Cook over a low heat for about
5 minutes, stirring occasionally, until
spinach is soft. Drain and purée in a blender.

Now make the cheese sauce. Melt the rest
of the butter in a heavy-bottomed pan and
add the flour, stirring. Gradually add the
milk, stirring continuously. Stir in the cheese
and season. Stir until sauce bubbles and
thickens, then turn down heat and cook for
a further minute. Mix thoroughly with the
spinach.

Separate the eggs. Beat the yolks into the
spinach mixture. Whisk the whites until
soft peaks have formed and fold into
mixture. Pour mixture into ring mould and
bake for 30-40 minutes until risen and
lightly set.

Meanwhile, make the tomato sauce.
Heat the oil in a frying pan and add the
onion and garlic. Fry, stirring, until
transparent. Add the tomatoes, reserving
the juice. Add the tomato paste and season.
Simmer for 5 minutes, adding more juice
and adjusting seasoning as necessary.

To turn out the spinach ring, dip mould
into ice-cold water for a few seconds. Run a
knife blade round edges of mould. Invert on
to a warmed plate. Spoon over the tomato
sauce and serve with wholewheat bread.

Chinese Eight Treasures

INGREDIENTS *serves 4*
15g/$\frac{1}{2}$oz dried bean curd skin sticks
$\frac{1}{3}$ cup/15g/$\frac{1}{2}$oz dried tiger lily buds
3-4 tbsp/15g/$\frac{1}{2}$oz dried wood ears
$\frac{1}{3}$oz/10g dried black moss
2oz/50g bamboo shoots
2oz/50g lotus root
2oz/50g straw mushrooms
2oz/50g cashews or almonds
4 tbsp/60ml oil
1$\frac{1}{2}$ tsp/7.5ml salt
1 tsp/5ml sugar
1 tbsp/15ml light soy sauce
1 tsp/5ml cornflour mixed with 1 tbsp/
    15ml cold water
2 tsp/10ml sesame seed oil

METHOD
Soak the dried vegetables separately in cold
water overnight or in warm water for at least
1 hour. Cut the bean curd sticks into short
lengths.

Cut the bamboo shoots and lotus root
into small slices. The straw mushrooms and
white nuts can be left whole.

Heat a wok or large frying-pan. When it
is hot, put in about half of the oil and wait
until it smokes. Stir-fry all the dried
vegetables together with a little salt for
about 1 minute. Remove and set aside.

Add and heat the remaining oil and stir-
fry the rest of the vegetables and the
remaining salt for about 1 minute. Add the
partly cooked dried vegetables, the sugar
and soy sauce, stirring constantly. If the
contents start to dry out, pour in a little
water. When the vegetables are cooked, add
the cornflour and water mixture to thicken
the gravy. Garnish with the sesame seed oil
just before serving. This dish can be served
hot or cold.

▶ Chinese eight treasures

▼ Spinach ring

Stir-Fried Mixed Vegetables

INGREDIENTS *serves 4*
4oz/100g Chinese cabbage
4oz/100g carrots
4oz/100g mange-tout
5-6 dried Chinese mushrooms
3 tbsp/45ml oil
1 tsp/5ml salt
1 tsp/5ml sugar
1 tsp/5ml water

METHOD
Soak the dried mushrooms in warm water for 25-30 minutes. Squeeze them dry, discard the hard stalks and cut into thin slices. Trim the mange-tout peas and cut the Chinese cabbage and carrots into slices.

Heat the oil in a pre-heated wok. Add the Chinese cabbage, carrots, mange-tout peas and dried mushroom and stir-fry for about 1 minute. Add the salt and sugar and stir for another minute or so with a little more water if necessary. Do not overcook or the vegetables will lose their crunchiness. Serve hot.

Chinese Mixed Vegetable Casserole

INGREDIENTS *serves 4-6*
2 tbsp/10g/^{1}/$_3$oz dried wood ears
1 cake bean curd
4oz/100g French beans or mange-tout
4oz/100g cabbage or broccoli
4oz/100g baby corn or bamboo shoots
4oz/100g carrots
3-4 tbsp/45-60ml oil
1 tsp/5ml salt
1 tsp/5ml sugar
1 tbsp/15ml light soy sauce
1 tsp/5ml cornflour mixed with 1 tbsp/
   15ml cold water

METHOD
Soak the wood ears in water for 20-25 minutes, rinse and discard the hard roots.

Cut the bean curd into about 12 small pieces and harden the pieces in a pot of lightly salted boiling water for 2-3 minutes. Remove and drain.

Trim the French beans or mange-tout.

Cut the vegetables into thin slices or chunks.

Heat about half of the oil in a flameproof casserole or saucepan. When hot, lightly brown the bean curd on both sides. Remove with a slotted spoon and set aside.

Heat the remaining oil and stir-fry the rest of the vegetables for about 1½ minutes. Add the bean curd pieces, salt, sugar and soy sauce and continue stirring to blend everything well. Cover, reduce the heat and simmer for 2-3 minutes.

Mix the cornflour with water to make a smooth paste, pour it over the vegetables and stir. Increase the heat to high just long enough to thicken the gravy. Serve hot.

Vegetarian Chop Suey

INGREDIENTS *serves 4-6*
2 cakes of bean curd
2 tbsp/10g/^{1}/$_3$oz wood ears, dried
6oz/175g broccoli or mange-tout
6oz/175g bamboo shoots
4oz/100g mushrooms
4-5 tbsp/60-75ml oil
1½ tsp/7.5ml salt
1 tsp/5ml sugar
1-2 spring onions, finely chopped
1 tbsp/15ml light soy sauce
2 tbsp/30ml rice wine or dry sherry
1 tsp/5ml cornflour mixed with 1 tbsp/
   15ml cold water

METHOD
Cut the bean curd into about 24 small pieces. Soak the wood ears in water for about 20-25 minutes, rinse them clean and discard any hard roots.

Cut the broccoli and bamboo shoots into uniformly small pieces.

Heat a wok over a high heat, add about half of the oil and wait for it to smoke. Swirl the pan so that its surface is well greased. Add the bean curd pieces and shallow-fry them on both sides until golden, then scoop out with a slotted spoon and set them aside.

Heat the remaining oil and add the broccoli. Stir for about 30 seconds and then add the wood ears, bamboo shoots and the partly cooked bean curd. Continue stirring for 1 minute and then add the salt, sugar, spring onions, soy sauce and wine. Blend well and when the gravy starts to boil, thicken it with the cornflour and water mixture. Serve hot.

◄▲ Stir-fried mixed vegetables
◄ Chinese mixed vegetable casserole

▲ Vegetarian chop suey

Chinese Three Precious Jewels

INGREDIENTS *serves 4*
2 cakes bean curd
8oz/225g broccoli or mange-tout
8oz/225g carrots
4 tbsp/60ml oil
1 tsp/5ml salt
1 tsp/5ml sugar
1 tbsp/15ml light soy sauce
1 tbsp/15ml rice wine or dry sherry

METHOD
Cut the bean curd into small pieces. Cut the broccoli into florets. Peel the stems and cut diagonally into small pieces. Peel the carrots and cut diagonally into small chunks.

Heat about half of the oil in a hot wok or frying-pan. Add the bean curd pieces and shallow-fry on both sides until golden. Remove and keep aside.

Heat the rest of the oil. When very hot, stir-fry the broccoli and carrots for about 1-1½ minutes. Add the bean curd, salt, sugar, wine and soy sauce and continue stirring, adding a little water if necessary. Cook for 2-3 minutes if you like the broccoli and carrots to be crunchy. If not, cook another minute or two. This dish is best served hot.

Sichuan Bean Curd Casserole

INGREDIENTS *serves 4*
2 tbsp/10g/¼oz dried wood ears or
    dried Chinese mushrooms
3 cakes bean curd
1-2 leeks or 2-3 spring onions
3 tbsp/45ml oil
1 tsp/5ml salted black beans
1 tbsp/15ml chilli bean paste
2 tbsp/30ml rice wine or dry sherry
1 tbsp/15ml light soy sauce
1 tsp/5ml cornflour mixed with 1 tbsp
    cold water
Sichuan pepper, freshly ground to garnish

METHOD
Soak the wood ears in water for 20-25 minutes, rinse them clean, discard any hard roots and then drain. If you use dried mushrooms, they should be soaked in hot or warm water for at least 30-35 minutes. Squeeze them dry, throw out the hard stalks and cut into small pieces, retaining the water for later use.

Cut the bean curd into ½in/1cm square cubes. Blanch them in a pan of boiling water for 2-3 minutes, remove and drain.

Cut the leeks or spring onions into short lengths.

Heat the oil in a hot wok until it smokes and stir-fry the leeks or spring onions and the wood ears or mushrooms for about 1 minute. Add the salted black beans, crush them with the scooper or spatula and blend well.

Now add the bean curd, the chilli bean paste, rice wine or sherry and soy sauce and continue stirring to blend. Add a little water and cook for 3-4 minutes more. Finally add the cornflour and water mixture to thicken the gravy.

Serve hot with freshly ground Sichuan pepper as garnish.

▲ Sichuan bean curd casserole
▶ Chinese three precious jewels

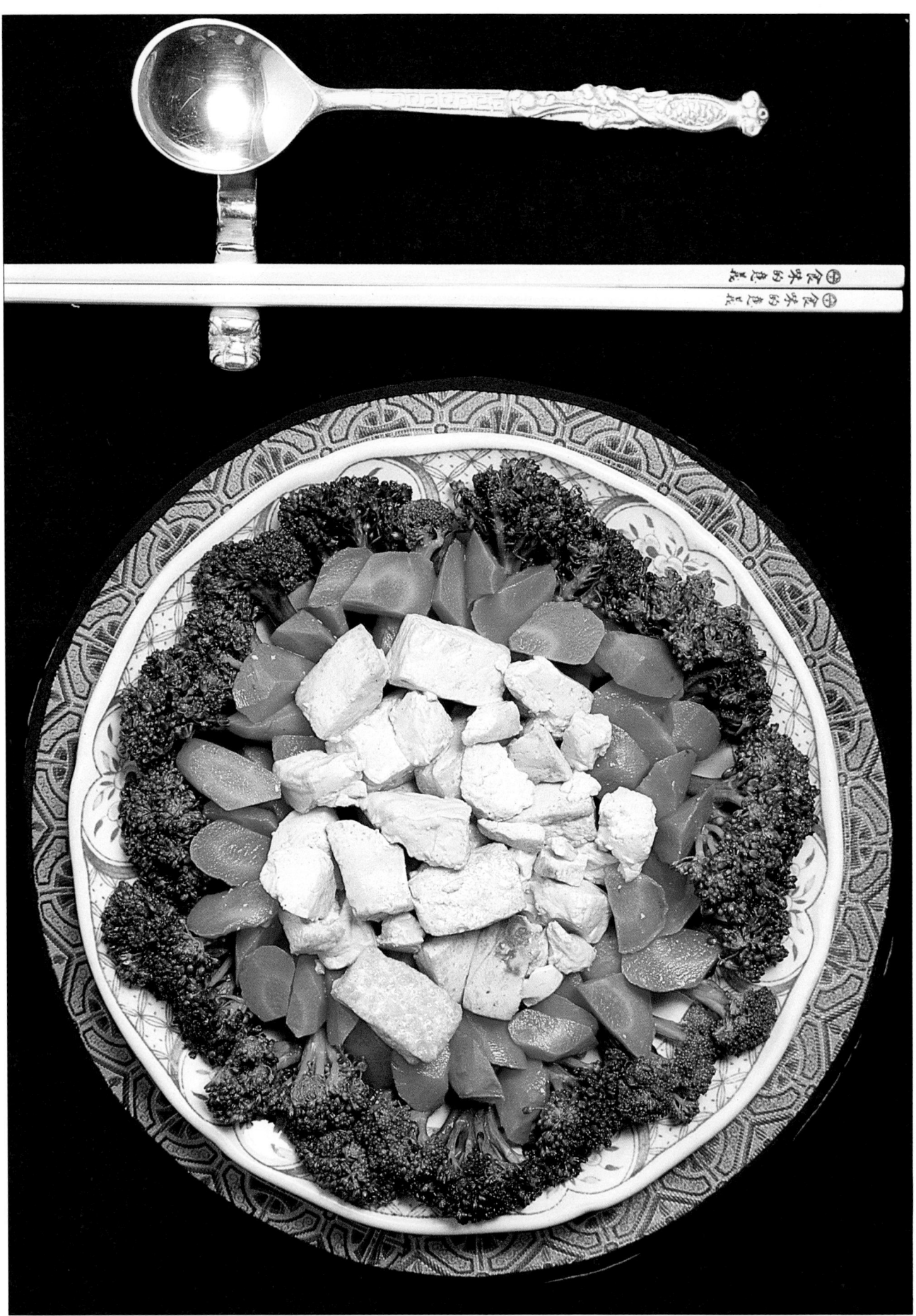

Kidney Bean, Artichoke and Mushroom Casserole

INGREDIENTS *serves 4*
1 cup/225g/8oz kidney beans
1-2 tbsp/15-30ml oil
1 large onion, chopped
1-2 cloves garlic, chopped
3 cups/175g/6oz mushrooms, sliced
1 cup/100g/4oz French beans, trimmed, cut in thirds and parboiled
1¾ cups/425g/15oz can artichoke hearts, drained
1¾ cups/425g/15oz can tomatoes, mashed
salt and freshly ground black pepper
parsley

METHOD
Soak the kidney beans overnight and cook until tender.

Pre-heat the oven to 350°F/180°C/Gas 4. Heat oil and fry onion and garlic until translucent. Add the mushrooms and stir-fry for 1-2 minutes until just soft.

Transfer all the ingredients to a casserole. Season well. Cover and bake for 30-40 minutes. Sprinkle with parsley and serve.

Bean Moussaka

INGREDIENTS *serves 4*
1 cup/225g/8oz rose cocoa beans
1 large aubergine, thinly sliced
oil
1 large onion, chopped
2 cloves garlic, chopped
1¾ cups/425g/15oz can tomatoes, mashed
1 tbsp/15ml tomato purée
2 tsp/10ml fresh thyme, chopped
salt and freshly ground black pepper

CHEESE SAUCE
2 tbsp/25g/1oz butter
4 tbsp/25g/1oz flour
1¼ cups/300ml/½pt milk
½ cup/50g/2oz grated Cheddar cheese
grated nutmeg to taste
salt and freshly ground black pepper

METHOD
Soak the beans overnight and cook until you can mash them with a fork. Drain.

Heat the oven to 350°F/180°C/Gas 4. Sprinkle the aubergine slices with salt and allow to stand in a colander for 30 minutes. Rinse and pat dry with kitchen paper. Heat some oil in a pan and fry aubergines gently until cooked. Set aside.

Add some more oil to the pan and fry the onion and garlic until translucent. Add the tomatoes, tomato purée, thyme and seasoning, and heat through, stirring. Mix in the beans. Set aside.

To make the cheese sauce, melt the butter in a thick-bottomed saucepan. Stir in the flour, then gradually add the milk, stirring all the time, until the sauce bubbles and thickens. Turn down the heat, add the cheese and stir till melted. Season with nutmeg and add salt and pepper to taste.

To assemble the dish, spread a layer of the bean mixture in the bottom of a casserole and top with aubergine slices. Spread thinly with cheese sauce. Continue to layer the ingredients until they are all used up, ending with a thick layer of the sauce. Bake in the oven to heat right through for 30-40 minutes and serve with a crisp green salad.

▶ Vegetable couscous
▼ Kidney bean, artichoke and mushroom casserole

Vegetable Couscous

INGREDIENTS *serves 4-6*
¾-1 cup/100-175g/4-6oz couscous
1 tsp salt
1¼ cups/300ml/½pt boiling water
3 tbsp/40g/1½oz butter

VEGETABLE TOPPING
1 tbsp/15ml oil
2 large onions, chopped
2 leeks, sliced
4 carrots, sliced
5 cups/1l/1½pts stock
salt and freshly ground black pepper
4 courgettes, sliced
6 tomatoes, sliced
½ cup/100g/4 oz peas
¾ cup/100g/4oz kidney beans, pre-
    soaked and cooked
¾ cup/100g/4oz chickpeas, pre-soaked
    and cooked
a few strands of saffron

HOT TOMATO SAUCE
Make this in advance (see page 127).

METHOD
Put the couscous in a bowl, add the salt and
pour over the boiling water. Let it soak for
20 minutes until the water has been
absorbed. Break up any grain that is sticking
together.

Meanwhile, make the vegetable topping.
Heat the oil in a large saucepan and stir-fry
the onions and leeks. Add the carrots and
stock and season well. Bring to the boil.

Place the couscous in a vegetable steamer
(or a sieve or colander) lined with muslin,
and put this over the saucepan. Put on the
lid and simmer for 30 minutes.

Remove the steamer and add the
remaining vegetables and the saffron to the
stock. Stir the couscous with a fork to break
up any lumps. Replace steamer, covered,
and continue cooking for 10 minutes.

Turn couscous into a bowl and stir in the
butter. Serve vegetables separately in a
tureen. Set the table with soup plates,
knives, forks and spoons and offer Hot
Tomato Sauce and pitta bread (page 151).

Curried Vegetables

INGREDIENTS *serves 4*
8oz/225g aubergine, cut in chunks
2 tbsp/30ml oil
¼ cup/50g/2oz cashew nuts
1 medium onion, chopped
1 clove garlic, crushed
2tsp/10ml curry powder
1 large potato, peeled and half cooked
4oz/100g green beans, trimmed
⅔ cup/150ml/¼pt water
4oz/100g tomatoes, quartered
1 tbsp/15ml garam masala
⅔ cup/150ml/¼pt yoghurt
2tsp cornstarch
1 tbsp water
salt

METHOD
Salt the aubergine and leave for 30 minutes.
Rinse and pat dry.

Heat the oil and fry the cashews to a
golden brown. Remove them from the pan
and put them to one side.

Stir the onions and garlic into the pan and
cook until they begin to soften. Add the
curry powder and stir in. Add the aubergine
and cook on a low heat for about 5 minutes,
stirring from time to time. Add a little more
oil if necessary.

Add the half cooked potato, cut into
large chunks, together with the green beans.
Pour on the water, cover and leave to cook
until the potatoes are ready.

Add the tomatoes and the garam masala,
stir round carefully and continue cooking
for a few more minutes.

Mix the cornstarch with the water to a
smooth paste, stir into the contents of the
pan and warm through for 3 minutes.

Serve hot, with the browned cashew nuts
sprinkled on top.

Paprika Mushrooms

INGREDIENTS *serves 4*
butter or margarine
1 medium onion, finely chopped
$\frac{1}{2}$ green pepper, finely chopped
1 tbsp/15ml paprika
6 cups/350g/12oz mushrooms, sliced
$\frac{2}{3}$ cup/150ml/$\frac{1}{4}$pt soured cream
salt and freshly ground black pepper
chopped parsley

METHOD
Heat the butter, add the onion and cook until it has just softened but not browned.

Add the green pepper and paprika and cook on a low heat for 3 minutes. Add the mushrooms, stir well and cook for a further 5 minutes until they are soft.

Stir in the soured cream, season to taste and warm through gently.

Serve, sprinkled with parsley, as on hors d'œuvre with hot French bread, as a filling for vol-au-vent, on fried bread or with a crisp salad.

▲ ▶ Savoury stuffed vine leaves
▶ Bulghar wheat stuffed peppers
◀ Paprika mushrooms

Savoury Stuffed Vine Leaves

INGREDIENTS *serves 4*
1 cup/225g/8oz brown rice
olive oil
1 small onion, chopped
2 cloves garlic, chopped
salt and freshly ground black pepper
8oz/225g peeled bottled or canned
    chestnuts
1-2 tbsp/15-30ml butter
4oz/100g mushrooms
2 tomatoes, peeled and chopped
1tsp/5ml dried mixed herbs
20 vine leaves

METHOD
Wash the rice in several changes of cold water. Heat 1 tbsp/15ml oil in a heavy-bottomed pan and fry the onion and garlic until translucent. Stir in the rice and cook for a few minutes before covering with boiling water. (Use about ²⁄₃ water to ¹⁄₃ rice by volume.) Bring back to the boil, then cover the pan and turn the heat down very low. The rice should be cooked in about 40 minutes.

Meanwhile, drain the chestnuts and chop them finely. Heat the butter in a pan and add the mushrooms. When they are tender, add the tomatoes, chestnuts and herbs. Stir once or twice and remove from the heat.

When the rice is cooked, mix it thoroughly with the nut stuffing and check the seasoning. Use it, by the spoonful, to stuff the vine leaves. Pack them into an ovenproof dish, brush with olive oil and cover the dish with foil. Heat through in the oven. Stuffed vine leaves are best eaten hot, but they're good cold too, if you have any left over.

Bulghar Wheat Stuffed Peppers

INGREDIENTS *serves 4*
5oz/150g bulghar wheat
2 red peppers, cut in half lengthways
    and seeded
2 yellow peppers, cut in half lengthways
    and seeded
1 tbsp/15ml sunflower oil
1 onion, chopped
¹⁄₂ cup/50g/2oz chopped hazelnuts
²⁄₃ cup/75g/3oz chopped dried apricots
¹⁄₂tsp/2.5ml powdered ginger
1tsp/5ml cardamon seeds, ground
2 tbsp/30ml coriander leaves, finely
    chopped
3 tbsp/45ml natural yoghurt
fresh coriander leaves

METHOD
Place the bulghar wheat in a bowl, pour over 1¹⁄₄ cups/300ml/¹⁄₂pt boiling water and leave to stand for 15 minutes.

Place the peppers in a shallow, lightly oiled ovenproof dish.

Place the remaining oil in a saucepan, add the onion and gently fry until softened.

Stir in the bulghar wheat, hazelnuts, apricots, ginger and cardamon. Cook for 1 minute, stirring continuously.

Add the coriander and yoghurt, mix together and use to fill the pepper shells. Cover the dish tightly with aluminium foil and bake in a pre-heated oven at 375°F/190°C/Gas 5 for 30-35 minutes.

Serve immediately, garnished with coriander leaves.

Potato Topped Vegetable Pie

INGREDIENTS *serves 4-6*
½ cup/75g/3oz green lentils
¼ cup/50g/2oz pot barley
1 onion, chopped
1¾ cups/425ml/15oz can chopped
    tomatoes
6oz/175g cauliflower florets
2 stalks celery, sliced
1 leek, thickly sliced
1 turnip, sliced
2 carrots, diced
2 tbsp/30ml fresh mixed herbs, chopped
1½lb/750g potatoes, scrubbed
3 tbsp/45ml semi-skimmed milk
salt and freshly ground black pepper
2 tbsp/25g/1oz grated reduced fat
    medium hard cheese

METHOD
Place the lentils, barley, onion, tomatoes, cauliflower, celery, leek, turnip, carrots and herbs in a large saucepan with 1¼ cups/300ml/½pt water.

Bring to the boil, cover and simmer for 40-45 minutes or until everything is soft.

Cover potatoes with boiling water and cook for about 15 minutes, or until soft.

Drain, peel and mash the potatoes with the milk and season to taste.

Place the lentil mix in a pie dish and either pipe or fork the potato on top.

Sprinkle with cheese and place in a pre-heated oven at 400°F/200°C/Gas 6 for 30-35 minutes.

Omelette Archie Williams

INGREDIENTS *serves 2*
½ cup/100g/4oz smoked cod or
    haddock
⅔ cup/150ml/¼pt milk
2 tbsp/15g/1oz butter
4 tbsp/15g/1oz flour
⅓ cup/40g/1½oz grated Cheddar cheese
3 eggs
salt and freshly ground black pepper

METHOD
Poach the fish in a little of the milk until cooked. Drain and reserve milk. Skin and flake fish.

Melt the butter in a pan and stir in the flour. Gradually stir in the milk, including the milk from the fish, until you have a smooth sauce. Add the cheese and stir until melted.

Beat the eggs and season well.

Put the fish in a shallow ovenproof dish about 8in/22cm across. Cover with cheese sauce, then pour over the beaten eggs. Cook under a pre-heated grill set at high for about 7 minutes until the egg is nearly set and the omelette is beginning to brown on top. Serve with salad. This omelette will make a light lunch for 2 people.

Avocado Soufflé Omelette

INGREDIENTS *serves 2*
1 green pepper
3 tbsp/40g/1½oz butter
1 ripe avocado
dash lemon juice
4 eggs, separated
salt and freshly ground black pepper

METHOD
De-seed and slice the green pepper. Heat a little of the butter in a pan and fry gently until soft. Set aside.

Cut the avocado in half. Remove the stone and remove the flesh from the shell in one careful movement with a palette knife. Slice the avocado and sprinkle with lemon juice.

Beat the egg yolks and season with salt and pepper. Whisk the whites and fold the two together.

Heat half the remaining butter in a pan and pour in half the omelette mixture. Arrange half the avocado and green pepper on one side of it. When lightly set, fold the omelette in two, slide out of the pan and keep hot until you have made the second omelette in the same way.

◄▲ Omelette Archie Williams
▲ Avocado soufflé omelette
► Mushroom omelette surprise

Mushroom Omelette Surprise

INGREDIENTS *serves 2*
4oz/100g mushrooms
about ²⁄₃ cup/150ml/5fl oz milk
1 tbsp/15ml butter
1 tbsp/5ml flour
1 tbsp/15ml grated Parmesan cheese
salt and freshly ground black pepper
4 eggs, separated

METHOD
Peel or wipe the mushrooms and slice. Put them in a small, heavy-bottomed pan with a little of the milk and poach gently until very black and juicy. Remove the mushrooms with a slotted spoon and arrange them in the bottom of a shallow greased heatproof dish about 7in/18cm in diameter.

Make a cheese sauce. Heat the butter in a pan and when it has melted, add the flour. Stir well and remove from the heat. Add the milk that the mushrooms have been cooked in and stir in enough extra milk (you may need a little more than ²⁄₃ cup/150ml/5fl oz) to make a thick sauce. Stir in the cheese and season well.

Beat the yolks into the cheese sauce. Whisk the whites until they form soft peaks and fold into the sauce.

Pour the mixture over the mushrooms and cook under a pre-heated grill until the omelette is nearly set and golden on top.

Fried 'Pocketed Eggs'

INGREDIENTS *serves 4*
4 eggs
2-3 tbsp/30-45ml oil
1 tbsp/15ml light soy sauce
1 spring onion, finely chopped

METHOD
Heat the oil in a hot wok or frying pan and fry the eggs on both sides. Add the soy sauce and a little water and braise for 1-2 minutes. Ganish with spring onion and serve hot.

Taking a bite of the egg and finding the yolk inside the white is rather like finding something in a pocket - hence the name of this dish.

Chinese Scrambled Eggs and Tomatoes

INGREDIENTS *serves 4*
9oz/250g hard tomatoes
5 eggs
1½ tsp/7.5ml salt
2 spring onions, finely chopped
1 tsp/5g finely chopped ginger root
   (optional)
4 tbsp/60ml oil

METHOD
Scald the tomatoes in a bowl of boiling water and peel off the skins. Cut each tomato in half lengthways and then crosscut each half into wedges.

Beat the eggs with a pinch of salt and about a third of the finely chopped spring onions.

Heat about half the oil in a hot wok or frying pan and lightly scramble the eggs over a moderate heat until set. Remove the eggs from the wok.

Heat the wok again over high heat and add the remaining oil. When the oil is hot, add the rest of the finely chopped spring onions, the ginger root (if used) and the tomatoes. Stir a few times and then add the scrambled eggs with the remaining salt. Stir for 1 minute more and serve hot.

NOTE
Other vegetables such as cucumber, green peppers or green peas can be substituted for the tomatoes.

Fu-Yung Bean Curd (Tofu)

INGREDIENTS *serves 4*
1 cake bean curd
4 egg whites
1 Cos lettuce heart
⅓ cup/50g/2oz green peas
1 spring onion, finely chopped
½ tsp/2.5ml grated ginger root
1 tsp/5g salt
1 tbsp/15g cornflour mixed with 2 tbsp/
   30ml water
⅓ cup/60ml/2fl oz milk
oil for deep-frying
1 tsp/5ml sesame seed oil

METHOD
Cut the bean curd into long, thin strips and blanch in a pan of salted boiling water to harden. Remove and drain.

Lightly beat the egg whites. Add the cornflour mixture and milk.

Wash and separate the lettuce heart. If you use frozen peas, make sure they are thoroughly defrosted.

Wait for the bean curd to cook and then coat with the egg whites, cornflour and milk mixture.

Heat the oil in a wok or deep-fryer until it is very hot. Turn off the heat and let the oil cool a bit before adding the bean curd coated with the egg whites and cornflour mixture. Cook for about 1-1½ minutes and then scoop out with a slotted spoon and drain.

Pour off the excess oil leaving about 1 tbsp in the wok. Increase the heat and stir-fry the lettuce heart with a pinch of salt. Remove and set aside on a serving dish.

Heat another tbsp of oil in the wok and add the finely chopped spring onion and ginger root followed by the peas, salt and a little water. When the mixture starts to boil, add the bean curd strips. Blend well, add the sesame oil, and serve on the lettuce heart.

▲ Fu-yung bean curd

▶ Chinese scrambled eggs and tomatoes

Leek and Stilton Bake

INGREDIENTS *serves 4*
1lb/450g small leeks
6 eggs
1 slice wholewheat bread, crumbed
2 tbsp/30ml cider vinegar
4oz/100g Stilton cheese

METHOD
Pre-heat the oven to 400°F/200°C/Gas 6.
Trim and wash the leeks. Steam for 10-15
minutes. Lay them in a greased ovenproof
dish.

Beat the eggs with the vinegar and
breadcrumbs and crumble in the Stilton.
Pour over the leeks and bake for 30 minutes
until risen and golden.

Eggs with Curly Kale

INGREDIENTS *serves 2-4*
1lb/450g curly kale
4 eggs
2tbsp/25g/1oz butter
¼ cup/25g/1oz plain untreated flour
1¼ cups/300ml/10fl oz milk
½ cup/50g/2oz Cheddar cheese, grated
salt and freshly ground black pepper

METHOD
Wash the kale and discard the stalks. Pack
into a saucepan with a very little water,
cover and cook slowly for about 20 minutes
until tender. Drain and cut up roughly with a
knife and fork. Put the kale in the bottom of

a heatproof serving dish and keep warm.
Soft-boil the eggs.

Meanwhile, make the cheese sauce. Melt
the butter in a pan and stir in the flour.
Cook, stirring for a few minutes. Gradually
add the milk. Continue to stir until the
sauce has thickened. Add the cheese. When
it melts, season.

Plunge the eggs in cold water and remove
the shells. Lay them on the bed of kale and
cover with the sauce. Heat the dish through
in the oven or under the grill.

Cheese Strudel

INGREDIENTS *serves 4*
12oz/350g packet puff pastry
1½ cups/175g/6oz grated Cheddar
    cheese
⅔ cup/100g/4oz cream cheese
⅔ cup/100g/4oz curd cheese
1 egg
chopped parsley or mint
salt and freshly ground black pepper
egg white for glazing

METHOD
Roll the pastry out as thinly as possible.

Mix the remaining ingredients except the
egg white until smooth. Spread the mixture
over the pastry.

Fold over to make a flattish strip, sealing
the edges well. Brush with the egg white.
Place on a moistened baking sheet and bake
at 400°F/200°C/Gas 6 for 20 minutes.

Serve hot, with soured cream if liked.

Broccoli and Tomato Cheesecake

INGREDIENTS *serves 4-6*
1 cup/100g/4oz wholewheat biscuit
    (cracker) crumbs
4tbsp/50g/2oz butter, softened

THE FILLING
8oz/250g broccoli florets
1 large tomato
1½ cups/350g/12oz curd cheese
salt and freshly ground white pepper
pinch nutmeg
2 eggs, separated

THE TOPPING
broccoli florets
a little gelatine, if liked

METHOD
Pre-heat the oven to 350°F/180°C//Gas 4.
Combine the crumbs and the butter and
press down well into a greased 8in/22cm
quiche pan with a loose bottom.

Steam the broccoli florets over boiling
salted water until tender. Carefully slice
some of the florets for decorating and
reserve the rest. Immerse the tomato in
boiling water for a minute, refresh in cold
water, peel and de-seed.

Mash the curd cheese with the broccoli
and tomato and season well with salt,
pepper and a good pinch of nutmeg. Beat in
the egg yolks.

Whisk the whites until they form soft
peaks and fold into the mixture. Pour the
filling over the crumb base and bake for
about 20-25 minutes until slightly risen and
just set.

Allow to cool. When cold, remove the
sides of the tin and decorate the top with the
remaining broccoli florets. Brush with
gelatine if you like and chill before serving.

◀▲ Leek and Stilton bake
▶ Cheese strudel

Savoury Cheesecake

INGREDIENTS *serves 4-6*
either a crumb base or a pie-shell
   shortcrust pastry case (8in/20cm)
butter
1 large onion, sliced
4 eggs
1⅓ cups/225g/8oz curd cheese
1⅓ cups/225g/8oz cream cheese
chopped chives
salt and freshly ground black pepper

METHOD
Put the pastry into the springform tin. Heat the butter, add the onion and cook until it has just softened but not browned.

Beat the eggs until they are very light and fluffy. Mix the cheeses with the cooked onion, chives, salt and pepper. Carefully fold the cheese mixture into the beaten eggs and spoon this into the prepared pie shell.

Bake at 350°F/180°C/Gas 4 for 40 minutes.

Serve cold (preferably the next day) with a crisp salad. This freezes very well. Leeks make a tasty addition with the onions, softened in a little butter.

Vegetable and Rice Hotch Potch

INGREDIENTS *serves 6*
oil
3 cups/350g/12oz onions, sliced
1 cup/225g/8oz rice
1 large green or red pepper, chopped
salt and freshly ground black pepper
1 tsp/5ml paprika
1¾ cups/425g/14oz canned tomatoes
⅔ cup/150ml/¼pt water
2½ cups/600ml/1pt yoghurt
4 eggs

METHOD
Heat the oil, add the onions and cook until they have just softened but not browned.

Add the rice and peppers and stir them round to colour them a little. Season well with salt, pepper and paprika.

Layer the rice mixture with the tomatoes in an ovenproof dish. Pour over a mixture of 4 tbsp/60ml oil and the water.

Cover and cook at 375°F/190°C/Gas 5 for 30 minutes (or on top of a medium heat).

Mix the yoghurt with the eggs. Pour over the vegetables and return the dish, uncovered, to the oven for a further 20 minutes.

VARIATION
This Bulgarian dish adapts to endless variations - add some more vegetables, such as aubergines, courgettes, mushrooms, fennel. Or salami, sausages or cooked meat can be added before the yoghurt topping.

▲ Vegetable and rice hotch potch

VEGETABLE AND RICE SIDE DISHES

Just as in non-vegetarian cookery, there are some dishes that satisfy as main courses and others which serve best as complements. They round out our enjoyment of a meal and fulfill nutritive requirements. Potatoes, rice and bean recipes, and a wide selection of green and root vegetables take to the table in styles Continental, Indian, Oriental and good old British.

Three peppers in tomato and garlic

Courgettes with Almonds

INGREDIENTS *serves 4*
6 large/700g/1½lb courgettes, sliced
   lengthways
1 medium onion, finely chopped
1 tbsp/15ml olive oil
salt and freshly ground black pepper
⅓ cup/50g/2oz flaked almonds
1 tsp/5ml cornstarch
1 tbsp/15ml water
1 cup/250ml/8fl oz yoghurt

METHOD
Place the courgettes in a shallow ovenproof
dish. Mix the onions, oil, salt and pepper
and spoon the mixture over the courgettes.
Bake uncovered at 350°F/180°C/Gas 4 for
40 minutes, or until tender.

Meanwhile toast the almonds: put them
into a heavy frying pan over a high heat and
shake the pan frequently; don't burn.

Mix the cornstarch with the water and
add it to the yoghurt with seasoning to taste.

Warm the mixture over a gentle heat,
stirring constantly, for 3 minutes.

Spoon it over the courgettes and scatter
the almonds on top.

Courgette Gratin

INGREDIENTS *serves 4*
oil
4 large/450g/1lb courgettes, sliced
1 large onion, chopped
1¾ cups/425g/15oz canned tomatoes
chopped basil, thyme or marjoram
sliver lemon peel
salt and freshly ground black pepper
1 cup/225g/8oz macaroni
2 eggs
⅔ cup/150ml/¼pt yoghurt
¾ cup/75g/3oz grated Cheddar cheese

METHOD
Heat the oil and fry the courgettes until they
are lightly coloured. Remove them from the
pan and reserve. Add the onion and fry until
golden, adding more oil if necessary. Add
the tomatoes, herbs, lemon peel, salt and
pepper and simmer for 10 minutes,
breaking up the tomatoes and stirring from
time to time.

Meanwhile, cook the macaroni and
drain it well. Put it into an ovenproof dish.

Pour the sauce over the macaroni and mix
it through well. Lay the cooked courgettes
on top. Mix the eggs, yoghurt and half the
cheese and pour the mixture over the
courgettes. Scatter the remaining cheese on
top.

Bake the dish at 375°F/190°C/Gas 5 for
30 minutes.

VARIATION
You could use aubergines instead of
courgettes, in which case slice and salt
them, leave them to drain for 20 minutes,
rinse and dry them and proceed as above.

▼ Courgette gratin

Courgettes with Dill

INGREDIENTS *serves 4*
1/4 cup/60ml/2fl oz olive oil
2 tbsp/25g/1oz butter
1 onion, chopped
1 garlic, crushed
450g/1lb courgettes topped, tailed and
    sliced in thickish rounds
salt and freshly ground black pepper
2 tsp/10ml paprika
1 tbsp/15ml dill, chopped (not the
    stalks)
1 small tub soured cream

METHOD
Heat oil and butter in a large frying pan.
Cook the onion and garlic gently until soft.
Turn up the heat.

Add the courgettes, garlic and black
pepper and toss.

Cook for 5-10 minutes, stirring to cook
both sides of the courgette slices.

When browning, add the paprika, dill
and soured cream. Season and serve.

▲ Courgettes with dill
► Chilli beans

Magyar Marrow or Squash

INGREDIENTS *serves 4*
1 medium to large marrow
2 tbsp/25g/1oz butter
2 tsp/10ml cornflour
1 tbsp/15ml water
1 tbsp/15ml dried dill weed
salt and freshly ground black pepper
2/3 cup/150ml/1/4pt soured cream

METHOD
Peel the marrow and either finely chop or
grate it. Cook the marrow with the butter,
stirring from time to time, just until it begins
to soften. Mix the cornflour with the water
until smooth and add it to the marrow. Stir
and cook for a further 3 minutes. Add the
dill, salt and pepper and finally stir in the
soured cream. Warm it through gently and
serve the marrow hot.

Chilli Beans

INGREDIENTS *serves 4*
1 cup/175g/6oz rose cocoa beans
2 tbsp/30ml olive oil
1/2 tsp/2.5g fennel seeds
1/2 tsp/2.5g mustard seeds
1 onion, chopped
2 cloves garlic, chopped
1 3/4 cup/100g/4oz sliced mushrooms
1/2 fresh green chilli, de-seeded and
    chopped
1 3/4 cups/425g/15oz can tomatoes,
    mashed
2 tbsp/30ml chopped fresh coriander or
    parsley
salt and freshly ground black pepper

METHOD
Soak the beans overnight and cook them in
salted water until tender. Cooking time will
vary depending on the age of the beans.
They could be ready in 20 minutes, or they
may take an hour, so keep testing.

Meanwhile, heat the oil in a pan and,
when hot, add the seeds. As soon as the
mustard seeds begin to pop, add the onion
and garlic. Cook gently until translucent.

Stir in the mushrooms. When they are
tender, add the chilli and tomatoes,
coriander and seasoning. If you can't get
coriander, use parsley instead, but the dish
will certainly lose some of its character.

Add the beans, heat through for 10
minutes and serve with toasted rarebit or an
omelette for a warming winter supper.

Stuffed Marrow or Squash

INGREDIENTS *serves 4-6*
1 marrow
salt and freshly ground black pepper
⅓ cup/75g/3oz brown rice
2 small carrots, diced
¼ cup/50g/2oz peas
1-2 tbsp/15-30ml oil
1 onion, chopped
1 clove garlic, chopped
1 stalk celery, chopped
1 handful parsley, chopped
2 tbsp hazelnuts, chopped

TOMATO SAUCE
1-2 tbsp/15-30ml oil
1 onion, chopped
2 cloves garlic, chopped
1¾ cups/425g/15oz can tomatoes, mashed
1 tbsp/15ml tomato purée
salt and freshly ground black pepper

METHOD
Pre-heat the oven to 350°F/180°C/Gas 4. Cut the marrow in half lengthways and scoop out the pith and seeds. Sprinkle the flesh with salt and leave the halves upside down to drain.

Meanwhile, make the filling. Simmer the rice in a covered pan of salted water until just tender (about 30 minutes). Drain.

Parboil carrots and peas and drain. Heat oil in a pan and fry onion and garlic until translucent. Add celery, carrots and peas. Stir in the rice, parsley and hazelnuts and season well. Dry the marrow and pile filling into one half of it. Top with second half.

Make the tomato sauce. Heat oil in a pan and add onion and garlic. Fry, stirring, until soft. Add tomatoes and tomato purée. Simmer for 5 minutes stirring occasionally, and season well.

Place marrow in a baking dish with a lid, if you have one big enough, otherwise use foil to cover. Surround it with the sauce. Cover and cook for 45 minutes until marrow is tender. Serve hot or cold with a crisp green salad.

Creamed Spinach

INGREDIENTS *serves 4*
3 cups/700g/1½lb fresh spinach, washed and picked over
1 egg yolk
grated nutmeg
salt and freshly ground black pepper
⅔ cup/150ml/¼pt yoghurt

METHOD
Cook the spinach without any excess water (the water adhering to it is sufficient) and a little salt. Drain the cooked spinach very well (press it between two plates for most effective drainage).

Whisk together the egg yolk, nutmeg and seasoning to taste, and yoghurt. Mix into the spinach. Warm through gently.

NOTE
If you prefer to use frozen spinach, use leaf, not chopped spinach.

Roasted Aubergine

INGREDIENTS *serves 4*
1 large aubergine
1 small onion, finely chopped
1-2 green chillis, finely chopped
½ tsp/2.5ml salt
2-3 tbsp/30-45ml mustard oil

METHOD
Place the aubergine under a pre-heated grill for about 15 minutes, turning frequently, until the skin becomes black and the flesh soft.

Peel the skin and mash the flesh.

Add the rest of the ingredients to the mashed aubergine and mix thoroughly.

La Lechuga

INGREDIENTS *serves 4*

1 tight head crisp lettuce, iceberg for
  preference
4 tbsp/60ml olive oil
4 cloves garlic, finely chopped

METHOD

Discard looser outer leaves of lettuce. With
a very sharp knife, cut lettuce in half from
stalk to tip. Cut each half into thirds. Keep
cold.

Heat oil in frying pan and when hot, add
garlic. Fry, stirring, until brown. Pour over
the lettuce and serve immediately. This is
best eaten with the fingers if you don't mind
the mess. Offer plenty of paper napkins.
Lettuce served this way makes an unusual
and appetising start to a summer meal.

Spicy Aubergine

INGREDIENTS *serves 4*

1lb/450g aubergines
3 tbsp/45ml oil
1 large onion, finely chopped
3 tomatoes, chopped
1 tbsp/15ml coriander leaves, chopped
1-2 green chillis, chopped
$\frac{1}{2}$ tsp/2.5ml ground turmeric
$\frac{1}{2}$ tsp/2.5ml chilli powder
$\frac{3}{4}$ tsp/4ml ground coriander
$\frac{3}{4}$ tsp/4ml salt

METHOD

Place the aubergines under a pre-heated grill
for about 15 minutes, turning frequently
until the skin turns black and the flesh soft.
Peel off the skin and mash the flesh.

Heat the oil in a karai over medium heat
and fry the onions until soft. Add the
tomatoes, coriander leaves and green chillis
and fry another 2-3 minutes.

Add the mashed aubergine, turmeric,
chilli, coriander and salt and stir.

Fry for another 10-12 minutes and serve
with Naan or Baktora (page 155).

◄▲ Stuffed marrow
▲► La lechuga
► Spicy aubergine

Caraway Cabbage

INGREDIENTS *serves 4*
2 tbsp/25g/1oz butter
9 cups/700g/1½lb finely sliced white or
   green cabbage
1 tbsp/15ml caraway seeds
salt and freshly ground black pepper
2 tsp/10ml flour
⅔ cup/150ml/¼pt soured cream

METHOD
Melt the butter and add the cabbage. Stir
well. Add the caraway seeds, salt and
pepper, cover and cook until the cabbage is
cooked but still crisp.

   Add the flour and stir it in well. Cook for
a further 2 minutes, stirring constantly. Add
the soured cream and warm it through.

Cabbage with Peas

INGREDIENTS *serves 4*
3 tbsp/45ml oil
2 bay leaves
¾ tsp/4ml whole cumin seeds
9 cups/700g/1½lb finely shredded
   cabbage
1 tsp/5ml ground turmeric
½ tsp/2.5ml chilli powder
1½ tsp/7.5ml ground cumin
1 tsp/5ml ground coriander
2 tomatoes, chopped
¾ tsp/4ml salt
½ tsp/2.5ml sugar
½ cup/100g/4oz peas

METHOD
Heat the oil in a karai over medium high
heat and add the bay leaves and the cumin
seeds. Let them sizzle for a few seconds.

   Add the cabbage and stir for 2-3 minutes.
Add the turmeric, chilli, cumin, coriander,
tomatoes, salt and sugar and mix with the
cabbage.

   Lower heat, cover and cook for 15
minutes. Add the peas and cover again.
Continue to cook for a further 15 minutes,
stirring occasionally.

   Remove the cover, turn heat up to
medium high and, stirring continuously,
cook until it is dry.

Shredded Carrot and Cabbage

INGREDIENTS *serves 4*
2 tbsp/30ml oil
1 tsp/5ml mustard seeds
1 tight head spring greens, finely
   shredded
1lb/450g carrots, grated
a little honey
salt and freshly ground black pepper

METHOD
Heat oil in a heavy pan with a lid. When it is
hot, add the mustard seeds.

   As soon as the mustard seeds begin to
pop, pile in the shredded vegetables, drizzle
over the honey and stir well. Turn down the
heat, put on the lid and cook for 3 minutes or
until just tender. Season and serve.

▲ ▲ Caraway cabbage
▲ Shredded carrot and cabbage

Brussels Sprouts with Garlic and Mushrooms

INGREDIENTS *serves 4*
2-3 tbsp/30-45ml oil
4 cloves garlic, chopped
1lb/450g Brussels sprouts, thinly sliced
1¼ cups/100g/4oz mushrooms, sliced

METHOD
Heat some oil in a wok or deep-sided frying pan. Add the garlic and fry quickly, stirring, until crisp and brown.

Add the sprouts and mushrooms and stir until coated with garlic and oil. Stir-fry for 1-2 minutes and eat while crisp and hot. A delicious accompaniment to bean dishes.

Cauliflower with Potatoes and Peas

INGREDIENTS *serves 4-6*
4 tbsp/60ml oil
2 medium onions, finely chopped
4 cups/450g/1lb diced potatoes in ¾in/
    2cm pieces
1 small cauliflower, cut into ¾in/2cm
    pieces
½ tsp/2.5ml ground turmeric
⅓ tsp/3ml chilli powder
1 tsp/5ml ground cumin
2 tomatoes, chopped
1 tsp/5ml salt
¼ tsp/1.5ml sugar
1 cup/200g/7oz peas
½ tsp/2.5ml Garam Masala (see Sauces
    and Dressings, page 126)

METHOD
Heat the oil in a karai over medium high heat. Add the onions and fry for 3-4 minutes until light brown.

Add the potatoes and cauliflower and stir. Add the spices, tomatoes, salt and sugar. Stir and fry for 2-3 minutes.

Add the peas, cover and lower heat to medium low and cook for about 20 minutes until the potatoes and cauliflower are tender. Stir the vegetables a few times to stop them sticking. Sprinkle with Garam Masala before serving.

▲ ► Carrots with yoghurt
◄ Cauliflower with potatoes and peas

Carrots with Yoghurt

INGREDIENTS *serves 4-6*
3½ cups/450g/1lb carrots, sliced
1 tsp/5ml sugar
½ tsp/2.5ml ground cumin
1 small onion, finely chopped
juice ½ lemon
⅔ cup/150ml/¼pt yoghurt
salt and pepper

METHOD
Cook the carrots with the sugar in boiling water just until they are al dente. Drain them and add the cumin and onion. Stir around.

Mix the lemon juice into the yoghurt, season to taste and spoon it over the carrots.

Serve immediately or leave it to cool and serve as a salad or an accompaniment to curry.

French Beans with Baby Corn

INGREDIENTS *serves 4-6*
8oz/225g French beans
8oz/225g baby corn
3-4 tbsp/45-60ml oil
1½ tsp/7.5ml salt
1 tsp/5ml sugar
2 tbsp/30ml water

METHOD
Wash and trim the beans. Depending on the size of the baby corns, leave them whole if small, or cut them into two or three diamond-shaped pieces if larger.

Heat a wok or large frying pan over a high heat until very hot, add the oil and swirl it so that the cooking surface is well greased. When the oil starts to smoke, add the French beans and baby corn and stir-fry for about 1 minute.

Add the salt and sugar and continue stirring for another minute or so. Add the water if the vegetables dry out before they are cooked.

Serve as soon as all the liquid has evaporated. If you prefer your vegetables slightly underdone, serve when there is still a little juice left in the wok.

Stir-Fried Asparagus

INGREDIENTS *serves 4*
1lb/450ml asparagus
2 tbsp/30ml oil
1 tsp/5ml salt
1 tsp/5ml sugar

METHOD
Wash the asparagus well in cold water and discard the tough end of the stalk. Cut the tender part of the shoots into 1in/2.5cm lengths, using the roll-cutting method: make a diagonal slice through the stalk, then roll it half a turn and slice again, so that you end up with diamond-shaped slices.

Heat the oil in a very hot wok or frying pan, swirling it to grease the pan well. Add the asparagus when the oil starts smoking. Stir-fry until each piece is coated with oil.

Add salt and sugar and continue stirring for 1-1½ minutes only. No extra liquid should be added because it would spoil the colour and texture.

This dish can be served either hot or cold.

▲ French beans with baby corn
◀ Stir-fried asparagus

113

Hot and Sour Cabbage

INGREDIENTS *serves 6*
1½lb/700g white cabbage
10 Sichuan peppercorns
5 small dried red chilli peppers
2 tbsp/30ml soy sauce
1½ tbsp/22.5ml vinegar
1½ tbsp/22.5ml sugar
1½ tsp/7.5ml salt
3 tbsp/45ml sunflower oil
1 tsp/15ml sesame seed oil

METHOD
Choose a round, pale green cabbage with a firm heart - never use looseleafed cabbage. Wash in cold water and cut the leaves into small pieces the size of a matchbox.

Cut the chillis into small bits. Mix the soy sauce, vinegar, sugar and salt to make the sauce.

Heat the sunflower oil in a pre-heated wok until it starts to smoke. Add the peppercorns and the red chillis and a few seconds later the cabbage. Stir for about 1½ minutes until it starts to go limp.

Pour in the prepared sauce and continue stirring for a short while to allow the sauce to blend in. Add the sesame seed oil just before serving.

This dish is delicious both hot and cold.

Stir Fried Green and Red Pepper

INGREDIENTS *serves 4*
1 large or 2 small green peppers, cored and seeded
1 large or 2 small red peppers, cored and seeded
3 tbsp/45ml oil
1 tsp/5ml salt
1 tsp/5ml sugar

METHOD
Cut the peppers into small diamond-shaped pieces; if you use one or two orange peppers, the dish will be even more colourful.

Heat the oil in a hot wok or frying pan until it smokes. Spread the oil with a scooper or spatula so that the cooking surface is well greased. Add the peppers and stir-fry until each piece is coated with oil. Add salt and sugar.

Continue stirring for about 1 minute and serve if you like your vegetables crunchy and crisp. If not, you can cook them for another minute or so until the skin of the peppers becomes slightly wrinkled. Add a little water if necessary during the last stage of cooking.

Green Beans in Garlic Sauce

INGREDIENTS *serves 4*
14oz/400g stringless beans
1 large or 2 small cloves of garlic
3 tbsp/45ml oil
1 tsp/5ml salt
1 tsp/5ml sugar
1 tbsp/15ml light soy sauce

METHOD
Trim the beans. Leave them whole if they are young and tender; otherwise, cut them in half.

Crush and finely chop the garlic.

Blanch the beans in a pan of lightly salted boiling water, drain and plunge in cold water to stop the cooking and to preserve the beans' bright green colour. Drain.

Heat the oil in a hot wok or frying pan. When it starts to smoke, add the crushed garlic to flavour the oil. Before the colour of the garlic turns dark brown, add the beans and stir-fry for about 1 minute. Add the salt, sugar and soy sauce and continue stirring for another minute at most. Serve hot or cold.

▶ Green beans in garlic sauce
▼ Hot and sour cabbage

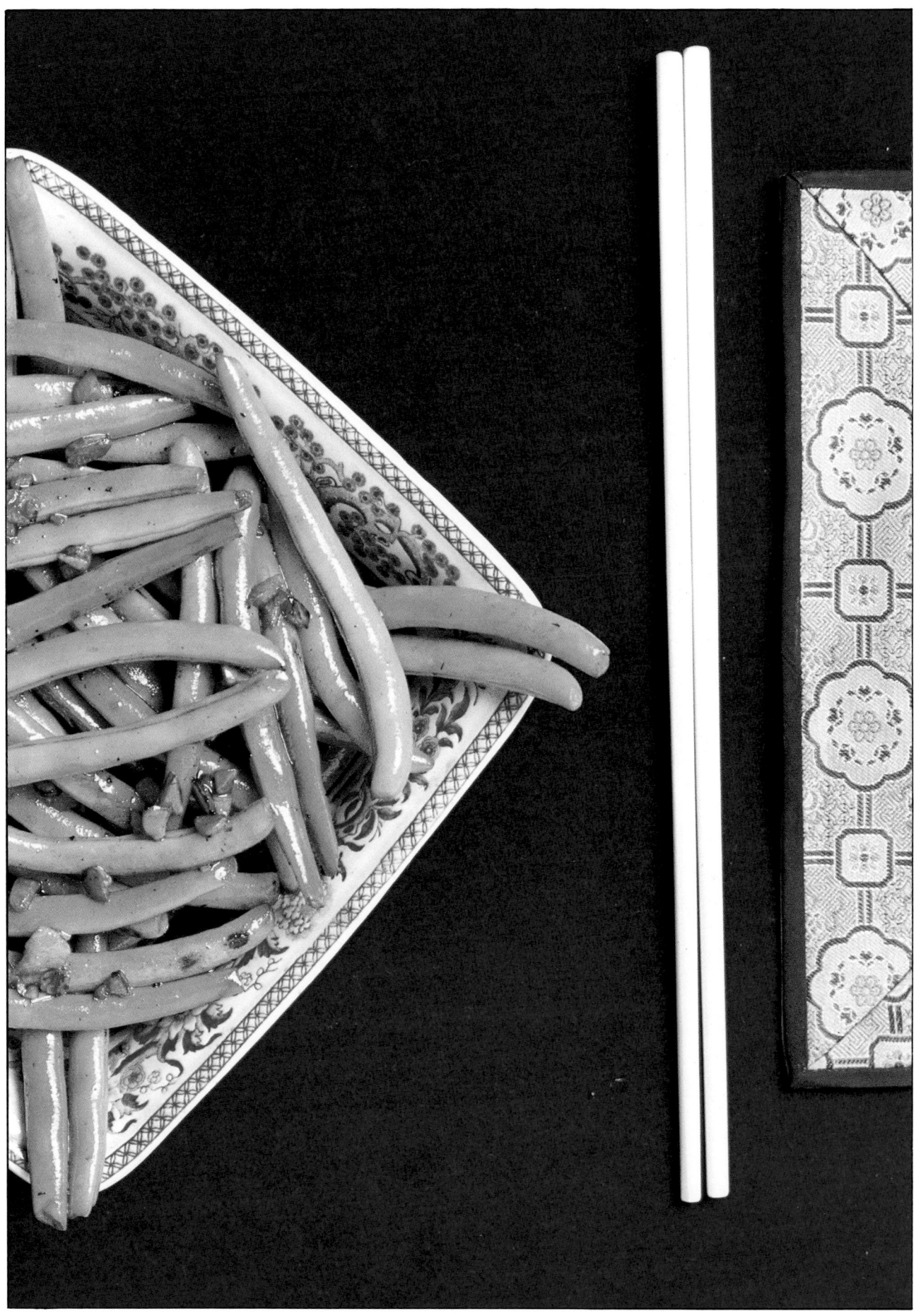

Savoury Vegetable Julienne

INGREDIENTS *serves 4*
1 tbsp/15ml sunflower oil
1 green chilli, de-seeded and finely
  chopped
1 clove garlic, crushed
1/2 head fennel, cut into thin strips
1 leek, cut into thin strips
1 green pepper, cut into thin strips
1/4 small red cabbage, shredded
1 tbsp/15ml lemon juice
salt and freshly ground black pepper

METHOD
Heat the sunflower oil in a large saucepan
and add the chilli and garlic. Cook for 1-2
minutes, then add the fennel, leek, pepper
and cabbage.

Stir and cook for 3-4 minutes. Add the
lemon juice and season to taste.

Roasted Cauliflower

INGREDIENTS *serves 4*
4 medium tomatoes
1 large onion
3 cloves garlic
1/2in/1cm root ginger
2 tbsp/30ml Ghee (see page 126)
3/4 tsp/4ml ground turmeric
1/2 tsp/2.5ml chilli powder
1/2 tsp Garam Masala (see page 126)
scant cup/175g/6oz peas
1/2 tsp/2.5ml salt
1 medium-sized cauliflower, blanched

METHOD
Blend the tomatoes, onion, garlic and
ginger in a blender until you have a paste.

Heat the Ghee in a frying pan over
medium heat and add the paste, turmeric,
chilli and Garam Masala and stir-fry until
the Ghee and spices separate, about 5-6
minutes.

Add the peas and salt and cook a further
5 minutes, stirring constantly. Remove from
the heat.

Place the cauliflower in a large ovenproof dish and pour the spices over it. Place
in a pre-heated oven at 375°F/190°C/Gas 5
for 30-35 minutes. Serve on a flat plate with
the peas and spices poured over.

Chestnuts and Vegetables

INGREDIENTS *serves 6-8*
1lb/450g chestnuts
4 tbsp/60ml olive oil
2 fat cloves garlic, chopped
6oz/175g mushrooms, sliced
12oz/350g Brussels sprouts
12oz/350g red cabbage
salt and freshly ground black pepper
small glass red wine

▲ ▲ Savoury vegetable julienne
▲ Roasted cauliflower
◀ Chestnuts and vegetables

METHOD
Pre-heat the oven to 400°F/200°C/Gas 6.
Make a nick in the top of the chestnuts with
a sharp knife and boil them for 10 minutes.
Plunge them in cold water and peel.

Heat the olive oil in a flameproof
casserole and fry the garlic. Add the
mushrooms, sprouts and red cabbage and
season. Cook, stirring occasionally, for
about 5 minutes until coated with oil and
beginning to soften.

Stir in the chestnuts and red wine. Cover
and bake in the oven for 40 minutes. Serve
with baked potatoes or a Purée of Root
Vegetables (see page 118).

Fennel Mornay

INGREDIENTS *serves 4*
3 bulbs fennel
bay leaf

THE SAUCE
2 tbsp/25g/1oz butter
1/4 cup/25g/1oz plain untreated flour
1 1/4 cups/300ml/10fl oz milk
2/3 cup/150ml/5fl oz single cream
1 cup/100g/4oz Cheddar cheese, grated
1/4-1/2 cup/25-50g/1-2oz breadcrumbs
salt and freshly ground black pepper

METHOD
Trim the fennel and simmer in salted water with a bay leaf for about 30 minutes until tender.

Meanwhile, make the sauce. Melt the butter in a pan and stir in the flour. Cook, stirring, for a couple of minutes and then gradually stir in the milk. Add the cream and most of the cheese and cook gently until the cheese has melted. Season well and keep warm.

Drain the fennel and cut each bulb in half. Lay the halves in a flameproof dish and pour the sauce over them. Sprinkle with the remaining cheese and the breadcrumbs. Put under a hot grill to brown and melt the cheese.

NOTE
For a tangier sauce, add a little powdered English mustard to taste.

Puée of Root Vegetables

INGREDIENTS *serves 4*
175g/6oz carrots
175g/6oz swede
1 turnip
1 parsnip
butter
salt and freshly ground black pepper

METHOD
Trim and peel the vegetables and simmer in salted water until tender.

Drain and mash to a fluffy purée with butter. Season with salt and plenty of black pepper. Serve with a dish that has a crunchy texture, such as Chestnuts and Vegetables (see page 117) or Nut Loaf (see page 84).

Corn Croquettes

INGREDIENTS *serves 4*
3 tbsp/45ml butter
3 tbsp/20g/3/4oz flour
1 1/4 cups/300ml/10fl oz milk
salt and freshly ground black pepper
1-2 tbsp/15-30ml finely chopped parsley
2 1/3 cups/400g/14oz corn kernels, cooked
2 egg yolks

THE COATING
2 eggs, beaten
seasoned flour
fine stale breadcrumbs
oil for frying

METHOD
To make the sauce, cut the butter into small pieces and melt in a heavy-bottomed pan. Stir in the flour and cook for a few minutes until the mixture is a pale gold.

Remove from the heat and pour in the milk. Stir well, return to the heat and stir until the sauce has thickened. Season with salt and plenty of pepper.

Stir the parsley, corn kernels and egg yolks into the mixture. Chill.

The mixture should have a heavy dropping consistency. Form it into croquettes. Dip each in the beaten egg, then roll in the flour and breadcrumbs.

Fry the croquettes in oil until crisp.

Corn on the Cob with Garlic Butter

INGREDIENTS *serves 4-6*
Corn on the cob
butter
garlic paste

METHOD
Remove the outer green leaves from the fresh corn. Place in boiling salted water with a drop of olive oil.

Simmer for 20 minutes, or until the corn is cooked and tender.

Remove from the heat and drain.

Smother liberally with butter and garlic paste.

Cheese and Potato Croquettes

INGREDIENTS *serves 6-8*
2lb/900g potatoes
2 egg yolks
4 tbsp/50g/2oz butter
salt and freshly ground black pepper
pinch nutmeg
dash sherry
1/2 cup/100g/4oz grated Parmesan
    cheese
pinch mustard
2 tbsp/30ml chopped parsley
seasoned flour
eggwash (egg beaten with a little milk)
breadcrumbs

METHOD
Wash and peel the potatoes, and cut to an even size. Cook in salted water until soft; then drain.

Put a lid on the pan of the potatoes and place over a low heat to dry out, stirring occasionally to prevent burning.

Place the potatoes in a food processor with the yolks, butter and seasoning.

Mix in the nutmeg, sherry, Parmesan cheese, mustard and parsley. The potatoes should be like a very firm mash. Overmixing will make them gluey, in which case some flour will have to be worked in by hand.

Check that the mix is seasoned well and mould into cylinder shapes (5×2in/13×5cm).

Roll in seasoned flour; dip in eggwash and coat with breadcrumbs.

Deep-fry in hot fat, 365°F/185°C. When golden, drain well and serve.

NOTE
If you want to keep the croquettes for cooking later, or the next day, place them carefully on a tray, cover with plastic film and refrigerate.

◄▲ Corn croquettes
◄ Purée of root vegetables
►▲ Split peas with vegetables
► Corn on the cob with garlic butter

Split Peas with Vegetables

INGREDIENTS *serves 4-6*
scant cup/200g/7oz split peas, washed
3 cups/750ml/25fl oz water
2 tbsp/30ml Ghee (see page 126)
1/2 tsp/2.5ml whole cumin seeds
2 bay leaves
2-3 green chillis, cut lengthways
2 1/2 cups/275g/10oz diced potatoes, cut
    into 1in/2.5cm pieces
1/3 cup/75g/3oz peas
3 cups/350g/12oz cauliflower, cut into
    large florets
1/2 tsp/2.5ml ground turmeric
1 tsp/5ml salt

METHOD
In a large saucepan bring the split peas and water to the boil. Cover and simmer for 30 minutes. Remove from heat.

Heat the ghee in a large saucepan over medium high heat. Add the cumin seeds, bay leaves and green chillis and let them sizzle for a few seconds.

Add the potatoes, peas, cauliflower and fry for 1-2 minutes.

Add the boiled split peas with the water, turmeric and salt. Mix thoroughly, lower heat and cook until the vegetables are tender. (If the dal gets too thick add a little more water.)

Egg-Baked Potatoes

INGREDIENTS *serves 6-8*
3 cups /900g/2lb sliced potatoes, peeled
salt
2 tsp/10ml paprika
4 eggs, hard-cooked and sliced
²⁄₃ cup/150ml/¹⁄₄pt soured cream
2 tbsp/30ml milk
butter

METHOD
Boil the potatoes until they are cooked but still firm. Drain off the water and slice them.

Put a layer of potatoes in the bottom of a greased ovenproof dish. Season with salt and paprika. Lay the sliced eggs over the potatoes. Mix the soured cream with the milk until smooth. Spoon over the eggs. Season again. Add the remaining potatoes.

Dot with butter and bake at 350°F/180°C/Gas 4 for 25 minutes, until golden.

VARIATION
To make this more substsantial you could add slices of cheese over the sliced eggs.

Russian Potatoes

INGREDIENTS *serves 6-8*
2lb/900g potatoes
salt and freshly ground black pepper
4 tbsp/50g/2oz butter
1 large onion, sliced
4oz/100g mushrooms, sliced
³⁄₄ cup/200ml/7fl oz soured cream
3 tbsp/45ml chopped chives

METHOD
Scrub the potatoes and cook in salted water until barely tender. Drain, peel and slice.

Heat some of the butter in a flameproof casserole and fry the onion until translucent. Add the mushrooms and cook gently until the juices run. Add the rest of the butter as necessary and stir in the potatoes. Let them gently brown on one side, season, turn over and add the cream.

When most of the cream has been absorbed, sprinkle over the chopped chives and a little more pepper and serve.

▼ Russian potatoes

Swiss Potato Cakes

INGREDIENTS *serves 4*
1lb/450g waxy potatoes
2 eggs
1 tbsp/15ml potato flour
salt and freshly ground black pepper
4 tbsp/60ml oil

METHOD
Peel the potatoes and grate them into a bowl of cold water. Drain. Squeeze the potato shreds dry in a cloth. Mix the potato with the eggs, flour and seasoning.

Heat 1 tbsp/15ml of the oil in a frying pan and make your first potato cake using a quarter of the mixture. Spread it out in the pan and flatten it. When the underside is crisp and golden, turn it over and brown the top. Keep it warm while you make the rest.

Patatas Bravas

INGREDIENTS *serves 2-3*
1 onion, chopped
2 tbsp/30ml olive oil
1 bay leaf
2 red chillies
2 tsp/10ml finely chopped garlic
1 tbsp/15ml tomato paste
¹⁄₂ tbsp/7.5ml sugar (up to 1 tbsp/15ml, if the sauce is too tart for your liking)
1 tbsp/15ml soy sauce
1lb/450g can plum tomatoes, chopped
1 glass white wine
salt and freshly ground black pepper
3 medium potatoes

METHOD
Sweat the onions in the oil with the bay leaf.

When soft, add the chillies, garlic, tomato paste, sugar and soy sauce. Sweat for a further 5 minutes on a low heat.

Add the chopped tomatoes and white wine. Stir and bring to the boil. Simmer for 10 minutes. Taste and season. (This sauce should be slightly sweet; the flavour of the tomatoes should not dominate it.)

Cut the potatoes like small roast potatoes. Grease a baking tray. Season the potatoes well and brush with melted butter.

Roast in a hot oven, 450°F/230°C/Gas 8, until golden. Pour over the tomato sauce and serve.

▲ ▲ Black eyed peas with onions   ▲ Patatas bravas

Black Eyed Peas with Onions

INGREDIENTS *serves 4-6*

1 good cup/200g/7oz black eyed peas,
  washed
5 cups/1.1l/2pts water
2 tbsp/30ml oil
1 large onion, finely chopped
2 cloves garlic, crushed
¼in/0.5cm root ginger, grated
1-2 green chillis, finely chopped
½ tsp/2.5ml salt
1 tsp/5ml molasses

METHOD

Soak the beans in the water overnight.

Boil the beans in the water and then cover
and simmer for 1 hour until tender. Drain.

Heat the oil in a large saucepan and fry
the onion, garlic, ginger and chilli until the
onions are soft. Add the beans, salt and
molasses and cook until all the moisture is
absorbed, about 15 minutes. Serve with
Baktoras (page 155).

Three Peppers in Tomato and Garlic

INGREDIENTS *serves 6*

¾ cup/175ml/6fl oz olive oil
2 yellow peppers, de-seeded and cut
  into thin strips
2 red peppers, de-seeded and vut into
  thin strips
2 green peppers, de-seeded and cut into
  thin strips
1 tbsp/15ml parsley, chopped
2 tsp/10ml finely chopped garlic
8oz/225g fresh or canned tomatoes
salt and freshly ground black pepper

METHOD

Heat the oil in a large frying pan and cook
the peppers gently for 2-3 minutes, stirring
frequently. Add the parsley and garlic and
cook for another couple of minutes.

Add the chopped tomatoes and their
juice to the pan. Stir and season.

Cover and simmer gently for about 20
minutes, until the peppers are tender.

The sauce should be quite thick - if
necessary, remove the peppers and boil
rapidly to reduce the liquid. Season.

◄ Egg-fried rice
► Perfect boiled rice

Egg-Fried Rice

INGREDIENTS *serves 6 - 8*
3 eggs
2 spring onions, finely chopped
1 tsp/5ml salt
4 tbsp/60ml oil
⅔ cup/100g/4oz green peas
4 cups/600g/20oz cooked rice
1 tbsp/15ml light soy sauce (optional)

METHOD
Lightly beat the eggs with about half of the finely chopped spring onions and a pinch of salt.

Heat about half of the oil in a hot wok or frying pan, pour in the beaten eggs and lightly scramble until set. Remove.

Heat the remaining oil and when hot, add the remaining spring onions followed by the green peas and stir-fry for about 30 seconds. Add the cooked rice and stir to separate each grain. Add the salt and soy sauce together with the eggs and stir to break the eggs into small pieces. Serve as soon as everything is well blended.

Perfect Boiled Rice

INGREDIENTS *serves 4*
1¼ cups/275g/10oz long grain rice
2½ cups/600ml/1pt water

METHOD
Wash and rinse the rice in cold water until clean.

Bring the water to the boil in a saucepan over high heat. Add the washed rice and bring back to the boil. Stir the rice with a spoon to prevent it sticking to the bottom of the pan and then cover the pan tightly with a lid and reduce the heat to very low. Cook gently for 15-20 minutes.

NOTE
It is best not to serve the rice immediately. Fluff it up with a fork or spoon and leave it under cover in the pan for 10 minutes or so before serving.

Chow Mein-Fried Noodles

INGREDIENTS *serves 4*
1oz/25g dried bean curd skin sticks
²/₃ cup/25g/1oz dried tiger lily buds
2oz/50g bamboo shoots
4oz/100g spinach or any other greens
8oz/225g dried egg noodles
2 spring onions, thinly shredded
3-4 tbsp/45-60ml oil
1 tsp/5ml salt
2 tbsp/30ml light soy sauce
2 tsp/10ml sesame seed oil

METHOD

Soak the dried vegetables overnight in cold water or in hot water for at least an hour. When soft, thinly shred both the bean curd skins and tiger lily buds.

Shred the bamboo shoots and spinach leaves into thin strips.

Cook the noodles in a pan of boiling water according to the instructions on the packet. Depending on the thickness of the noodles, this should take 5 minutes or so. Freshly made noodles will take only about half that time.

Heat about half the oil in a hot wok or frying pan. While waiting for it to smoke, drain the noodles in a sieve. Add them with about half the spring onions and the soy sauce to the wok and stir-fry. Do not overcook, or the noodles will become soggy. Remove and place them on a serving dish.

Add the rest of the oil to the wok. When hot, add the other spring onions and stir a few times. Then add all the vegetables and continue stirring. After 30 seconds or so, add the salt and the remaining soy sauce together with a little water if necessary. As soon as the gravy starts to boil, add the sesame seed oil and blend everything well. Place the mixture on top of the fried noodles as a dressing.

NOTE

Of course you can use substitutes for any of the ingredients in the dressing. For instance, instead of dried bean curd skin, you can use dried Chinese mushrooms or fresh mushrooms. Instead of tiger lily buds, why not use fresh bean sprouts or shredded celery. It is the contrast of texture and colour that is important.

Vegetarian Special Fried Rice

INGREDIENTS *serves 4*
4-6 dried Chinese mushrooms
1 green pepper, cored and seeded
1 red pepper, cored and seeded
4oz/100g bamboo shoots
2 eggs
2 spring onions, finely chopped
2 tsp/10ml salt
4-5 tbsp/60-75ml oil
6 cups/900g/30oz cooked rice
1 tbsp/15ml light soy sauce (optional)

▲ Vegetarian special fried rice

METHOD

Soak the dried mushrooms in warm water for 25-30 minutes, squeeze dry and discard the hard stalks. Cut the mushrooms into small cubes.

Cut the green and red peppers and the bamboo shoots into small cubes

Lightly beat the eggs with about half of the spring onions and a pinch of the salt.

Heat about 2 tbsp/30ml of oil in a hot wok, add the beaten eggs and scramble until set. Remove.

Heat the remaining oil. When hot, add the rest of the spring onions followed by all the vegetables and stir-fry until each piece is covered with oil. Add the cooked rice and salt and stir to separate each grain of rice. Finally add the soy sauce, blend everything together and serve.

Pilau with Coconut

INGREDIENTS *serves 4-6*

1½ cups/325g/12oz basmati rice, rinsed
   and drained

2 tbsp/10ml dessicated coconut

2-3 green chillies

1 tsp/5ml salt

½ tsp sugar

2 tbsp/30ml raisins

1 tbsp/15ml pistachio nuts, skinned and
   cut into thin strips

2 baby leaves

2in/5cm cinnamon stick

4 cardamons

3 tbsp/45ml Ghee (see page 126)

2½ cups/600ml/1pt milk

1¼ cups/275ml/10fl oz water

METHOD

Mix the rice with all the dry ingredients.

Heat the Ghee in a large saucepan over medium heat. Add the rice mixture and sauté for 5 minutes, stirring constantly.

Add the milk and water, increase the heat to high and bring to the boil. Stir.

Lower heat to very low, cover and cook for about 20 minutes until all the liquid has evaporated. Fluff the pillau with a fork and serve hot.

Fried Rice

INGREDIENTS *serves 4*

3 tbsp/45ml Ghee (see page 126)

2 bay leaves

2in/5cm cinnamon stick

4 cardamoms

3 large onions, finely sliced

3 green chillies, cut lengthways

1½ cups/350g/12oz basmati rice,
   cooked and cooled

1 tsp/5ml salt

½ tsp/2.5ml sugar

2 tbsp/30ml raisins (optional)

METHOD

Heat the Ghee in a large frying pan over medium high heat. Add the bay leaves and spices; let them sizzle a little.

Add the onions and chillies and fry until the onions are golden brown. Add the rice, salt, sugar and raisins and continue frying until the rice is thoroughly heated up.

▼ Pilau rice with coconut and milk

SAUCES AND DRESSINGS

Sauces and dressings are invaluable to the vegetarian cook, since they can turn a plainly-prepared vegetable or salad into something altogether more interesting. They can save time – and vitamins – allowing the vegetables to be lightly-cooked or served raw, and then dressed.

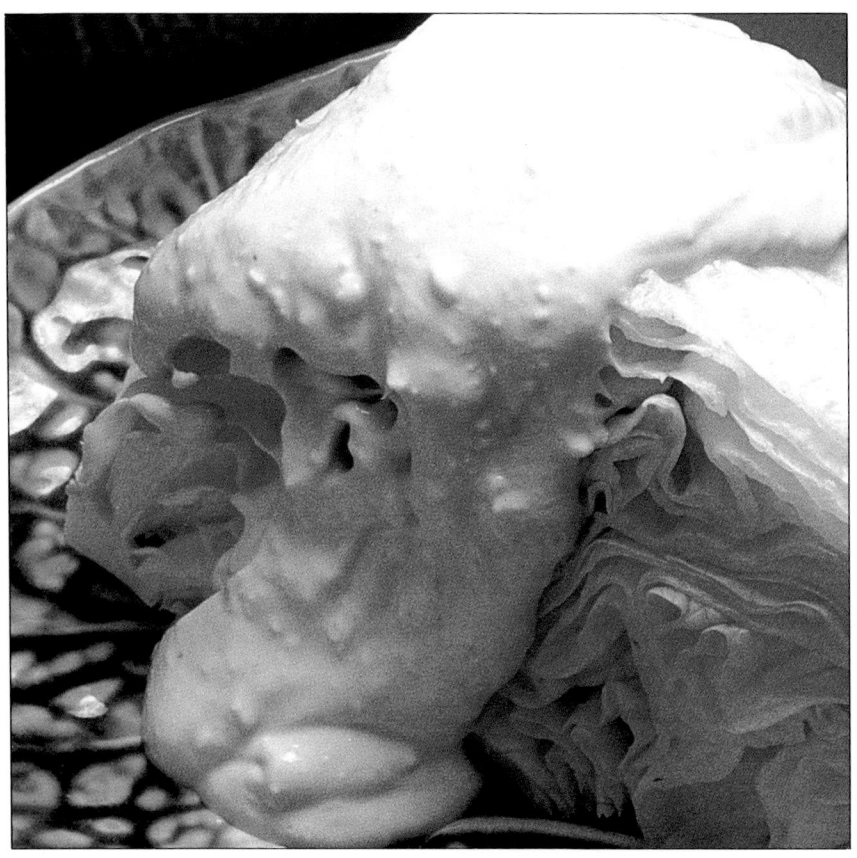

Blue cheese dressing

Yoghurt

INGREDIENTS *makes about 5 cups*
5 cups/1.1l/2pts milk
2 tbsp/30ml unflavoured commercial yoghurt at room temperature

METHOD

Scald the milk. Heat it until it is ready to boil. Just before boiling point, remove the pan from the heat and allow to cool until lukewarm. Test by dripping a little milk on your wrist. It should feel warm, not hot.

Put the yoghurt in the chosen container and stir in a little milk until smooth. Now stir in the remaining milk.

Cover and place container in the incubator. Be careful not to disturb the yoghurt for about 4 hours. When the consistency is right, chill in the fridge to set before using.

NOTE

Yoghurt can be made in any sterile container with a tightly fitting lid inside any sort of incubator, such as an oven with the pilot light on or a styrofoam box, but because the secret of successful yoghurt making is a constant lukewarm temperature, it is best to use a special yoghurt maker. Don't put incubating yoghurt near a heat source regulated by a thermostat that switches on and off. Use 2 tbsp/30ml of the home-made yoghurt to start the next batch. The cost of making yoghurt at home is minimal and the method is easy.

Ghee-Clarified Butter

INGREDIENTS *makes about 2 cups/ 450ml/¾pt*
1lb/450g unsalted butter

METHOD

Heat the butter in a saucepan over low heat. Let it simmer for 15-20 minutes until all the white residue turns golden and settles at the bottom.

Remove from the heat, strain and cool.

Pour into an airtight bottle and store in a cool place.

Homemade Garam Masala

INGREDIENTS *makes about ⅓ cup/2oz/ 4 tbsp*
3 tbsp/45ml cardamom seeds
3in/7.5cm cinnamon sticks
½ tbsp/7.5ml cumin seeds
½ tsp/2.5ml black peppercorns
½ tsp/2.5ml cloves
¼ nutmeg

METHOD

Grind all the spices together until they are finely ground. Store in a spice bottle until required. (The ingredients may be added in different proportions to suit individual tastes.)

Béchamel Sauce

INGREDIENTS *makes about 3¼ cups/ 900ml/1½pts*
2½ cups/600ml/1pt milk
1 small onion, peeled
1 small carrot, peeled and sliced
1 bay leaf
6 slightly crushed peppercorns
1 blade mace
1 stalk parsley
3 tbsp/40g/1½oz butter
6 tbsp/40g/1½oz flour
salt and white pepper

METHOD

Pour milk into a saucepan. Add the onion cut into quarters with 2 slices of carrot, bay leaf, peppercorns, mace and parsley stalk.

Cover and allow to heat on a low heat without boiling for about 10 minutes. Remove from the heat and allow to infuse for a further 10 minutes, covered.

Make a roux (a blend of butter and flour) by melting the butter in a saucepan. Do not allow the butter to brown. Add the flour and stir well over a medium heat.

Gradually add the strained milk and stir briskly or whisk until a smooth creamy sauce is made, season to taste.

Cold Horseradish Sauce

INGREDIENTS *makes about ¼ cup/ 200ml/7 fl oz*
2 tbsp/30ml prepared horseradish cream
⅔ cup/150ml/¼pt soured cream

METHOD

Stir the horseradish cream into the soured cream. Refrigerate for an hour before use if possible.

Use this sauce for potatoes and beetroot dishes.

▲ Homemade garam masala

Cucumber Dill Sauce

INGREDIENTS *makes about 2¹/₂ cups/ 600ml/1pt*
1 medium cucumber, peeled
2 tbsp/25g/1oz butter
²/₃ cup/150ml/¹/₄pt vegetable stock
²/₃ cup/150ml/¹/₄pt dry white wine
2 tbsp/30ml fresh dill, chopped or
    1 tbsp/15ml dried dill
4 tsp/20ml cornflour
2 tbsp/30ml water
¹/₂ cup/120ml/4fl oz soured cream or
    yoghurt
salt and pepper

METHOD
Coarsely grate the cucumber and put it into a saucepan. Add the butter and cook on a gentle heat just to soften the cucumber. Add the stock, wine and dill and simmer for 5 minutes. Mix the cornflour with the water. Add it to the pan, cook gently until the sauce begins to thicken, stirring constantly. Add the soured cream or yoghurt and warm it through. Season to taste.

Serve hot or cold, with salmon or other fish. Also good with poached eggs, boiled potatoes, rice or pasta.

Marinara Sauce

INGREDIENTS *makes about 5 cups/ 1.1l/1³/₄pts*
4 tbsp/60ml olive oil
2 cloves garlic, crushed
4¹/₂ cups/1¹/₂kg/3lb ripe beef tomatoes,
    peeled and chopped
salt and freshly ground black pepper
6 basil leaves

METHOD
Heat the oil in a saucepan, add the garlic and stir for 1 minute. Add the tomatoes roughly chopped and seasoning and allow to simmer for 6 minutes.

Chop the basil leaves and add to the tomatoes, stir the sauce for a further minute. Serve on freshly cooked pasta. This sauce is a simple accompaniment to pasta which is very good to eat and easy to prepare but the secret is that the tomatoes should be simply heated through, not cooked to a pulp.

Hot Tomato Sauce

INGREDIENTS *makes about 1³/₄ cups/ 400ml/14fl oz*
1 tbsp/15ml oil
1 onion, finely chopped
2-3 cloves garlic, finely chopped
1³/₄ cups/425g/15oz can tomatoes,
    mashed, with juice
2 tbsp/30ml tomato purée
1 tsp/5ml ground cumin
1 tsp/5ml ground coriander
¹/₂ tsp/2.5ml ground chilli
salt

METHOD
Heat oil in a pan, add onion and garlic and stir-fry till soft.

Add remaining ingredients, simmer until thickened and check seasoning. Serve with vegetable couscous (page 95).

▲ Cucumber dill sauce

Creamy Mustard Vinaigrette

INGREDIENTS *makes about ²/₃ cup/ 150ml/¹/₄pt*
3 tbsp/45ml olive oil
2 tbsp/30ml double cream
2 tbsp/30ml red wine vinegar
1 tbsp/15ml Dijon mustard
¹/₂ tsp/2.5ml dried thyme
1¹/₂ tsp/7.5ml soy sauce
salt and freshly ground black pepper

METHOD
Put the olive oil, cream, vinegar and mustard in a small bowl. Stir with a fork or whisk until the mixture is somewhat foamy.

Stir in the thyme, soy sauce, salt and pepper.

Modern Vinaigrette

INGREDIENTS *makes 1 cup/250ml/ 8fl oz*
2 tbsp/30ml wine vinegar
1 tbsp/15ml lemon juice
1 tsp/5ml prepared mustard
salt and freshly ground black pepper
³/₄ cup/175g/6fl oz pure olive oil

METHOD
Put the vinegar, lemon juice, mustard, salt and pepper in a jar with a tightly fitting lid.

Cover the jar tightly and shake until the salt dissolves.

Add the olive oil to the jar and shake until well mixed.

Tofu Dressing

INGREDIENTS *makes about 2 cups/ 475ml/16fl oz*
1²/₃ cups/300g/10oz silken tofu
2 tbsp/30ml lemon juice
3 tbsp/45ml oil
pinch salt
1 tsp/5ml soy sauce
1 clove garlic, crushed

METHOD
Blend all the ingredients together in a liquidiser.

Mayonnaise

INGREDIENTS *makes 1³/₄ cups/400ml/ 14fl oz*
2 egg yolks
¹/₂ tsp/2.5ml salt
1 tsp/5ml Dijon mustard
1¹/₄ cups/300ml/¹/₂pt olive oil
2 tsp/10ml cider vinegar

METHOD
All the ingredients must be at room temperature. Put the egg yolks in a bowl with the salt and mustard and whisk together with a balloon whisk.

Beating constantly and evenly, add the olive oil at a very slow trickle. A bottle with a nick cut in the cork can be used to ensure that only a very little oil dribbles out at a time. The aim is to break up the oil into very small globules so that it can be absorbed by the egg yolks. When all the oil has been added you should have a thick glossy emulsion that will cling to the whisk.

Gradually beat in the cider vinegar. For a thinner mayonnaise, beat in 1 tbsp/15ml hot water.

Mayonnaise Maltaise

INGREDIENTS *makes 1¹/₄ cups/400ml/ 14fl oz*
1³/₄ cups/400ml/14fl oz mayonnaise (see above)
grated rind and juice of 2 oranges

METHOD
Combine the ingredients and serve with cooked vegetables such as asparagus and artichokes, or use as a salad dressing.

Blue Cheese Dressing

INGREDIENTS *makes about 1¹/₄ cups/ 400ml/14fl oz*
1 cup/250ml/8fl oz yoghurt
¹/₂ cup/50g/2oz blue cheese
3 tbsp/45ml olive oil
salt and freshly ground black pepper

METHOD
Blend all the ingredients together thoroughly.

Tomato Yoghurt Dressing

INGREDIENTS *makes ³/₄ cup/175ml/ 6fl oz*
²/₃ cup/150ml/¹/₄pt yoghurt
4 tsp/20ml tomato ketchup
dash Worcestershire sauce
dash Tabasco
salt and freshly ground black pepper

METHOD
Mix all the ingredients together well. Serve on crisp lettuce or as a seafood dressing.

VARIATION
Add finely chopped green or red pepper, chopped hard-boiled egg, chopped spring onions.

Rich French Dressing

INGREDIENTS *makes about 1¹/₄ cups/ 400ml/14fl oz*
1 egg
¹/₂ cup/120ml/4fl oz oil
2 tbsp/30ml lemon juice
1 clove garlic, crushed
fresh herbs
salt and freshly ground black pepper
1 cup/250ml/8fl oz yoghurt

METHOD
Blend together the egg, oil, lemon juice, garlic, herbs, salt and pepper. Slowly add the yoghurt, with the blender running. Refrigerate until required - it should thicken as it stands.

VARIATION
This makes a delicious salad dressing but if you want to make it thicker, for piping, you can add some gelatin and let it set. Use chives, fennel, parsley, tarragon or any other fresh herb you have on hand - or a mixture.

NOTE
For a less rich dressing omit the egg.

▲ ► Tomato yoghurt dressing
► Blue cheese dressing

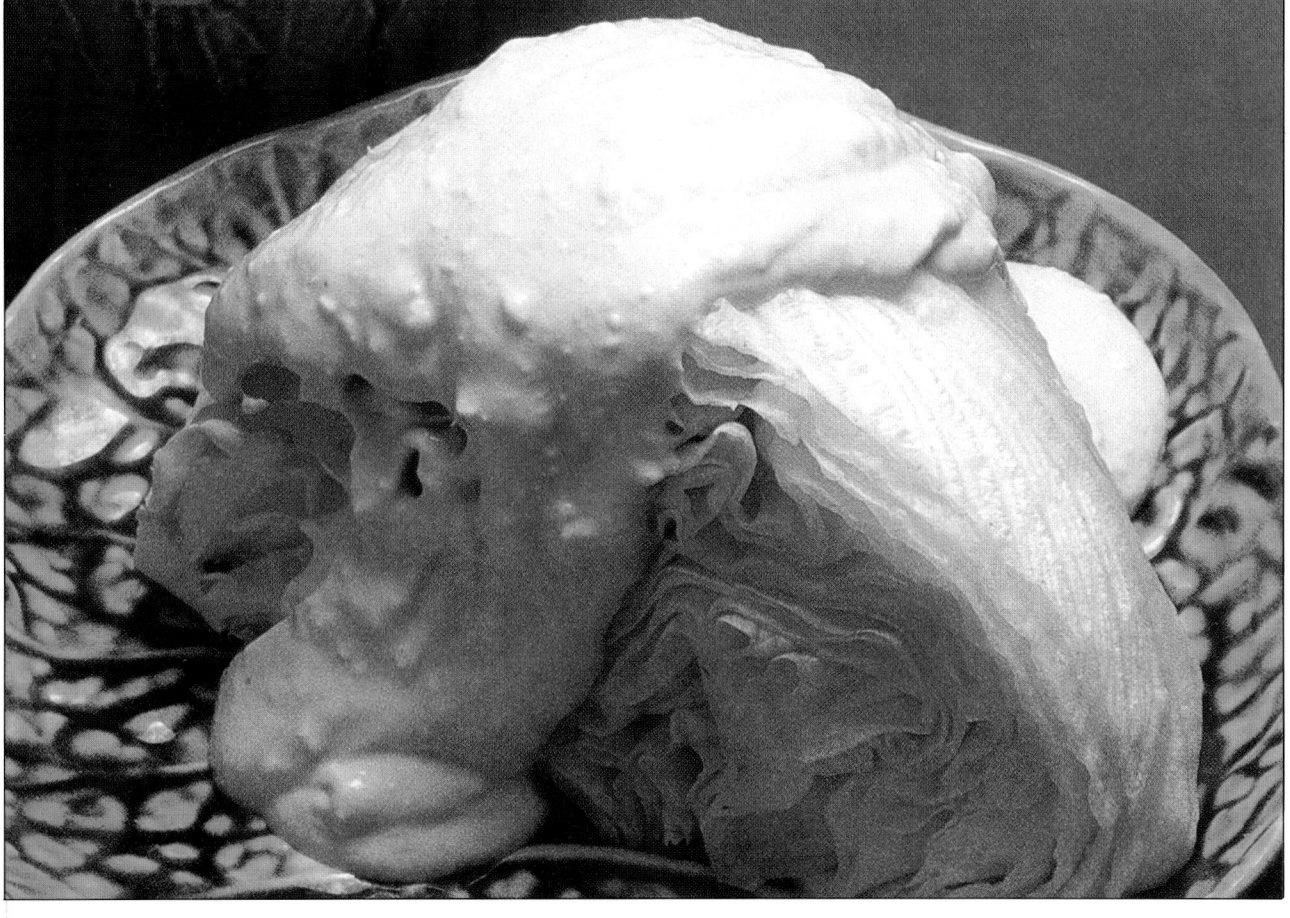

Tomato Dressing

INGREDIENTS *makes ¼ cup/175ml/ 6fl oz*
4 tbsp/60ml tomato purée
3 tbsp/45ml olive oil
4 tbsp/60ml lemon juice
2 cloves garlic, crushed
1 small onion, finely chopped
1 tbsp/15ml honey
pinch salt

METHOD
Blend all the ingredients together thoroughly.

Cheese Herb Dressing

INGREDIENTS *makes 2 cups/475ml/ 16fl oz*
1⅓ cups/225g/8oz curd cheese or quark
¾ cup/200ml/7fl oz soured cream
2 spring onions, finely chopped
1 tbsp/15ml chopped parsley
1 tbsp/15ml chopped dill
1 tbsp/15ml sugar
1 tbsp/15ml chopped onion

METHOD
Combine everything together, mixing well to blend the cheese and soured cream.
 Serve over plain poached fish or as a salad dressing.

VARIATION
Use ricotta instead of curd cheese, if preferred.

◀ Tomato dressing

Green Mayonnaise

INGREDIENTS *makes about 1½ cups/ 350ml/12fl oz*
3 tbsp/45ml chopped fresh spinach
3 tbsp/45ml chopped watercress
3 tbsp/45ml chopped spring onion
3 tbsp/45ml chopped parsley
1 cup/250ml/8fl oz mayonnaise
½ tsp/2.5g grated nutmeg
salt to taste

METHOD
Put the spinach, watercress, spring onion and parsley in a small saucepan. Add water to cover them.

Quickly bring to the boil. Remove the saucepan from the heat. Let stand for 1 minute.

Drain the greens well. Rub them through a sieve or purée them in a blender. Drain off excess liquid.

Put the mayonnaise in a blender or medium-sized bowl. Add the purée, nutmeg and salt to taste. Blend until evenly mixed.

Touch of Asia Dressing

INGREDIENTS *makes 1 cup/250ml/ 8fl oz*
2 tsp/10ml soy sauce
2 tsp/10ml water
1 whole spring onion, chopped
½ tsp/2.5ml sesame oil
¼ tsp/1.5ml hot pepper chilli oil
1 garlic clove, finely chopped
¼ tsp/1.5ml ground black pepper
6fl oz/175ml peanut oil
2½ tbsp/38ml rice wine vinegar

METHOD
Put the soy sauce, water, spring onion, sesame oil, hot pepper oil, garlic and black pepper in a jar with a tightly fitting lid. Cover and shake until the ingredients are blended.

Add the peanut oil to the jar, cover tightly and shake again. Let the mixture stand for 2 minutes.

Add the vinegar to the jar. Cover tightly and shake well again. Pour over the salad immediately.

Lemon Dressing

INGREDIENTS *makes ¼ cup/175ml/ 6fl oz*
1 tsp/5ml water
large pinch salt
large pinch grated lemon rind
2 tsp/10ml dried mint
4 tbsp/60ml/2fl oz fresh lemon juice
½ cup/120ml/4fl oz pure olive oil
large pinch ground black pepper

METHOD
Put the water, salt and lemon rind in a jar with a tightly fitting lid. Let stand for 2 minutes.

Add the mint and lemon juice. Cover the jar tightly and shake.

Add the olive oil and black pepper. Cover the jar tightly, shake again and serve.

Yoghurt Mayonnaise

INGREDIENTS *makes 1 cup/250ml/ 8fl oz*
½ cup/4fl oz/120ml unflavoured yoghurt
1 tbsp/15ml honey
1 tsp/5ml fresh lemon juice
4½ tbsp/3fl oz/90ml mayonnaise
¼ tsp/1.5ml salt
1 tsp/5ml poppy seeds

METHOD
Combine the yoghurt, honey and lemon juice in a bowl. Stir with a wooden spoon until well blended.

Add the mayonnaise, salt and poppy seeds. Stir until thoroughly mixed. Chill for 1 hour and serve.

Basil Dressing

INGREDIENTS *makes 1 cup/250ml/ 8fl oz*
1 cup/250ml/8fl oz yoghurt
10 basil leaves, finely chopped
1 large clove garlic, crushed
salt and freshly ground black pepper

METHOD
Blend everything together well. Serve over green or mixed salad or tomato and onion salad.

NOTE
This also makes a good sauce for pasta, in which case double the quantity.

Herb Dressing

INGREDIENTS *makes 1½ cups/350ml/ 12fl oz*
½ cup/75g/3oz cream cheese
1 cup/250ml/8fl oz yoghurt or
 buttermilk
salt and freshly ground black pepper
finely chopped fresh herbs

METHOD
Blend everything together well. Refrigerate until required. Use on salads or fish.

Tahini Dressing

INGREDIENTS *makes 1¼ cups/400ml/ 14fl oz*
1 cup/250ml/8fl oz tahini
4 tbsp/60ml water
4 tbsp/60ml lemon juice
3 cloves garlic, crushed
pinch salt

METHOD
Blend all the ingredients together thoroughly.

Thousand Island Dressing

INGREDIENTS *makes 1¹/₃ cups/325ml/ 11fl oz*

1 cup/250ml/8fl oz mayonnaise
4 tbsp/60ml Tabasco or chilli sauce
2 tbsp/30ml finely chopped pimento-
   stuffed green olives
1 hard-boiled egg, finely chopped
1 tbsp/15ml double cream
¹/₂ tsp/2.5ml fresh lemon juice
1¹/₂ tsp/7.5ml finely chopped spring
   onion
2 tbsp/30ml finely chopped sweet green
   pepper
2 tbsp/30ml finely chopped fresh parsley
¹/₄ tsp/1.5ml paprika
large pinch freshly ground black pepper

METHOD

Put the mayonnaise and chilli sauce in a medium-sized bowl. Stir with a wooden spoon until well blended.

Add the olives, egg, cream and lemon juice. Continue stirring.

Add the remaining ingredients. Stir until well blended. Refrigerate for at least 1 hour before serving. It goes well on tossed green salad.

Chutney Dressing

INGREDIENTS *makes about 1¹/₂ cups/ 350ml/12fl oz*

¹/₂ cup/120ml/4fl oz soured cream
¹/₂ cup/120ml/4fl oz buttermilk
2 tbsp/30ml mango chutney
1 tbsp/15ml lemon juice
2 tsp/10ml oil
2 tsp/10ml mustard
salt and freshly ground black pepper

METHOD

Blend everything together well. Refrigerate until required.

Serve on salad or cold vegetables. Use as a dressing for hard-cooked eggs, cold fish or meat.

Fruit Salad Syrup Dressing

INGREDIENTS *makes 1¹/₄ cups/300ml/ ¹/₂pt*

1 tbsp/15ml flour
²/₃ cup/150ml/¹/₄pt water
¹/₂ tsp/2.5ml pure vanilla essence
1 egg
5 tbsp/75ml sugar
2 tsp/10ml butter
large pinch ground nutmeg
3 tbsp/45ml double cream

METHOD

Put the flour and 2 tbsp/30ml water into a saucepan. Stir to form a thin paste. Add the vanilla and egg. Beat well until smooth.

Put the sugar, remaining water and butter in another saucepan. Bring to the boil over a low heat.

Add the boiling syrup to the vanilla and egg mixture. Stir well. Cook over low heat, stirring constantly, until thick and smooth.

Remove the saucepan from the heat. Allow the dressing to cool.

Stir in the nutmeg and cream. Beat until well blended and pour over the fruit salad.

Soured Cream Anchovy Dressing

INGREDIENTS *makes about ²/₃ cup/ 150ml/¹/₄pt*

²/₃ cup/150ml/¹/₄pt soured cream
1 clove garlic, crushed
4 anchovy fillets, finely chopped
3 spring onions, finely chopped
chopped dill
juice of 1 lemon
salt and freshly ground black pepper

METHOD

Mix everything together well. Refrigerate until required.

Serve as a salad dressing or on hot or cold fish or grilled meats.

▲ Thousand island dressing

132

DRINKS, PICKLES AND CHUTNEYS

*The emphasis on healthy eating – and less alcohol consumption
– has bought the attractions of fresh fruit drinks to a wide public,
while pickles and chutneys are a much-treasured legacy from
earlier days. The following recipes are the stock of an
international store cupboard.*

Orange yoghurt drink

Mint and Chilli Cucumber

INGREDIENTS *makes 1¹/₃ cups/ 325ml/11fl oz*

1 cucumber, grated, sprinkled with
    salt and placed in a sieve to remove
    excess moisture
1 beef (large) tomato, peeled by placing
    in boiling water for 10 seconds and
    then plunged into cold water to
    remove skin
¹/₂ tsp/2.5ml garlic, chopped
bunch mint, chopped
²/₃ cup/150ml/5fl oz tub plain yoghurt
²/₃ cup/150ml/5fl oz tub soured cream
1 tsp/5ml cumin
2 red chillies, seeded and chopped
salt and freshly ground black pepper

METHOD
Wash the excess moisture off the cucumber
and drain well, squeezing any moisture out.

Chop the tomato into little squares;
discard the seeds.

Mix all the ingredients together in a
bowl, season well and chill.

Mint Chutney

INGREDIENTS *makes 1 cup/250ml/ 8fl oz*

¹/₄ cup/2oz/50g tamarind juice
2oz/50g/¹/₂ cup mint leaves, washed
2 tbsp/30ml onions, chopped
2 cloves garlic
³/₄in/2cm root ginger
2-3 green chillis
¹/₂ tsp/2.5ml salt
¹/₂ tsp/2.5ml sugar

METHOD
Make the tamarind juice by soaking 1 dried
tamarind in boiling water for 10 minutes.

Blend all the ingredients together until
you have a smooth paste. Serve with any
fried foods (Can be stored in an airtight jar
in the refrigerator for one week.)

Coriander Chutney

INGREDIENTS *makes 1¹/₄ cups/300ml/ ¹/₂pt*

³/₄ cup/75g/3oz coriander leaves
4 cloves garlic
3 tbsp/45ml desiccated coconut
2 green chillies
2-3 tbsp/30-45ml lemon juice
¹/₂ tsp/2.5ml salt
¹/₄ tsp/1.5ml sugar

METHOD
Chop the sprigs of coriander and throw
away the roots and lower stalk.

Blend the coriander with all the other
ingredients until you have a smooth paste.
Serve with any fried foods. (Can be stored in
an airtight jar in the refrigerator for one
week.)

▲ ▲ Mint and chilli cucumber
▲ Mint chutney
▲ ▶ Coriander chutney

134

Fresh Tomato, Cucumber and Onion Sambal

INGREDIENTS *makes about 3 cups/ 750ml/1¼pts*
¾ cup/225g/8oz tomatoes, chopped
  into ¼in/0.5cm pieces
1 cup/225g/8oz cucumber, cut into ¼in/
  0.5cm pieces
½ cup/100g/4oz onions, chopped
2-3 green chillis
½ tsp/2.5ml salt
¼ tsp/1.5ml sugar
3 tbsp/45ml lemon juice
2 tbsp/30ml coriander leaves, chopped

METHOD
Mix all the ingredients together in a small
bowl. Cover and set aside to chill. Serve
with any Indian meal.

Pineapple Chutney

INGREDIENTS *makes about 1 cup/ 250ml/8fl oz*
½ tbsp/7.5ml oil
½ tsp/2.5ml whole mustard seeds
1 cup/237g/8oz canned pineapple,
  crushed and drained
big pinch salt
1 tsp/5ml cornflour mixed with a little
  milk

METHOD
Heat the oil in a small pan over medium
heat. Add the mustard seeds and let them
sizzle for a few seconds.

Add the drained pineapple and salt and,
stirring occasionally, cook for about 10
minutes.

Thicken with the cornflour mixture and
remove from the heat. Chill.

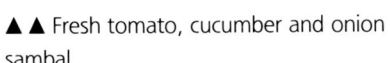

▲▲ Fresh tomato, cucumber and onion
sambal
▲ Pineapple chutney

Cucumber Raita

INGREDIENTS *makes about 2½ cups/ 600ml/1pt*
½ cucumber, peeled and chopped
1 small onion, chopped
2 cups/500ml/17fl oz yoghurt
squeeze lemon juice
salt and freshly ground black pepper
coriander leaves

METHOD
Mix all the ingredients together, seasoning
to taste, and garnish with the coriander
leaves. Use parsley if coriander is not
available.

Chill well before serving.

Tea Eggs

INGREDIENTS *serves 12*
12 eggs
2 tsp/10ml salt
3 tbsp/45ml light soy sauce
2 tbsp/30ml dark soy sauce
1 tsp/5ml five-spice powder
1 tbsp/15ml red tea leaves

METHOD
Boil the eggs in water for 5-10 minutes. Remove and gently tap the shell of each egg with a spoon until it is cracked finely all over.

Place the eggs back in the pan and cover with fresh water. Add the salt, soy sauces, five-spice powder and tea leaves (the better the quality of the tea, the better the result). Bring to the boil and simmer for 30-40 minutes. Leave the eggs to cool in the liquid.

Peel off the shells - the eggs will have a beautiful marbled pattern. They can be served either on their own or as part of a mixed hors d'œuvre, whole or cut into halves or quarters.

Pickled Radishes

INGREDIENTS *serves 4-6*
24 radishes
2 tsp/10ml sugar
1 tsp/5ml salt

METHOD
Choose fairly large radishes that are roughly equal in size, if possible, and cut off and discard the stalks and tails. Wash the radishes in cold water and dry them thoroughly. Using a sharp knife, make several cuts from the top about two-thirds of the way down the sides of each radish.

Put the radishes in a large jar. Add the sugar and salt. Cover the jar and shake well so that each radish is coated with the sugar and salt mixture. Leave to marinate for several hours or overnight.

Just before serving, pour off the liquid and spread out each radish like a fan. Serve them on a plate on their own or as a garnish with other cold dishes.

Chinese Pickled Vegetables

INGREDIENTS *use four to six of the following vegetables or more:*
cucumber
carrot
radish or turnip
cauliflower
broccoli
green cabbage
white cabbage
celery
onion
fresh ginger root
leek
spring onion
red pepper
green pepper
string beans
garlic
5qt/4.5l/8pt cold boiled water
¾ cup/175g/6oz salt
2oz/50g chilli peppers
3 tsp/15g/½oz Sichuan peppercorns
¼ cup/60ml/2fl oz Chinese distilled spirit
   (or white rum, gin or vodka)
4oz/100g root ginger
½ cup/100g/4oz brown sugar

METHOD
Put the cold boiled water into a large, clean earthenware or glass jar. Add the salt, chillies, peppercorns, spirit, ginger and sugar.

Wash and trim the vegetables, peel if necessary and drain well. Put them into the jar and seal it, making sure it is airtight. Place the jar in a cool place and leave the vegetables to pickle for at least five days before serving.

Use a pair of clean chopsticks or tongs to pick the vegetables out of the jar. Do not allow any grease to enter the jar. You can replenish the vegetables, adding a little salt each time. If any white scum appears on the surface of the brine, add a little sugar and spirit. The longer the pickling lasts, the better.

◀ Tea eggs with pickled radishes
▶ Pickled vegetables

Tomato Cocktail

INGREDIENTS *serves 4*
3-4 medium/450g/1lb ripe tomatoes, skinned
1¼ cups/300ml/½pt yoghurt
fresh basil
salt and freshly ground black pepper
pinch sugar
2 ice cubes

METHOD
Squeeze out the seeds of the tomatoes (reserve them for use in a soup) and place the flesh in a blender, together with the remaining ingredients. Blend everything together well. Serve immediately in tall glasses. Garnish with additional basil leaves.

VARIATION
This also makes a good salad dressing, in which case halve the quantity.

Orange Yoghurt Drink

INGREDIENTS *serves 2*
¾ cup/175ml/6fl oz yoghurt
½ cup/120ml/4fl oz milk
grated rind and juice of 1 orange
grated lemon peel
1 tsp/5ml honey
1½ tbsp/25g/1oz hazelnuts (optional)

METHOD
Blend all the ingredients together well. Serve immediately or refrigerate until required.

VARIATION
A simpler citrus yoghurt drink can be made by liquidizing either the flesh of an orange or that of a small grapefruit together with ⅔ cup/150ml/¼pt yoghurt and sugar to taste.

Green Beech Liqueur

INGREDIENTS *makes 1 bottle*
tender young beech leaves
vodka
fruit sugar
brandy

METHOD
Pick young beech leaves in late spring or early summer. Make sure they are tender. (What you don't use in this recipe you can eat in a salad.)

Pack the leaves into a jar and press them well down. Fill the jar with vodka. Seal and leave for two weeks in a dark place.

Strain off the vodka, which will now be a bright green in colour.

To make the liqueur, prepare a syrup of 1 cup/225g/8oz fruit sugar and 10fl oz/300ml boiling water to every pint of vodka. Stir the sugar into the water until dissolved. When cool, add 1 tbsp/15ml brandy for each 10fl oz/300ml of water and sugar and combine with the vodka. Bottle and seal.

Sloe Gin

INGREDIENTS *makes 1 bottle*
ripe sloes
the best Dutch gin

NOTE
Sloes are the blue-black fruit of the blackthorn bush and can be harvested in October. Pick over them and remove the stalks.

METHOD
Half fill a bottle with sloes and fill it to the top with gin. Seal the bottle and store in a dark place.

The gin will take on a beautiful pink colour and a tangy fruity flavour within about two weeks. You can leave it longer if you want a stronger, fruitier taste, or you can decant the gin and top up the bottle with fresh gin a second time. Sloe gin makes an ideal Christmas drink.

◀ Tomato cocktail

BREADS AND PASTRIES

This is a large section comprising breads of all colours and textures, sweet and savoury biscuits, rolls and muffins, yeast pastries, tarts and cakes. The home baker and patissiere will find a wealth of inspiration and counsel here.

Fruit tartlets

Quick White Bread

INGREDIENTS *makes 2 large or 4 small loaves*
2 tbsp/50g/2oz fresh yeast or 4 tbsp/
  25g/1oz dried yeast and ¹/₂ tsp/2.5ml
  sugar
3³/₄ cups/750ml/1¹/₂pts warm water
2×25mg tablets vitamin C
12 cups/1.5kg/3lb white flour
2 tsp/10ml salt
2 tbsp/30ml sugar
¹/₄ cup/50g/2oz butter or margarine

METHOD
Oven temperature 450°F/230°C/Gas 8.

Grease two large (or four small) bread tins. Mix the yeast with a few tbsp water adding the 1tsp/5ml sugar if dried yeast is used. Set the dried yeast liquid aside for 10 minutes until frothy. Crush the vitamin C tablets in a little water; add to the yeast liquid.

Mix the flour and salt together in a large warm bowl. Add the sugar and rub in the fat. Stir in the yeast liquid and the rest of the warm water and mix to a soft dough. Turn on to a lightly floured board and knead the dough until it is smooth, elastic and non-sticky. Divide the dough in half, shape into 2 or 4 loaves and put them into the bread tins. Cover the tins with clingfilm and prove until doubled in size, about 1 hour.

Preheat the oven. Remove the clingfilm and bake the loaves for about 45 minutes (30-35 minutes for small loaves). Cool the bread on a wire rack.

White Bread

INGREDIENTS *makes 3 large loaves*
1 tbsp/25g/1oz fresh yeast or 2 tbsp/
  15g/¹/₂oz dried yeast and 1 tsp/5ml
  sugar
3³/₄ cups/900ml/1¹/₂pts warm water
12 cups/1.5kg/3lb white flour
2-3 tsp/10-15ml salt
1 tbsp/5ml sugar
¹/₄ cup/50g/2oz butter or margarine

METHOD
Oven temperature 450°F/230°C/Gas 8.

Grease three large bread tins. Stir the yeast with a few tbsp water, adding 1tsp/5ml sugar if dried yeast is used. Put the bowl of dried yeast liquid aside for 10 minutes until frothy.

Mix the flour and salt together. Add the sugar, rub in the fat, stir in the yeast liquid and the rest of the warm water to make a soft dough. Turn the dough on to a lightly floured board and knead until it becomes smooth, elastic and non-sticky.

Return the dough to the bowl, cover it with clingfilm and allow to prove until doubled in size, about 1¹/₄ hours.

Knock back the dough and divide it into 3 portions. Knead and shape into loaves to fit into the three bread tins. Cover the bread tins with clingfilm. Allow to prove until doubled in size, about 45 minutes.

Remove the film and bake the loaves for 45-50 minutes. Cool on a wire rack.

White and Brown Rolls

COB LOAF
Shape the dough into a large ball. Flatten it slightly and place on a greased baking sheet. Slash the top of the dough with a sharp knife to make a cross. Cover and prove for about 45 minutes in a warm place. Bake for 30-40 minutes.

ROLLS
(makes 12) Baking time for rolls is 10-15 minutes after shaping, proving and glazing.

CLOVER LEAF ROLLS
Divide each 2oz/50g piece of dough into 3 equal parts. Shape into 3 balls. Place on the baking sheet in the shape of a clover leaf and press lightly together.

THREE-STRAND PLAITED ROLLS
Cut off 2oz/50g pieces of risen dough. Divide and roll each piece into three 4in/10cm strands. Plait (braid) as above.

TWO-STRAND PLAITED ROLLS
Divide the 2oz/50g dough pieces in half. Roll each piece into a strand 8in/20cm long. Place the strands in the form of a cross on the work surface. Take the two ends of the lower strand and cross them over the middle of the upper strand so that they lie side by side. Repeat this with the remaining strand and repeat alternately until all the dough has been used. Pinch the ends firmly together. Place on the baking sheet, glaze and decorate, cover, prove and bake.

KNOT ROLLS
Roll 2oz/50g pieces of dough into a thick 6in/15cm strand. Tie into a simple knot.

PLAIT
Divide the dough into three equal pieces. Roll each piece into a strand 12-14in/30-35cm long. Pinch together one end of the three strands and then plait them. Pinch the remaining ends together and lift the plait on to a greased baking sheet. Cover, prove and glaze as for the flowerpot loaf. Decorate with poppy seeds, if desired. Bake for 25-30 minutes.

◀ Bread rolls

W *holewheat* B*read*

INGREDIENTS *makes 1 loaf*

4½ cups/450g/1lb wholewheat flour

2 tbsp/30ml seeds (sesame, caraway or
poppy)

1½ heaped tsp/7.5ml salt

1½ cups/300ml/½pt warm water

1 tbsp/15g/1oz fresh yeast or 1½ tsp/
7g/⅛oz/15g dried yeast

½ tsp/2.5ml molasses

1 tbsp/15ml oil

1 tbsp/15ml malt extract

beaten egg to glaze

1 tsp/5ml seeds (sesame, caraway or
poppy) to top the loaf

METHOD

Mix the flour, seeds and salt together in a warm bowl. Pour a little of the water into a small bowl and add the yeast. Put in a warm place for 10 minutes. If using dried yeast, make up according to manufacturer's instructions.

Add the oil, the malt extract and the molasses to the rest of the water in a jug.

Pour the yeast mixture into the flour and stir. Add enough of the other liquid to make a soft dough, but don't allow it to get too sticky. As different brands of flour absorb different amounts, it may not be necessary to add all this liquid, so don't add it all at once. Gather it with your hands into a ball.

Knead the dough for 20 minutes, then place in a greased plastic bag to rise. Put it in a warm place, such as the airing cupboard or a sunny window sill. Leave it there for an hour.

Pre-heat the oven to 400°F/200°C/Gas 6. Punch down the dough with the heel of the hand to redistribute the raising agent and knead it for a minute. Put it in an oiled loaf tin 8½×4½in/22×12cm. Brush the top with beaten egg and sprinkle over the remaining seeds. Cover the loaf with a clean damp tea towel and leave it to rise on top of the stove.

Bake for 35 minutes. Turn out of the tin and flick the bottom of the loaf with your fingernail. It should sound hollow. The sides of the loaf should spring back when pressed. Allow it to cool on a wire rack.

VARIATION/WALNUT BREAD

For a very good flavoursome loaf with added texture, add ½ cup/50g/2oz roughly chopped walnuts to the flour and use walnut oil instead of olive oil. Omit the molasses. This loaf will fill the kitchen with its delicious nutty aroma and taste marvellous with jam for breakfast. Or try Cheddar and watercress sandwiches in walnut bread with tomato soup for supper.

VARIATION/MARMITE BREAD

For a tangy savoury loaf, omit the molasses and replace the malt extract with Marmite (yeast extract spread). Add 1-2 tbsp caraway seeds to the flour and sprinkle the top of the loaf with the seeds, too. This bread is good with strong Cheddar or simply with butter as an accompaniment to a lunchtime bowl of soup.

▲ Wholewheat bread

Milk Bread

INGREDIENTS *makes 2 loaves*
2 tsp/15g/½oz fresh yeast or 1 package
   dried yeast and ½ tsp sugar
2 cups/450ml/¾pt warm skimmed milk
   or whole milk and water mixed
6 cups/675g/1½lb white flour
1½ tsp/7.5ml salt
1½ tsp/7.5ml sugar
6 tbsp/75g/3oz butter or margarine
beaten egg or milk for glazing

METHOD
Oven temperature 400°F/200°C/Gas 6.

Grease 1 large and 1 small bread tin. Stir
the yeast into the liquid, adding sugar if
dried yeast is used. Allow 15 minutes in a
warm place for dried yeast to become frothy.

Mix the flour, salt and sugar and rub in
the butter or margarine. Stir in the yeast
liquid and mix to a soft dough. Turn the
dough on to a lightly floured board and
knead until it becomes smooth and loses its
stickiness. Return the dough to the warm
mixing bowl and cover it with oiled
polythene. Leave to rise until doubled in
size, about 1½ hours.

Knock back the dough, divide it into 1
large and 1 small piece and shape to fit the
bread tins. Brush the loaves with beaten egg
or milk. Cover the tins with oiled polythene
and allow to rise until doubled in size, about
1 hour.

Preheat the oven. Bake for about 50
minutes and cool on a wire rack.

VARIATION/OLIVE BREAD
Omit the 1½ tsp/7.5ml sugar and stir in 5-6
tbsp/75-90ml olive oil instead of rubbing in
the butter or margarine. Add 1½ cups/
225g/½lb pitted, sliced black olives to the
dough with the dough liquid. The olive
loaves may be shaped into 2 or 3 rounds and
baked on greased baking sheets instead of
being baked in bread tins if preferred.

Potato Bread

INGREDIENTS *makes 3 loaves*
1 (225-250g/8-9oz) large raw potato
2 cups/450ml/¾pt milk
2 tbsp/30g/1oz fresh yeast or 1 package
   dried yeast and 1 tsp/5ml sugar
8 cups/900g/2lb flour
2 tsp/10ml salt
1 egg
3 tbsp/45ml soured cream

METHOD
Oven temperature 350°F/180°C/Gas 4.

Grease three 6½×3½×3in/16×9×7.5cm
bread tins. Grate the peeled potato finely.
Bring the milk to the boil and pour it over the
potato in a bowl. Cool until lukewarm and
add the fresh yeast. If dried yeast is used stir
it, with the sugar, into 3 tbsp warm milk or
water and leave for 8-10 minutes until
frothy.

Add the dried yeast mixture to the
potato-milk mix. Beat in half the flour until
well mixed. Add the salt, egg, soured cream
and the rest of the flour. Beat the mixture
thoroughly.

Cover the bowl with clingfilm and set
aside in a warm place for 2-2½ hours. Knead
thoroughly and divide between the 3 bread
tins.

Prove once again, covered, for about 40
minutes. Preheat the oven and bake for 45
minutes until cooked.

▶▲ Herb bread
▶ Bagels
▲ Milk bread
◀▲ Potato bread

Herb Bread

INGREDIENTS *makes 2 loaves*
2 cups/225g/8oz wholewheat flour
2 cups/225g/8oz plain flour
2 tsp/10g/¼oz margarine
1 tsp/5ml salt
1 tsp/5ml sugar
½ tsp/2.5ml dried dillweed
1 tsp/5ml dill seed
1 tsp/5ml dried savory
2 tsp/15g/½oz fresh yeast or 1 package
    dried yeast and ½ tsp/2.5ml sugar
1¼ cups/300ml/10fl oz warm water
cracked wheat for decoration

METHOD
Oven temperature 450°F/230°C/Gas 8.
    Grease two 7in/18cm loaf tins. Mix the flours and rub the fat into them. Add the salt, sugar and dried herbs. Cream the fresh yeast with the water and add to the flour mixture. If dried yeast is used, stir ½ tsp (2.5ml) sugar into half the dough liquid, sprinkle the yeast on top and leave for 10 minutes in a warm place until frothy. Add with the rest of the water to the flour mixture. Mix to a soft dough and knead on a lightly floured board until smooth. Sprinkle the greased tins evenly with cracked wheat. Half-fill each tin with bread dough.

    Cover the tins with lightly oiled clingfilm or polythene bags. Allow the dough to rise in a warm place until doubled in size. Uncover the dough and bake in the heated oven for about 35 minutes. Remove the loaves from the tins and serve warm.

Bagels

INGREDIENTS *makes 18*
1 tbsp/25g/1oz fresh yeast or 2 tbsp/
    15g/½oz dried yeast and ½ tsp brown
    sugar
2 cups/450ml/¾pt warm milk
1 tsp/5ml brown sugar
¼ cup/50ml/2fl oz vegetable oil
2 tsp/10ml salt
5 cups/550g/1¼lb wholewheat flour (a
    little extra flour may be needed)
2 quarts/2 litres/3¼pts water
2 tbsp/25g/1oz brown sugar
egg wash for glazing (1 egg yolk plus 1
    tbsp/15ml water)
toasted sesame seeds, poppy seeds, or
sautéed chopped onions for decoration

METHOD
Oven temperature 375°F/190°C/Gas 5.
    Grease 2 baking sheets. Dissolve the yeast in the warm milk, adding the sugar if dried yeast is used. Allow about 10 minutes for dried yeast to rehydrate and the liquid to become frothy.

    Add the brown sugar, oil and salt to the yeast liquid and work in the flour by degrees, beating at first and then kneading the stiffer dough. When all the flour has been incorporated, knead the dough on a floured board for 10 minutes. Return the dough to the warm bowl, cover with oiled clingfilm and allow to rise for about 1 hour until doubled in size. Knock back the dough, cover and prove until doubled in size once again.

    Knock back the dough and divide it into 18 equal pieces. Roll each piece into a strand 6in/15cm long, 1in/2.5cm thick, tapering at each end. Shape into rings, pinching the ends firmly together. Cover the shaped bagels and prove for 10-15 minutes. Bring the water to the boil and add the 2 tbsp brown sugar.

    Put 2 or 3 bagels at a time into the boiling water and cook until they rise to the surface (takes 1 or 2 minutes). Lift out the bagels with a perforated spoon. Place them on the greased baking sheets.

    Glaze the bagels with egg wash and sprinkle with seeds or onions.

    Bake until browned, about 20 minutes.

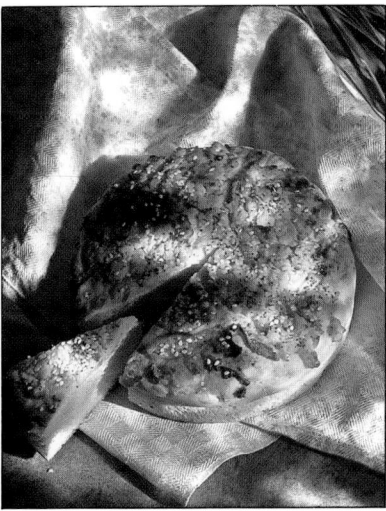

Malt Bread

INGREDIENTS *makes 2 small loaves*
1 tsp/15g/¹⁄₂oz fresh yeast or 2 tsp dried
    yeast and 1 tsp/5ml sugar
2¹⁄₂ cups/600ml/1pt warm water
4 cups/450g/1lb wholewheat flour
1 tsp/5ml salt
2 tbsp/10ml malt
1 tbsp/15ml honey or syrup
2 tbsp/30ml vegetable oil
1 cup/150g/5oz sultanas
honey or syrup for glazing

METHOD
Oven temperature 400°F/200°C/Gas 6
then reduced to 350°F/180°C/Gas 4.

Grease two 6¹⁄₂×3¹⁄₂×3in/16×9×7.5cm
bread tins. Mix the yeast (and sugar) in the
warm water.

Add the malt, honey, oil and sultanas to
the warmed flour. Stir in the yeast liquid and
mix thoroughly. Put the mixture into the
two bread tins.

Set aside for 1 hour in a warm place,
covered with clingfilm. Preheat the oven
and bake at the higher temperature for 15
minutes then reduce to the lower
temperature and bake for a further 20
minutes until cooked. A skewer inserted
into the centre of the loaf should emerge
clean. Place the loaves on a wire rack. Warm
a little honey or syrup and brush the tops of
the loaves while they are still hot.

Onion Bread

INGREDIENTS *makes 1 round loaf*
one quarter of the Quick White Bread
    dough (page 140)
2 cups/225g/8oz onions, sliced
¹⁄₄ cup/50g/2oz butter or margarine
2 tbsp/15g/¹⁄₂oz white flour
²⁄₃ cup/150ml/¹⁄₄pt milk
¹⁄₄ tsp/1.5ml salt or garlic salt
pinch freshly ground black pepper
1 tsp/5ml poppy or sesame seeds

METHOD
Oven temperature 375°F/190°C/Gas 5.

Grease and flour a round cake tin 8in/
20cm in diameter. Roll out the dough to fit
the tin. Put the dough into the tin, cover
with clingfilm and prove until doubled in
size, about 30 minutes.

Cook the onions in the fat in a heavy pan
until transparent and softened. Stir in the
flour and cook for a couple of minutes. Add
the milk, stirring constantly. Bring to the
boil and simmer for another minute. Add
the salt and pepper.

Preheat the oven. Spread the onion
mixture over the dough and sprinkle with
the seeds. Bake for 30 minutes. Serve hot or
cold with soup or salad.

Oatmeal Bread

INGREDIENTS *makes 2 small loaves*
1 tbsp/25g/1oz fresh yeast or 1 package
    dried yeast and 1 tsp/5ml brown
    sugar
2¹⁄₄ cups/550ml/18fl oz warm water
4¹⁄₂ cups/500g/1lb 2oz mixed flour (¹⁄₂
    wholewheat, ¹⁄₂ white flour)
¹⁄₄ cup/25g/1oz gluten (high gluten)
    flour
2 tbsp/30ml brown sugar
2 cups/175g/6oz rolled oats (fine
    oatmeal)
4 tbsp/60ml wheatgerm
4 tbsp/60ml soya flour
2 tbsp/30ml vegetable oil
1¹⁄₂ tsp/7.5ml salt

METHOD
Oven temperature 350°F/180°C/Gas 4.

Grease two small bread tins. Put the yeast
into a bowl (with the sugar, if dried yeast is
used) and stir with ¹⁄₂ cup of the warm water.
Set aside for up to 10 minutes until foamy.
Add the gluten (high gluten) flour, sugar
and half the mixed flours to the rest of the
water and beat well for 5 minutes. Add the
yeast liquid and beat thoroughly. Stir in the
rolled oats and set the mixture aside in a
warm place for about 30 minutes to make a
sponge batter.

Add the wheatgerm, soya flour, oil, salt
and the rest of the mixed flours to the
sponge batter. Turn out on to a floured
board and knead well until smooth. Return
the dough to the bowl and cover with oiled
clingfilm. Set aside in a warm place until
doubled in size, about 30 minutes.

Knock back the dough on a floured board
and divide into 2 pieces. Shape into loaves
and place them in the bread tins. Cover with
oiled clingfilm and allow to rise until double
in size once again. Preheat the oven and
bake for about 1 hour. Cool on a wire rack.

◀▲ Malt bread
▲ Onion bread

Pumpernickel Bread

INGREDIENTS *makes 2 large loaves*
1 tbsp/25g/1oz fresh yeast or 2 tbsp/
    15g/½oz dried yeast and 1 tsp/5ml
    brown sugar
5 cups/1.2l/2pts warm water
1 tbsp/15ml molasses
6 cups/675g/1½lb wholewheat flour
1 cup/100g/4oz dark rye flour
⅔ cup/65g/2½oz buckwheat flour
⅓ cup/50g/2oz cornmeal
2 tsp/10ml salt
1 cup/225g/8oz cooked, mashed potato
1 tsp/5ml caraway seeds
1 cup/100g/4oz wholewheat flour (if
    needed)

METHOD
Oven temperature 375°F/190°C/Gas 5.

Grease two large bread tins. Stir the yeast into one cup of the warm water, adding the brown sugar in the case of dried yeast. Set the dried yeast liquid aside for 10 minutes until frothy.

Mix the wholewheat flour, molasses, yeast liquid and the rest of the warm water to make a very wet dough. Beat well, knead in the bowl until it becomes smooth and less sticky. Add the rest of the ingredients and mix well. Turn on to a floured board and knead, working in the last cup of wholewheat flour if required. Knead until the dough is smooth and elastic. Return it to the bowl and cover with a sheet of clingfilm. Prove in a warm place until doubled in size, 1¼-1½ hours.

Knock back the dough, divide it into 2 pieces. Shape into loaves and put the dough into the bread tins. Cover the tins with oiled polythene and prove once again until doubled in size, about 1 hour. Preheat the oven and bake for about 1 hour, remove the loaves from the tins and bake for a further 10-15 minutes. Cool the bread on a wire rack. Keep the bread for 1 or 2 days before slicing.

▲ ► Oatmeal bread
▲ Pumpernickel bread

Cornbread

INGREDIENTS *makes 16 squares*
1 cup/100g/4oz wholewheat flour
1 cup/100g/4oz cornmeal
½ tsp/2.5ml salt
1 tsp/5ml bicarbonate of soda
¾ tsp/4ml cream of tartar
1½ cups/350ml/12fl oz buttermilk or half
    yoghurt, half skimmed milk
3 tbsp/45ml sunflower oil
2 eggs, beaten
1 tbsp/15ml brown sugar or honey

METHOD
Oven temperature 425°F/220°C/Gas 7.

Grease an 8in/20cm square baking tin. Mix together the flour, cornmeal, salt, soda, and cream of tartar. Stir the buttermilk with the oil, eggs and sugar or honey. Pour the liquid ingredients into the dry mixture and stir together.

Preheat the oven. Put the batter into the baking tin and bake for about 35 minutes. Cut into 2in/5cm squares and serve warm.

Cheese Bread

INGREDIENTS *makes 1 large loaf*
2 tsp/15g/¹/₂oz fresh yeast or 1 tbsp/
    10g/¹/₄oz dried yeast and ¹/₂ tsp/2.5ml
    sugar
1¹/₄ cups/300ml/¹/₂pt warm water
4 cups/450g/1lb white flour
1 tsp/5ml salt
¹/₄ tsp/1.5ml cayenne pepper
¹/₂ tsp dry mustard powder or 2 tsp/10ml
    creamed horseradish
2 tbsp/30ml chives
1 tbsp/15g/¹/₂oz butter or margarine
1 cup/100g/4oz finely grated Cheddar
    cheese
beaten egg or milk for glazing
1-2 tbsp/15-30ml grated cheese for
    decorating (optional)

METHOD

Oven temperature 400°F/200°C/Gas 6.

Grease one large or two small bread tins. Stir the yeast into the warm water, adding sugar if dried yeast is used.

Stand the dried yeast liquid for 10 minutes to become frothy.

Put the flour, salt, cayenne pepper, mustard and chives into a bowl and rub in the fat. Stir in the cheese and then the yeast liquid (and horseradish if used). Work together to make a dough. Turn the dough on to a floured board and knead until smooth and non-sticky.

Return to the bowl, cover with clingfilm and leave to prove for 1 hour until doubled in size. Knock back the dough and shape into 1 large or 2 small loaves. Place the shaped dough in the tin. Brush the dough with beaten egg or milk. Cover the tin with clingfilm and prove in a warm place for about 45 minutes.

Preheat the oven and sprinkle the bread dough with grated cheese if desired.

Bake for about 40 minutes until brown. Turn out and cool the bread on a wire rack.

This bread makes delicious toast and may be used as a quick pizza base.

Swiss Buns

INGREDIENTS *makes 8 buns*
2 tsp/15g/¹/₂oz fresh yeast or 1 tbsp/
    10g/¹/₄oz dried yeast and 1 tsp/5ml
    sugar
²/₃ cup/150ml/¹/₄pt warm milk
2 cups/225g/¹/₂lb white flour
2 tsp/10ml sugar
¹/₂ tsp/2.5ml salt
2 tbsp/25g/1oz butter or margarine

GLACÉ ICING
1¹/₂ cups/175g/6oz icing sugar
3 tbsp/45ml water
colouring (optional)

METHOD

Oven temperature 425°F/220°C/Gas 7.

Grease one or two baking sheets (according to size). Stir the yeast with the milk, adding 1 tsp/5ml of sugar in the case of the dried yeast. If the latter, allow the yeast liquid to stand for 10 minutes or so until frothy.

Mix the flour with the sugar and salt and rub in the fat. Stir in the yeast liquid and mix to a soft dough. Turn on to a lightly floured board and knead thoroughly until the dough loses its stickiness and becomes smooth. Return the dough to the warm bowl, cover with oiled clingfilm and allow to rise until doubled in size, about 1 hour.

Knock back the dough, divide it into 8 pieces and shape each piece into an oblong 5in/12cm long.

Place the buns on the greased baking sheet(s). Cover with oiled clingfilm and allow to prove in a warm place for about 20 minutes. Preheat the oven, uncover the buns and bake for about 15 minutes until browned. Lift on to a wire rack to cool. Combine the icing ingredients and ice the buns with it.

◀▲ Cheese bread
◀ Swiss buns

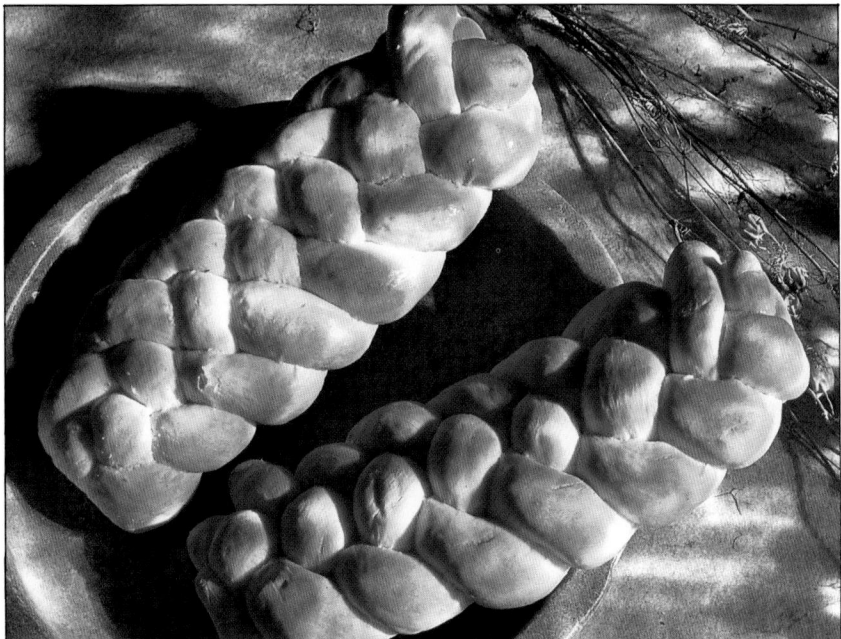

Irish Soda Bread

INGREDIENTS *makes 1 loaf*
4 cups/450g/1lb plain white flour
1 tsp/15ml salt
2 tsp/10ml bicarbonate of soda
1½ tsp/7.5ml cream of tartar
2 tbsp/25g/1oz lard
1¼ cups/300ml/½pt buttermilk

METHOD
Oven temperature 425°F/220°C/Gas 7.

Sift the flour, salt, bicarbonate of soda and cream of tartar into a bowl. Rub in the lard and add enough buttermilk to make a soft dough. Turn the mixture on to a lightly floured board and knead for a minute. Shape into a round and place on the baking sheet. Mark with a cross, cutting deep into the dough.

Preheat the oven and bake for 40-50 minutes, until lightly browned and firm when tapped on the base. Cool the bread on a wire rack.

VARIATIONS
You can use plain milk instead of buttermilk, but if you do, double the quantity of cream of tartar. You can also use a mixture of white and wholewheat flours.

Jewish Chollah Bread

INGREDIENTS *makes 2 loaves*
2 tsp/15g/½oz fresh yeast or 1 tbsp/
   10g/¼oz dried yeast and ½ tsp sugar
1 cup/225ml/8fl oz milk or water
4 cups/450g/1lb white flour
1 tsp/5ml salt
¼ cup/50g/2oz butter or vegetable
   margarine or 2 tbsp/30ml vegetable
   oil
1 tbsp/15ml liquid honey
1 egg, beaten, for glazing

METHOD
Oven temperature 400°F/200°C/Gas 6.

Grease 2 baking sheets. Stir the yeast into the milk, adding the sugar in the case of the dried yeast. Set aside the dried yeast liquid for 5-10 minutes to become frothy. Stir in 1 cup/25g/4oz of the flour and leave in a warm place to ferment.

Add the salt to the rest of the flour. Rub the fat into the flour or stir the oil into the yeast batter. Add the fat and flour (or flour only, if oil has been used) to the yeast batter and honey. Mix to a soft dough. Turn the mixture on to a floured board and knead vigorously until the dough is smooth, elastic and non-sticky, for about 10 minutes. Put the dough back into the bowl and cover it with a sheet of oiled clingfilm. Leave to rise in the warm until doubled in size, about 1 hour.

Knock back the dough and knead it thoroughly. Divide the dough into 2 halves and then slice each half into 4 pieces. Allow the 8 pieces of dough to rest for 5 to 10 minutes covered with oiled clingfilm. Roll 4 pieces of dough into individual lengths of 15in/38cm. Keep the other 4 pieces covered with oiled polythene while the first 4 lengths are plaited. Put the bread plait on to a greased baking sheet, brush with beaten egg and cover with oiled clingfilm. Plait the other four pieces.

When both plaits have rested and proved to double size, preheat the oven and bake them for 30-40 minutes. The chollah loaves should look golden brown and shiny. They keep moist for several days.

▲ ▲ Jewish chollah bread
▲ Irish soda bread

Italian Panettone

INGREDIENTS *makes 1 loaf*

1 tbsp/25g/1oz fresh yeast or 2 tbsp/
   15g/¹/₂oz dried yeast and 1 tsp/5ml
   sugar
³/₄ cup/175ml/6fl oz warm milk
4 cups/450g/1lb white flour
1 tsp/5ml salt
5 tbsp/60g/2¹/₂oz sugar
5 tbsp/60g/2¹/₂oz butter
2 eggs plus 2 egg yolks, beaten
2 tsp/10ml ground cardamom
rind of 2 small lemons, finely grated
¹/₂ cup/75g/3oz mixed dried citrus peel,
   chopped
³/₄ cup/100g/4oz raisins, chopped and
   soaked in 2 tbsp/30ml rum
beaten egg for glazing

METHOD

Oven temperature 425°F/220°C/Gas 7 for
20 minutes, then reduce to 375°F/190°C/
Gas 5 for 30 minutes.

Grease a deep, round cake tin, 20cm/8in
in diameter. Stir the yeast into the milk,
adding 1 tsp/5ml of sugar if dried yeast is
used. Set the dried yeast liquid aside for
about 10 minutes until frothy. Add a quarter
of the flour to the yeast liquid and set aside
in a warm place for ¹/₂ hour. Add to the yeast
batter the rest of the flour, the melted butter,
the beaten eggs and egg yolks, cardamom,
lemon rind, mixed peel and the raisins in
rum. Mix thoroughly to form a heavy
dough. Knead well, cover with oiled
clingfilm and leave to prove for 1¹/₂-2 hours
until risen.

Knock back the dough and knead well.
Put the dough into the greased cake tin.
Brush the top of the loaf with egg wash.
Cover with oiled clingfilm and prove for
about 40 minutes. Preheat the oven, remove
the covering and bake for 50 minutes (see
temperatures above). Turn out of the tin
after 10 minutes and cool on a wire rack.

Walnut, Apricot and Orange Bread

INGREDIENTS *makes 1 large or 2 small loaves*

2 tsp/15g/¹/₂oz fresh yeast or 1 tbsp/
   10g/¹/₄oz dried yeast and 1 tsp honey
1¹/₄ cups/300ml/¹/₂pt warm water
4 cups/450g/1lb wholewheat flour
1 tsp/5ml salt
¹/₄ cup/50g/2oz sugar
¹/₄ cup/50g/2oz butter or margarine
¹/₂ cup/50g/2oz chopped walnuts
1¹/₄ cups/175g/6oz dried apricots,
   soaked and chopped
2 tbsp/30ml grated orange rind

METHOD

Oven temperature 425°F/220°C/Gas 7.

Grease one large or two small bread tins.
Dissolve the yeast (and sugar) in the warm
water leaving the dried yeast to become
frothy (10 to 15 minutes). Mix the flour
with the sugar and salt and rub in the fat. Stir
in the yeast liquid and mix to a dough. Turn
on to a floured board and knead until
smooth. Return the dough to the bowl,
cover it with oiled clingfilm and let it prove
for about 1 hour until doubled in size.
Knead again, working in the nuts, apricots
and orange rind. Shape into a loaf (or 2
loaves) and place them in the prepared
tin(s). Cover the dough and prove once
more for 40-50 minutes.

Preheat the oven and bake for about 45-
50 minutes, depending on the size of the loaf
(loaves).

Allow to cool on a wire rack.

▲ Italian panettone
◀ Walnut, apricot and orange bread

Sally Lunn

INGREDIENTS *makes 2 cakes*
1 tbsp/15g/¹/₂oz fresh yeast or 2 tsp/10g/
  ¹/₂oz dried yeast and 1 tsp/5ml sugar
1¹/₄ cups/300ml/¹/₂pt warm milk
4 cups/450g/1lb flour
1 tsp/5ml salt
2 eggs, beaten
¹/₄ cup/50g/2oz butter or margarine,
  melted and cooled

TO GLAZE
2 tbsp/30ml water
2 tbsp/1oz sugar

METHOD
Oven temperature 425°F/220°C/Gas 7.
  Grease two 6in/15cm cake tins. Stir the
fresh yeast (or dried yeast and sugar) into the
warm milk. If dried yeast is used, set the
bowl aside for 10 minutes until foamy.
  Mix in 1 cup/100g/4oz of the flour and
leave in a warm place for about 20 minutes
until the yeast batter is frothy.
  Mix the remaining flour with the salt and
stir into the yeast with the eggs and melted
butter. Beat well until a smooth batter is
produced. Pour the batter into the cake tins,
cover them with oiled clingfilm and leave in
a warm place for about 1¹/₂ hours until
doubled in size.
  Preheat the oven and bake the cakes for
about 20 minutes until nicely browned.
Turn the cakes on to a wire rack and brush
them with the hot glaze made by boiling the
sugar and water together. Allow to cool a
little before serving warm with clotted
cream or butter.

Swiss Pear Bread

INGREDIENTS *makes 2 small
or 1 large loaf*
5 cups/1kg/2lb dried pears
1¹/₂ cups/225g/8oz sultanas
⁷/₈ cup/100g/4oz hazelnuts, chopped
6 tbsp/50g/2oz thick candied lemon
  peel, diced small
1 cup/225g/8oz sugar
7 tbsp/110ml/4¹/₂fl oz rosewater
¹/₂ glass Kirsch
1 tbsp/15ml powdered cinnamon
2lb/900g White Bread dough, (see page
  140)

METHOD
Oven temperature 425°F/220°C/Gas 7.
  Grease two baking sheets.
  Soak the pears overnight in water to
cover, then stew them in the water in which
they were soaked.
  Drain and mash the pears, removing any
stems or cores. Mix the mashed pears with
the sultanas, nuts, lemon peel, sugar,
rosewater, Kirsch and cinnamon. Knead
half the bread dough with the pear mixture
and shape into two oblong loaves.
  Preheat the oven. Roll out the other half
of the dough on a floured board. Divide it in
two and wrap each pear loaf inside a sheet
of plain dough. Brush the edges of the
dough with milk and seal them. Prick the
loaves with a fork. Bake for 50-60 minutes.

◄▲ Sally Lunn
▲ Swiss pear bread
▲► Almond bread

Almond Bread

INGREDIENTS *makes about 4/5 slices*
3 cups/350g/12oz white flour
2 tsp/10ml baking powder
¹/₄ tsp/1.5ml salt
2 large eggs
¹/₂ cup/120ml/4fl oz sunflower oil
5-6 tbsp/75-90ml honey or brown sugar
2 tsp/10ml grated orange or tangerine
  rind
2 tsp/10ml almond essence
³/₄ cup/100g/4oz chopped almonds

METHOD
Oven temperature 350°F/180°C/Gas 4.
  Sift together the flour, baking powder
and salt. Beat together in an electric blender
or a bowl the eggs, oil, honey, citrus rind and
almond essence. Transfer the mixture into a
large bowl and beat in the flour mixture a
little at a time.
  Stir the almonds into the stiff dough then
divide it into six oblong rolls about 2in/5cm
wide. Place the rolls well apart on a foil
covered baking sheet and bake for 20
minutes.
  Lift out the baking sheet and cut each roll
into seven or eight slices ¹/₂in/1cm thick.
Return the slices to the oven on the baking
sheet and bake for a further 15-20 minutes
until brown. Cool on a wire rack, then store
in a cake tin.

Muffins

INGREDIENTS *makes 12*

1 tbsp/15g/¹/₂oz fresh yeast or 1 tbsp/
   10g/¹/₄oz dried yeast and 1 tsp/5ml
   honey
1 cup/250ml/8fl oz warm water
4 cups/450g/1lb white flour
1 tsp/5ml salt
2 tbsp/25g/1oz butter, melted
2 small eggs, beaten

METHOD

Oven temperature 450°F/230°C/Gas 8 for oven-baked muffins.

Grease two baking sheets and dust them well with rolled oats or wheatgerm or with cornmeal or semolina. Or heat a greased and floured griddle (or heavy frying pan) if the muffins are to be cooked over top heat.

Stir the yeast into the warm milk, adding the honey if dried yeast is used. Set the dried yeast liquid aside for 10 minutes until foamy.

Mix the flour and salt and add the yeast liquid, melted butter and the eggs. Mix to a soft dough in the bowl then turn it out on to a floured board. Knead the dough until it becomes smooth, non-sticky and elastic. Return the dough to the warm bowl. Cover with oiled clingfilm and prove for about 1¹/₄ hours, until doubled in size. Turn the dough on to a lightly floured surface, knead and then roll the dough to ¹/₂in/1cm thickness. Cover with oiled clingfilm and rest for 5 minutes. Cut into 3in/7.5cm rounds with a plain cutter.

Put the muffins on the baking sheets and dust the tops with semolina. Cover with oiled clingfilm and leave to prove for about 40 minutes. Cook the muffins by baking them in the oven for about 10 minutes, turning the muffins over with a palette knife after 5 minutes. Or cook the muffins for 5 minutes on each side on the heated griddle. Stack the muffins on a wire rack.

To serve the muffins, pull them open all around the edges. Leave the halves joined in the centre. Toast them slowly on both sides. Pull the muffins fully apart and place a slice of chilled butter inside. Put the muffin halves together again and serve them hot.

Crumpets

INGREDIENTS *makes about 20*

2 tsp/15g/¹/₂oz fresh yeast or 1 package
   dried yeast and ¹/₂ tsp sugar
1¹/₄ cups/300ml/¹/₂pt warm water
3 cups/350g/12oz white flour
1 tsp/5ml salt
¹/₂ tsp/2.5ml bicarbonate of soda
³/₄ cup/200ml/7fl oz warm milk (more, if
   required, to make a pouring batter)

METHOD

Heat a greased griddle or heavy frying pan. When ready to cook the batter, grease crumpet rings, egg-poaching rings or plain biscuit cutters 3in/7.5cm in diameter. Stir the yeast into the water, adding the sugar if dried yeast is used.

Let the dried yeast liquid stand for 5-10 minutes until frothy. Mix in half the flour and beat well. Set the batter aside in a warm place for about 30 minutes until foamy.

Add the rest of the ingredients to the batter, stirring thoroughly. Beat well, adjusting the milk quantity if necessary.

Place the crumpet rings on the heated griddle and pour 2 tbsp/30ml batter into each ring. Cook until set underneath and holes appear on the upper surface. Take away the rings and turn the crumpets with a palette knife. Lightly cook the second side. Cool the crumpets stacked on a wire rack. Serve freshly made with butter or toast them on both sides, serving them hot with butter, later on.

▲ Crumpets
▼ Muffins

Oatcakes

INGREDIENTS *makes about 22*
½ cup/100g/4oz soft brown sugar
½ cup/50g/2oz plain untreated flour
1 cups/100g/4oz wheat flour
1⅓ cups/100g/4oz porridge oats
pinch bicarbonate of soda
pinch salt
8 tbsp/100g/4oz butter
1 egg yolk

METHOD
Pre-heat the oven to 350°F/180°C/Gas 4.
Mix the dry ingredients together in a bowl.
Cut the butter into small pieces in the bowl
and rub in with the fingertips.

Mix in the egg yolk and form into a
dough. Knead for a few minutes and then
roll out thinly on a lightly floured surface
and cut into rounds with a biscuit cutter.

Leaving plenty of space between each
one, arrange the rounds on a greased baking
sheet and bake for 10-15 minutes until crisp
and golden. Allow to cool slightly before
transferring to a wire rack. When cool, store
in an airtight tin. Serve with cheese.

Pitta Bread

INGREDIENTS *makes 8*
Use the same ingredients and follow the
recipe for Wholewheat Bread, up to and
including paragraph 4 (page 141).

METHOD
Pre-heat the oven to 450°F/230°C/Gas 8.
Punch down the dough with the heel of the
hand and kneed for a minute. Divide the
dough into 8 and roll out into thin ovals.
Place on baking sheets and cover with clean
damp cloths. Leave on top of the stove for
20 minutes.

Bake for 5-7 minutes. Allow to cool.
These pitta breads freeze very successfully.

▲ Pitta bread

151

Bran and Sultana Muffins

INGREDIENTS *makes 12*
2 tbsp/30ml oil
2 tbsp/30ml honey
1 egg
150ml/5fl oz milk
1¼ cups/125g/5oz wholewheat flour
75g/3oz bran
2 tsp/10ml baking powder
pinch salt
⅓ cup/50g/2oz sultanas

METHOD
Pre-heat the oven to 375°F/190°C/Gas 5. Beat together the oil and honey. Beat in the egg. Gradually beat in the milk until smooth.

Combine the dry ingredients and stir these into the liquid ones. When the bran has soaked up the liquid, you should have a soft dough.

Spoon into an oiled muffin tin and bake for about 20 minutes.

Spiced Buttermilk Scones

INGREDIENTS *makes 8*
2 cups/225g/8oz plain untreated flour
2 cups/225g/8oz wholewheat flour
2 tsp/10ml bicarbonate of soda
2 tsp/10ml cream of tartar
1 tsp/15ml fruit sugar
1 tsp/5ml mixed spice
8 tbsp/100g/4oz butter
300ml/10fl oz buttermilk
3 tsp baking powder

METHOD
Pre-heat the oven to 425°F/220°C/Gas 7. Sift the flours together and mix thoroughly with the other dry ingredients. Cut the butter into the flour mix and rub in well.

Stir in the buttermilk and mix to form a soft dough. Knead the dough lightly on a floured board. Divide in half, form each half into a round and cut each round into four wedges. Place the wedges on a greased baking sheet, dust with flour and bake for about 12 minutes.

Cool on a wire rack. While still warm, slice in half and fill with butter and jam.

▲ ▲ Bran and sultana muffins
▲ Spiced buttermilk scones

Sesame Snaps

INGREDIENTS *makes about 20*
1 cup/100g/4oz wholewheat flour
½ cup/50g/2oz sesame seeds
1 tsp/5ml baking powder
1-2 tsp/5-10ml salt
2 tsp/10ml tahini paste
1 tbsp/15ml olive oil
3-5 tbsp/45-75ml tepid water

METHOD
Pre-heat the oven to 425°F/220°C/Gas 7. Combine the dry ingredients in a bowl. Add the tahini paste and olive oil and mix with the fingertips until crumbly. Gradually add enough water to form a soft dough.

Knead gently on a floured board and then roll out thinly. Press out rounds with a biscuit cutter and arrange on a greased baking sheet. Bake in the oven for 15 minutes until crisp and golden.

Cool on a wire rack, store in a tin and serve with cheese.

Rye Savoury Biscuits

INGREDIENTS *makes about 20*
2tbs/25g/1oz butter
1 cup/100g/4oz rye flour
pinch salt
a little milk, heated

METHOD
Pre-heat the oven to 350°F/180°C/Gas 4. Rub the butter into the flour with a pinch of salt, and bind with a little milk to form a dough. Knead for about 7 minutes.

Form the dough into about 20 small balls and roll flat on a floured surface.

Bake on a biscuit tray for about 10 minutes, until the edges are just beginning to brown. Cool on a wire rack. Store in a tin and serve with butter and cheese.

▶ Sesame snaps

Stuffed Potato Paratha

INGREDIENTS *makes about 20*
5 cups/450g/1lb potatoes, boiled and
    mashed
1 small onion, finely chopped
1-2 green chillies, finely chopped
1 tbsp/15ml coriander leaves, chopped
¾ tsp/4ml salt
¾ tsp/4ml ground roasted cumin

DOUGH
2¾/325g/12oz cups plain flour
½ tsp/2.5ml salt
4 tbsp/60ml oil
¾ cup/175ml/6fl oz hot water
Ghee (see page 126) for frying

METHOD
Mix all the ingredients of the filling together
and set aside.

To make the dough, sieve the flour and
salt together. Rub in the oil. Add enough
water to form a stiff dough. Knead for about
10 minutes until you have a soft smooth
dough. Divide into 20 balls.

Roll out two balls into 4in/10cm rounds
each. Place about 1½-2 tbsp/20-30ml of the
filling on one of the rounds and spread it
evenly. Place the other round over the filling,
sealing the edges with a little water.

Roll out gently into 7in/18cm rounds,
and be careful that no filling comes out. Roll
out all the parathas in a similar manner.

Heat a frying pan over medium heat.
Place a paratha in the frying pan and cook
for about 1 minute until brown spots
appear. Turn and cook the other side.

Add 2 tsp/10ml Ghee and cook for 2-3
minutes until golden brown. Turn and cook
the other side, adding more Ghee if
required. Make all the parathas in the same
way. Serve warm.

Indian Lucchi Bread

INGREDIENTS *makes about 40*
2¾ cups/350g/12oz plain flour
½ tsp/2.5ml
2 tbsp/30ml oil
¾ cup/175ml about 6fl oz hot water
oil for deep-frying

METHOD
Sieve the flour and salt together. Rub in the
oil. Slowly add enough water to form a stiff
dough. Knead for about 10 minutes until

you have a soft pliable dough.

Divide the dough into about 40 small
balls and flatten each ball.

Roll out a few balls on a slightly oily
surface into rounds of 4in/10cm across (do
not roll out all the balls at the same time as
they tend to stick).

Heat oil in a karai or cast-iron frying pan
over high heat. Put in a lucchi and press the
middle with a slotted spoon as this causes
the lucchi to puff up. Turn and cook the
other side for a few seconds. Drain and serve
hot.

▲ ◄ Stuffed potato paratha
◄ Indian lucchi bread

154

N *aan*

INGREDIENTS *makes 12*
1 tsp/5ml dried yeast
1 tsp/5ml sugar
³/₈ cup/75ml/3fl oz lukewarm water
2³/₄ cups/275g/10oz plain flour
¹/₂ tsp/2.5ml salt
³/₄ tsp/4ml baking powder
1 tbsp/15ml oil
about 3 tbsp/45ml plain yoghurt

METHOD
Stir the yeast and sugar into the water and
set aside for 15-20 minutes until frothy.

Sieve together the flour, salt and baking
powder. Make a well in the middle, add the
yeast liquid, oil and yoghurt and knead for
about 10 minutes till soft and not sticky.

Place the dough in an oiled plastic bag
and set aside in a warm place for 2-3 hours
until double in size.

Knead again for 1-2 minutes and divide
into 12 balls. Roll into 7in/18cm rounds.

Place as many as possible on a baking
sheet and put in a pre-heated oven 400°F/
200°C/Gas 6 for 4-5 minutes each side until
brown spots appear. Place them for a few
seconds under a hot grill until slightly
browned. Keep warm to serve.

▲ Naan   ▼ Baktora yoghurt bread

B *aktora* Y *oghurt* B *read*

INGREDIENTS *makes 12-14*
2¹/₄ cups/225g/8oz plain flour
1¹/₂ tsp/7.5ml baking powder
¹/₂ tsp/2.5ml salt
1 tsp/5ml sugar
1 egg, beaten
about 3 tbsp/45ml yoghurt
oil for deep-frying

METHOD
Sieve the flour, baking powder and salt
together. Mix in the sugar.

Add the beaten egg and enough yoghurt
to form a stiff dough. Knead for 10-15
minutes until you have a soft, smooth
dough. Cover with a cloth and let it rest for
3-4 hours.

Knead again on a floured surface for 5
minutes. Divide into 12-14 balls.

Roll out on a floured surface into 5in/
12.5cm rounds.

Heat the oil in a karai over high heat. Fry
the batora, pressing in the middle with a
slotted spoon so that it puffs up. Turn and
cook the other side for a few seconds until
lightly browned. Drain.

Hazelnut and Apricot Crunch

INGREDIENTS *makes about 16*
8 tbsp/100g/4oz butter
$\frac{1}{3}$ cup/50g/2oz soft brown sugar
2 tbsp/30ml maple syrup
1$\frac{1}{3}$ cups/100g/4oz porridge (rolled) oats
$\frac{1}{2}$ cup/50g/2oz chopped hazelnuts
$\frac{1}{3}$ cup/50g/2oz dried apricots, chopped

METHOD
Pre-heat the oven to 350°F/180°C/Gas 4. Put the butter, sugar and syrup in a heavy pan and stir over a low heat until combined.

Stir in the remaining ingredients. Press into a Swiss roll pan lined with greaseproof paper. Bake for about 45 minutes, until golden. Cut into bars in the pan using an oiled knife. Cool in the tin.

Amarett Biscuits

INGREDIENTS *makes about 20*
2 egg whites
$\frac{1}{2}$ cup/100g/4oz fruit sugar
$\frac{2}{3}$ cup/100g/4oz ground almonds
1 tsp/5ml kirsch (optional)
few drops vanilla essence
almond slivers for decorating

METHOD
Pre-heat the oven to 350°F/180°C/Gas 4. Whisk the egg whites until they form soft peaks. Gradually add the sugar, whisking continuously until the mixture is thick and lustrous. Stir in the ground almonds, kirsch and vanilla.

Line baking sheets with sheets of rice paper. Take a spoonful of mixture about the size of a plum and roll it into a ball in the palms of your hands. With a sticky mixture, you will find it easier if your hands are wet. Flatten the balls and arrange them on the baking trays with plenty of space for them to expand during cooking.

Decorate each biscuit with a sliver of almond and bake for 20-30 minutes. Allow to cool slightly, then carefully remove biscuits with their rice paper bases (which are edible) and cool them completely on a wire rack. Store in an airtight tin.

◄ Hazelnut and apricot crunch

Courgette and Cream Cheese Loaf

INGREDIENTS *makes 1 loaf*
4 baby courgettes
1 egg, beaten
4 tbsp/60ml oil
2 tbsp/30ml honey
2 tbsp/30ml molasses
2 tbsp/30ml cream cheese
1½ cups/175g/6oz wholewheat flour
½ cup/50g/2oz soya flour
pinch salt
2 tsp/10ml baking powder
1 tsp/5ml bicarbonate of soda

METHOD
Pre-heat the oven to 325°F/170°C/Gas 3. Cut the courgettes into thin strips, leaving on the peel, then cut into ½in/1cm pieces.

Put the egg in a bowl and beat in the oil, honey and molasses. Beat in the cream cheese until smooth.

In another bowl, combine the dry ingredients, stirring well. Mix in the courgettes. Gradually stir the dry ingredients into the cream cheese mixture.

Transfer batter to a greased and floured loaf tin and bake for 50-60 minutes.

Muesli Biscuits

INGREDIENTS *makes 15-20*
1 cup/175g/6oz sultanas or raisins
⅜ cup/50g/2oz dried apricots, chopped
1 egg, beaten
2 tbsp/25g/1oz butter, melted with
2 tbsp/30ml hot water
1½ cups/175g/6oz muesli
1 heaped tbsp/25g/1oz chopped nuts

METHOD
Pre-heat the oven to 350°F/180°C/Gas 4. Pick over dried fruit and wash in boiling water. Drain. In a bowl beat the fruit with egg and butter. Stir in muesli and nuts.

Line a biscuit tray with greased waxed paper and spread the mixture thinly over it. Mark into fingers and bake for 45 minutes.

Cut fingers through and allow to cool for 10 minutes before removing from the tray. Finish cooling on a wire rack.

◄ Courgette and cream cheese loaf

Wholewheat Pastry

INGREDIENTS
3/4 cup/75g/3oz wholewheat flour
3/4 cup/75g/3oz wholewheat self-raising
flour
pinch salt
6 tbsp/75g/3oz polyunsaturated
margarine
water

METHOD
Mix the flours and salt together in a bowl.
Cut the fat into small pieces in the flour and
rub in with your fingertips until the mixture
is fine and crumbly. Add enough water to
bind together and roll into a smooth ball.
Chill in the fridge for 20 minutes.

To use, roll the pastry out on a floured
surface.

▲ Wholewheat pastry
▶ Cheese pastries

Shortcrust Pastry

INGREDIENTS
1 cup/100g/4oz flour
pinch salt
4 tbsp/50g/2oz butter or a mixture of
butter and margarine
2 tbsp/30ml cold water

METHOD
Sift the flour and salt into a bowl. Cut up the
butter and crumble it into the flour. Mix in
just enough water with a knife to make a
firm dough and gather it into a ball. On a
floured surface, knead the dough gently
until smooth. Wrap it in plastic wrap and
refrigerate for a short while to firm.

To line a pie plate, roll out the pastry on a
floured surface to a thickness of 2.5-5mm/
1/8-1/4in and about 5cm/2in bigger than the
pie plate. Grease the pie plate and lay the
pastry gently in it, pressing it down to fit the
bottom and sides. Prick the bottom lightly
and leave to rest in a cool place for 30
minutes.

Soured Cream Pastry

INGREDIENTS
2 3/4 cups/275g/10oz flour
scant 1 cup/200g/7oz butter or
margarine
1 egg
1 tbsp/15ml rum (optional)
2 tbsp/30ml soured cream
1/3 cup/75g/3oz castor sugar

METHOD
Rub the flour and butter together. Mix in the
remaining ingredients to make a firm
dough. Knead well and let it rest for half an
hour before using.

This is excellent for any pie or tart that
requires a sweet pastry. You can make
delicious cookies from any trimmings when
using the pastry (or make some specially for
cookies).

Yoghurt Pastry

INGREDIENTS
1/2 cup/100g/4oz butter or margarine,
cut into small pieces
1 1/2 cups/175g/6oz flour
1 tsp/5ml baking powder
3/8 cup/75ml/3fl oz yoghurt

METHOD
Combine the butter, flour and baking
powder, rubbing them together until the
mixture is like fine breadcrumbs. Add the
yoghurt and stir it in well. Gather the pastry
together and knead it gently. Refrigerate it
for an hour or more. Use as required. This
recipe makes a nice soft pie (shortcrust)
pastry, suitable for sweet or savoury pies.

Cheese Pastry

INGREDIENTS
1 1/3 cups/225g/8oz curd cheese
1/2 cup/100g/4oz butter
1/2 cup/100g/4oz margarine
2 1/4 cups/225g/8oz flour
1 tsp/5ml baking powder

METHOD
Mix the cheese and fats together and rub
them into the flour and baking powder.
Refrigerate for a minimum of 3 hours.

VARIATION
For a strudel, roll out and spread with
chopped apples, jam, raisins, crushed
cornflakes and sugar. Roll up and bake.

For individual pastries, cut pastry into
squares measuring about 5cm/2in. Fill with
apricot jam, finely chopped apples with
raisins, or cheese filling. Fold over to make a
triangle or bring the corners together in the
middle. Brush with beaten egg and bake at
350°F/180°C/Gas 4 for 30 minutes.

CHEESE FILLING
2/3 cup/100g/4oz cream cheese
1/2 beaten egg
1 tbsp/15ml sugar
grated lemon rind

METHOD
Mix everything together well and use as
required.

Apricot Tart

INGREDIENTS *serves 4-6*
2½ cups/600ml/1pt yoghurt
   shortcrust pastry to line a pan
   approximately 19cm/7½in
1½ cups/400g/14oz canned apricots
⅜ cup/90ml/3½fl oz whipping cream
2 tbsp/30ml cornflour
¼ cup/50g/2oz castor sugar
1 tbsp/15ml lemon juice
2 tsp/10ml vanilla extract
1 egg, separated

METHOD
Drain the yoghurt for 3 hours. Bake the pastry case for 10 minutes. Drain the fruit (save the juice for use in a fruit salad) and lay the apricot halves on the pastry. When the yoghurt has drained, mix it together with the whipped cream and remaining ingredients except the egg white, beating everything to a smooth mixture.

Whisk the egg white until it is stiff and fold it into the other mixture. Spoon it over the apricots and bake at 325°F/170°C/Gas 3 for 50 minutes.

VARIATION
Use curd cheese or quark (1¼ cups/225g/8oz) instead of the yoghurt if preferred.

▲ Apricot tart
▶ French apple tart

Danish Apple Pie

INGREDIENTS *serves 4-6*
shortcrust pastry to line a pan
   approximately 19cm/7½in
5 medium/700g/1½lb cooking apples,
   peeled, cored and sliced
¼ cup/50ml/2oz water
¼ cup/50g/2oz sugar
1 tbsp/½oz butter
1 tsp/5ml ground cinnamon
1 cup/250ml/8fl oz soured cream
2 tbsp/30ml castor sugar

METHOD
Bake the pastry for 10 minutes at 350°F/180°C/Gas 4. Make a thick apple sauce using the apples, water, sugar, butter and half of the cinnamon. There shouldn't be any excess liquid when the apples are cooked, but if there is, cook for a few minutes more without a lid, stirring to prevent the apples sticking.

Let the apple sauce cool a little before turning into the pie shell. Spoon the soured cream over the apples. Mix the rest of the cinnamon with the sugar and sprinkle this over the soured cream. Bake at 400°F/200°C/Gas 6 for 30 minutes.

This is best served warm, rather than straight from the oven, but it is also good cold.

French Apple Tart

INGREDIENTS *serves 6*
¾ cup/75g/3oz plain untreated flour
¾ cup/75g/3oz wholewheat flour
⅓ cup/50g/2oz ground almonds
8 tbsp/100g/4oz butter, softened
1 egg
¼ cup/50g/2oz fruit sugar
pinch salt

THE FILLING
6 cooking apples
10 tbsp/150g/5oz butter
2-3 tbsp/30-45ml fruit sugar
2 tsp/10ml mixed spice

METHOD
Pre-heat the oven to 400°F/200°C/Gas 6. To make the pastry, sift the flours and almonds together onto a board and make a well in the middle. Put the remaining ingredients into the well and work in with your fingertips until you have a smooth dough. Knead for a few minutes, then leave for half an hour in the fridge.

Meanwhile, peel, core and slice the apples. Heat the butter in a pan and fry the apples gently until soft and golden.

Add the sugar and spice and cook, stirring, until the apple is coated with syrup.

Line a greased 8in/22cm loose-bottomed quiche pan with the pastry and fill with the apple. Bake for 25-30 minutes and serve with whipped cream.

Chocolate Cake

INGREDIENTS *serves 6*
1/2 cup/100g/4oz butter or soft margarine
3/4 cup/175g/6oz sugar
2 eggs, beaten
2 1/4 cups/225g/8oz flour
1 tsp/5ml baking powder
4 tbsp/50g/2oz cocoa
1 tsp/5ml bicarbonate of soda
1 cup/225ml/8fl oz yoghurt
1 tsp/5ml vanilla extract

METHOD
Beat the butter and sugar together until light. Add the eggs and continue beating. Sieve the flour, baking powder, cocoa and bicarbonate, and mix it into the butter mixture. Add the yoghurt and vanilla extract, mix in thoroughly.

Turn the mixture into a well greased cake pan, measuring approximately 8in/20cm. (Use two sandwich pans or a large ring mould if preferred.) Bake at 350°F/180°C/Gas 4 for 25 minutes. Insert a knife to test and cook a little longer if necessary. Timing obviously depends on the type of pan used.

Cool and ice with Cream Cheese Frosting (see page 165) or serve sprinkled with icing sugar.

Fruit Tartlets

INGREDIENTS *serves 6-8*
6-8 small pie shells, baked
2/3 cup/100g/4oz cream cheese
1/2 tsp/2.5ml vanilla extract (optional)
1-2 tsp/5-10ml castor sugar
3-4 cups/450g/1lb fresh fruit (raspberries, grapes, strawberries, redcurrants etc)
apricot jam to glaze

METHOD
Mix the cream cheese with the vanilla and just enough sugar to make a mixture the consistency of thick cream. Spoon into the baked and cooled pie shells. Cover the cream cheese with fresh fruit (de-pip the grapes). Melt a little apricot jam in a saucepan and brush over the fruit to glaze it.

Use a selection of different fruits to make an attractive plate of pastries. You could also make one large pie and fill the pie shell with alternate rings of different fruits.

Buttermilk Spice Cake

INGREDIENTS *serves 6*
2 1/4 cups/300g/10oz flour
1 cup/225g/8oz sugar
1 1/2 tsp/7.5ml bicarbonate of soda
1 tsp/5ml baking powder
pinch salt
1 tsp/5ml ground cinnamon
1/2 tsp/2.5ml ground cloves
1/2 cup/100g/4oz butter, melted
1 1/2 cups/350ml/12fl oz buttermilk
2 eggs

METHOD
Sift the dry ingredients together. Add the butter and buttermilk and beat the mixture until it is smooth. Pour the batter into a greased and floured cake pan measuring approximately 8in/20cm. Bake at 350°F/180°C/Gas 4 for 40 minutes.

Pumpkin, Sunflower and Raisin Cake

INGREDIENTS *serves 6-8*
2 1/4 cups/350g/12oz pumpkin
2 1/4 cups/225g/8oz wholewheat flour
pinch salt
2 tsp/10ml baking powder
1 tsp/5ml bicarbonate of soda
1/3 cup/50g/2oz sunflower seeds, chopped
1/3 cup/50g/2oz raisins
2 eggs
2 tbsp/30ml honey
2 tbsp/30ml molasses
1 tbsp/15ml warm water

METHOD
Pre-heat the oven to 375°F/190°C/Gas 5. Peel the pumpkin, cut into smallish pieces and boil until tender. Drain and cut up finely.

Combine flour, salt, baking powder, sunflower seeds and raisins and mix well.

In another bowl, beat the eggs and stir in the honey and molasses. Add 1 tbsp/15ml of warm water with the pumpkin and beat well.

Mix all the ingredients together thoroughly and pour into a greased and floured tin. Bake for 50-60 minutes until done. Allow to stand for 10 minutes in the tin, then cool on a wire rack.

Pecan Pie

INGREDIENTS *serves 4-6*
1 1/2 cups/250g/8oz pastry (see page 158)
4 tbsp/50g/1oz butter, softened
2 tbsp/30ml honey
2 tbsp/30ml maple syrup
3 eggs
1 tsp/5ml vanilla essence
1 cup/100g/4oz pecan halves
whipped cream

METHOD
Pre-heat the oven to 425°F/220°C/Gas 7. Line a 8 1/2in/22cm tin with the chosen pastry. Prick and bake blind for 10 minutes.

Meanwhile, make the filling. Beat the butter together with the honey and syrup until smooth. In another bowl, beat the eggs and vanilla essence thoroughly with a wire or rotary whisk. Pour in the syrup, beating constantly with a fork.

Scatter the nuts evenly over the pastry base and pour the custard over. Bake in the middle of the oven for 10 minutes. Reduce the heat to 325°F/160°C/Gas 3 and bake for a further 25-35 minutes until the filling is set, but not dry. Serve warm (but not hot) or cold with whipped cream.

Yoghurt Cake

INGREDIENTS *serves 4*
5/8 cup/150ml/1/4pt yoghurt
2 1/2 cups/250g/9oz flour
3 tsp/15ml baking powder
1/4 cup/60ml/2 1/2fl oz oil
3/4 cup/175g/6oz sugar
1 tsp/5ml vanilla extract
2 eggs

METHOD
Mix everything together well. Beat until smooth. Turn the mixture into a well-greased cake pan measuring approximately 20cm/8in. Bake at 180°C/350°F/Gas 4 for 45 minutes. Insert a knife to test and cook a little longer if necessary.

This is a good basic recipe with many variations. To make an upside-down fruit cake sprinkle the bottom of the pan with brown sugar and lay sliced apples, pears or canned pineapple on the sugar, cover with the cake mixture and cook as directed.

▲ Pecan pie   ▼ Pumpkin, sunflower and raisin cake

Continental Cheesecake

INGREDIENTS *serves 6 - 8*
Soured Cream Pastry (see page 158)
6 tbsp/75g/3oz butter or margarine
4 tbsp/75g/3oz castor sugar
1/3 cup/50g/2oz raisins
grated lemon rind
1 1/3 cups/225g/8oz curd cheese
2 tbsp/30ml soured cream
2 eggs, separated
1 tsp/5ml vanilla essence

METHOD
Line a 9in/23cm pie plate with the pastry and bake for 5 minutes. Reserve some pastry to decorate the top of the cake. Mix the remaining ingredients except the egg whites together well. Beat the whites until they are stiff and fold them into the mixture.

Turn it into the prepared pie shell and decorate with the reserved pastry in a criss-cross pattern. Bake at 350°F/180°C/Gas 4 for 30 minutes.

Greek Cheesecake

INGREDIENTS *serves 6*
shortcrust pastry to line a pan
    approximately 7 1/2/19cm
2 2/3 cups/450g/1lb curd cheese
4 eggs
3/8 cup/100g/4oz clear honey
1 tsp/5ml ground cinnamon

METHOD
Bake the pastry for 15 minutes at 350°F/180°C/Gas 4. Mix the curd cheese, eggs, honey and cinnamon together well (in a blender or food processor is excellent). Fill the partially baked pie shell with the mixture and bake it at 350°F/180°C/Gas 4. for 30 minutes.

VARIATION
The Greek name for this cake is siphnopitta (literally cake from the island of Siphnos). It is very easy to make and a nice variation on the cheesecake theme. You can use ricotta cheese if you prefer.

▲ ▶ Carrot cake
◀ Continental cheesecake

Carrot Cake

INGREDIENTS *serves 6*
6 tbsp/75g/3oz butter
generous 1 cup/250g/9oz castor sugar
3 eggs
2 3/4 cups/300g/10oz flour
2 tsp/10ml bicarbonate of soda
1/2 tsp/2.5ml salt
1/2 tsp/2.5ml ground cinnamon
2/3 cup/150ml/1/4pt yoghurt
4 cups/350g/12oz carrots, finely grated
3/4 cup/100g/4oz chopped walnuts or
    mixed nuts

METHOD
Cream the butter and sugar. Add the eggs one at a time. Sift the flour, bicarbonate of soda, salt and cinnamon, and add this mixture to the creamed mixture alternately with the yoghurt. Fold in the carrots and nuts and mix them in thoroughly but gently.

Turn into a greased and floured cake pan measuring approximately 8in/20cm. Bake at 350°F/180°C/Gas 4 for 45 minutes. Insert a knife to test and cook a little longer if necessary.

Ice the cake with the Cream Cheese Frosting (see next column) for the all-American cake. It is very good on its own if you find the frosting too rich.

Cream Cheese Frosting

INGREDIENTS *Ices an 8in/20cm cake*
2 tbsp/25g/1oz unsalted butter
2/3 cup/75g/3oz icing sugar
grated lemon rind
1 1/3 cups/225g/8oz cream cheese

METHOD
Mix everything together until smooth - a blender or food processor speeds the work. Refrigerate until required. Spread on top or as a filling for cakes.

This is the classic American icing for carrot cake (preceeding recipe). It is also good with the Chocolate Cake (see page 162) or indeed any cake which you want to ice.

VARIATION
To make frosting with different flavours, omit the lemon rind and substitute:
1 tsp/5ml vanilla extract;
or 1 tbsp/15ml orange juice and grated orange rind;
or 1/2 tsp/2.5ml ground cinnamon;
or 2 tbsp/25g/1oz melted bitter chocolate;
or 2 tbsp/30ml very strong coffee.

Apple Cake

INGREDIENTS *serves 6*
3 medium cooking apples, peeled, cored
  and sliced
a little cider
1 clove
2 tbsp/30ml butter, softened
2 tbsp/30ml honey
2 tbsp/30ml molasses
1 egg
1 tsp/5ml mixed spice
pinch salt
2 tsp/10ml baking powder
1 tsp/5ml bicarbonate of soda
½ cup/75g/3oz raisins
1½ cups/175g/6oz wholewheat flour
4 tbsp/15g/1oz wheatgerm
1 tsp/5ml mixed spice

METHOD
Pre-heat the oven to 350°F/180°C/Gas 4.
Poach the apple slices in a little cider with
the clove until soft. Remove clove. Drain
and reserve cider. Purée apples in a blender.

In a large bowl mix butter, honey,
molasses and 1 tbsp/15ml reserved cider.
Beat in egg. Stir in apples and remaining
ingredients and mix well.

Pour batter into a greased and floured
loaf tin, 9×4in/22×10cm, and bake for
about an hour until firm. Allow to stand for
10 minutes, then turn out of the tin and cool
completely on a wire rack.

Fresh Fruit Dessert Cake

INGREDIENTS *serves 8*
2 eggs
¼ cup/75ml/⅛ milk
2 tbsp/30ml honey
2 tbsp/30ml molasses
1½ cups/175g/6oz wholewheat flour
1 tsp/5ml baking powder
1 tsp/5ml bicarbonate of soda
1 tsp/5ml cinnamon
pinch salt
500g/1lb peaches
250g/½lb plums

250g/½lb cherries
1 cup/100g/4oz walnuts, chopped
a little butter
fresh fruit to decorate
whipped cream

METHOD
Pre-heat the oven to 400°F/200°C/Gas 6.
Beat the eggs with the milk. Stir in the honey
and molasses. Stir in the rest of the dry
ingredients and mix well.

Stone and chop the fruit. Mix it into the
batter with the nuts. Pour into a greased and
floured 9in/22cm cake tin with a removable
bottom (spring form cake pan) and bake for
50-60 minutes until set in the middle. Dot
with butter towards the end of the cooking
time to prevent the top drying out.

Allow to cool in the tin. Chill in the
fridge, decorate with fresh fruit and serve
with whipped cream.

▲ Apple cake

166

DESSERTS AND PUDDINGS

Fruit fools and trifles, souffles and mousses, rich ice creams and low-calorie ices are on the menu. There is something for everyone here; from the most sweet-toothed to the carefully diet- and health-conscious.

Rose petal trifle

Blackcurrant Froth

INGREDIENTS
²/₃ cup/150ml/¹/₄pt yoghurt
2 eggs, separated
1 tbsp/15ml crème de cassis (or
    blackcurrant syrup)
¹/₄ cup/50g/2oz castor sugar
2 cups/225g/8oz blackcurrants

METHOD
Stir the yoghurt and egg yolks together with
the crème de cassis and sugar until the sugar
is dissolved.

Just before serving, whisk the egg whites
until stiff and fold them into the yolk
mixture. Fold the blackcurrants in gently.
Spoon into individual dishes.

Serve with sponge fingers or cookies.

VARIATION
Change the flavours by using a different
liqueur: orange liqueur with a little grated
orange rind; chocolate liqueur with some
grated chocolate. If you want to prepare this
some time before serving it, refrigerate the
yolk mixture and add the whites and
currants at the last minute.

▲ Blackcurrant froth

Orange Chiffon

INGREDIENTS *serves 4-6*
1 tbsp/15ml gelatine
¹/₂ cup/100ml/4fl oz orange juice
5 tbsp/75ml castor sugar
2 eggs, separated
1 cup/250ml/8fl oz buttermilk
grated orange peel

METHOD
Soak the gelatine in orange juice. Heat this
gently until the gelatine is dissolved.
Remove the pan from the heat. Beat 3 tbsp/
45ml sugar with the yolks until light and
fluffy. Add this to the gelatine mixture and
stir it over a very low heat until it begins to
thicken. Pour the thickened mixture into a
bowl and add the buttermilk and orange
peel. Mix together and chill until it is
beginning to set.

Beat the egg whites until they are stiff.
Fold in the remaining sugar. Combine the
egg whites and the gelatine mixture, stirring
gently.

Turn the chiffon into a serving dish (or use
individual glasses) and refrigerate until
required.

VARIATION
If you prefer you can make a pie by turning
this mixture into a baked pie crust and
refrigerating it in the crust. Decorate the
chiffon with slivers of candied fruit or
chocolate.

Orange Cream

INGREDIENTS *serves 4*
2 eggs, separated
2 tbsp/30ml castor sugar
juice and grated rind of 1 orange
1¹/₃ cups/225g/8oz cream cheese
2 tbsp/30ml orange-flavoured liqueur

METHOD
Beat the yolks with the sugar until they are
thick and creamy. Add the orange juice and
rind and mix it in well. Soften the cheese and
add it to the egg mixture. Add the liqueur.

Beat the whites until they are stiff. Fold in
a little of the beaten whites to the cheese
mixture and then gently fold in the rest.
Spoon into four glasses and serve

immediately.

If you want to prepare this in advance,
leave the egg whites until just before you are
going to serve, and whisk the whites and
fold them into the cheese mixture at the very
last minute. If you make it in advance with
the egg whites it may separate - if this
happens, stir through before serving.

VARIATION
Use curd cheese or quark for a less rich
version.

Rhubarb Cream Jelly

INGREDIENTS *serves 6*
2¹/₂ cups/600ml/1pt yoghurt
4 cups/450g/1lb rhubarb
sugar to taste
1 tsp/5ml vanilla essence
¹/₂ tsp/2.5ml ground cinnamon or a
    small piece of cinnamon stick
1 cup/250ml/8fl oz whipping cream,
    whipped
2 tbsp/15g/¹/₂oz gelatine
2 tbsp/30ml boiling water

METHOD
Drain the yoghurt for about 3 hours.

Cook the rhubarb with the sugar, vanilla
essence and cinnamon with just enough
water to stop it from burning. You will need
1¹/₄ cups/300ml/¹/₂pt of cooked rhubarb.
Mix the cooked rhubarb with the drained
yoghurt and the whipped cream. Mix
gently until everything is combined.

Dissolve the gelatine in the boiling water,
mixing well until smooth. Add to the
rhubarb mixture, stirring the gelatine in
quickly.

Turn the mixture into a moistened small
ring mould and chill until set. Serve with
more whipped cream if desired.

VARIATION
Use 1¹/₃ cups/225g/8oz quark, fromage
blanc or curd cheese if preferred instead of
the drained yoghurt.

Crème Caramel

INGREDIENTS *serves 6*
4 tbsp/60ml fruit sugar
4 tbsp/60ml water

THE CUSTARD
600ml/20fl oz milk
few drops vanilla essence
4 eggs
3 tbsp/45ml fruit sugar

METHOD
Pre-heat the oven to 350°F/180°C/Gas 4. For the caramel, put the sugar and the water in a heavy saucepan and stir over a low heat until the sugar has dissolved. Bring to the boil and boil until the syrup is golden. Pour the caramel into six individual moulds (or one large one) and swirl it around so that it coats the bottom and sides.

Bring the milk and vanilla essence to the boil in a saucepan. Remove from the heat.

Beat the eggs and sugar together in a bowl. Gradually add the hot milk, stirring all the while.

Strain or ladle the custard into the moulds. Stand them in a roasting tin half filled with hot water and bake for 45 minutes until set. Allow to cool and then chill. Don't turn out the crème caramel until you are ready to serve or it will lose its gloss.

▼ Crème caramel

169

Russian Pashka

INGREDIENTS *serves 6*
¾ cup/175g/6oz castor sugar
¾ cup/175g/6oz unsalted butter
2 egg yolks
2 cups/350g/12oz cottage cheese,
   drained and sieved
⅔ cup/150ml/¼pt soured cream or thick
   cream
1⅓ cups/225g/8oz mixed dried fruit
1 tsp/15ml vanilla essence

METHOD
Cream the sugar and butter together until it
is light and fluffy. Beat in the egg yolks one at
a time. Add the drained and sieved cottage
cheese to the butter mixture and mix well
together. Add the remaining ingredients,
mixing them all in well.

   Turn the mixture into a serving dish and
refrigerate for a minimum of 2 hours.

Damson Mousse

INGREDIENTS
1lb/450g damsons or other plums
sugar to taste
1 cup/250ml/8fl oz water
1 tbsp/15ml gelatine
3 tbsp/45ml boiling water
⅔ cup/150ml/¼pt yoghurt
2 egg whites

METHOD
Cook the damsons with sugar and water.
Rub the cooked fruit through a sieve to
make a thick purée. Check the sweetness
and add more sugar if necessary.

   Dissolve the gelatine in the boiling water
and add it to the purée. Leave the mixture to
cool and when it is beginning to set fold in
the yoghurt. Beat the egg whites until they
are stiff. Add a little of the beaten whites to
the damson mixture to lighten it and then
fold in the rest of the whites.

   Refrigerate for a minimum of 6 hours -
overnight if possible. The longer you leave
it, the better the flavour.

VARIATION
Try this with other fruit - well flavoured
plums or other stewed fruit.

Chestnut Whips

INGREDIENTS *serves 4*
1¼ cups/425g/15oz can unsweetened
   chestnut purée
2 tbsp/30ml dark rum
1 tbsp/15ml dark muscovado sugar
⅔ cup/150ml/5fl oz strained Greek
   yoghurt
2 egg whites
chopped chestnuts or pistachio nuts

METHOD
Beat the chestnut purée, rum, sugar and
yoghurt together until smooth.

   Whisk the egg whites until stiff and fold
into the chestnut mixture.

   Spoon into 1 large or 4 individual serving
dishes.

   Chill for 1 hour, decorate with chopped
nuts and serve.

▲ ▲ Russian pashka
▲ Chestnut whips
◀ Damson mousse

Rose Petal Trifle

INGREDIENTS *serves 6*

2 eggs
4 tbsp/50g/2oz dark brown muscovado
    sugar
½ tsp/2.5ml ground cinnamon
4 tbsp/25g/1oz wholemeal flour
4 tbsp/25g/1oz plain flour
1 tbsp/15g/½oz polyunsaturated
    margarine, melted
2 egg yolks
2 tbsp/15g/½oz cornflour
2 tbsp/25g/1oz light muscovado sugar
1¼ cups/300ml/½pt skimmed milk
1 tbsp/15ml triple strength rose water
4 passion fruit, halved
6oz/175g raspberries
2 tbsp/30ml whipping cream, whipped
    or strained Greek yoghurt
rose petals

METHOD

Line and lightly grease an 18cm/7in
sandwich tin. Whisk the eggs and dark
muscovado sugar together, until thick and
creamy.

Fold in the cinnamon, flours and melted
margarine. Pour into the tin and bake in a
pre-heated oven at 350°F/180°C/Gas 4 for
20 minutes, or until risen and firm. Turn out
and cool.

Beat the egg yolks, cornflour and light
muscovado sugar together. Heat the milk
until boiling and pour on to the egg mix.
Return to the saucepan and cook, stirring
continuously, over a gentle heat until
thickened.

Add the rose water, cover and set aside
until cold.

Cut the sponge into cubes and place in
the base of a serving dish. Scoop the flesh
from the passion fruit and spoon over the
sponge. Top with raspberries.

Pour over the custard and pipe the cream,
or spoon the yoghurt on top. Garnish with
rose petals and serve.

Raspberry and Apple Layer

INGREDIENTS *serves 6*

1lb/450g dessert apples, peeled, cored
    and chopped
8oz/225g ripe raspberries, puréed
1 tbsp/15ml light muscovado sugar
2 tbsp/25g/1oz polyunsaturated
    margarine
2oz/50g wholemeal breadcrumbs
4oz/100g muesli biscuits, crushed
1 tsp/5ml mixed spice
raspberries
green apple slices

METHOD

Place the apples in a saucepan with 1 tbsp/
15ml water, cover and gently cook until
tender. Beat or process in a liquidizer or food
processor to a purée.

Mix with the raspberry purée and sugar.
Leave to cool.

Melt the margarine in a saucepan, add
the breadcrumbs and stir over a low heat
until browned. Stir in the muesli biscuits
and mixed spice. Place the fruit purée and
crumb mix in alternate layers in glass bowls.
Decorate with fruit and serve.

Banana and Cherry Yoghurt

INGREDIENTS *serves 4*

4 very ripe bananas, cut into pieces
2 tsp/10ml lemon juice
1¼ cups/300ml/½pt natural low fat
    yoghurt
8oz/225g fresh cherries, pitted
cherry pairs with stalks

METHOD

Mash the bananas with the lemon juice.
Mix in the yoghurt.

Divide the pitted cherries between four
tall glasses and top with the banana
yoghurt.

Hang a pair of cherries over the edge of
each glass to decorate. Serve chilled, alone
or with wholemeal biscuits.

Berry Meringue

INGREDIENTS *serves 4-6*

crushed meringues to line a 7in/18cm
    baking dish
2½ cups/350g/12oz blackberries
⅔ cup/150ml/¼pt soured cream
2 tsp/10ml castor sugar
½ tsp/2.5ml vanilla essence

METHOD

Line the baking dish with the crushed
meringues. Cover with the blackberries.
Mix the soured cream, sugar and vanilla
essence together and spoon this over the
berries. Bake at 350°F/180°C/Gas 4 for 20
minutes.

NOTE

If you are a frequent baker of meringues you
may well suffer from a surfeit of crushed
meringues - here is the answer to the
problem. Other berries would do but
blackberries have the particular acidity
which contrasts with the sweetness of the
meringues.

▲ ▲ Banana and cherry yoghurt
▲ Raspberry and apple layer
► Berry meringue

Cheese Blintzes

INGREDIENTS *makes 8-9 pancakes*
1 recipe Pancakes (see page 68)
2 cups/350g/12oz curd cheese
1 egg yolk
1tbsp/15ml sugar
butter

METHOD

Make the pancakes. Mix the cheese, egg yolk and sugar together well. Put a spoonful of the mixture onto the cooked side of each pancake and make a square parcel by folding two edges to the middle and then folding the remaining two edges over.

Melt a little butter and fry the filled pancakes, folded side down first, turning over to fry the second side until lightly browned. Keep the cooked pancakes hot while frying the remaining ones. Serve hot.

NOTE

Blintzes freeze very well. Cook them and, when cold, wrap in foil and freeze. Cook them from frozen in the oven with a dab of butter on each one, or if defrosted, warm through in a frying pan. You can make a less rich filling by using cottage cheese, or a richer one by using cream cheese.

▶ Cheese blintzes

Buckwheat Pancakes with Bilberries

INGREDIENTS *makes 9 small pancakes*
³/₈ cup/40g/1¹/₂oz wholewheat flour
¹/₈ cup/40g/1¹/₂oz buckwheat flour
pinch salt
1 egg
²/₃ cup/150ml/5fl oz milk
1tbsp/15ml melted butter

THE FILLING
500g/1lb bilberries
4tbsp/60ml honey
whipped cream to serve

METHOD
To make the pancake batter, sift the flours and salt into a bowl. Make a well in the middle of it and add the egg.

Gradually beat in the milk. When half of the milk has been added, beat in the melted butter. Continue beating in the milk until you have a thin batter. Allow the batter to stand for half an hour.

Meanwhile, prepare the filling. Wash and pick over the bilberries. Put them in a heavy-bottomed pan over a very low flame. It is best to add no water at all. When the fruit is submerged in its own juice, add the honey and stir until dissolved. The syrup should be thick and fruity.

To make the pancakes, oil a heavy-bottomed pan 7in/18cm in diameter. Place it on the flame and when it is very hot, add 2tbsp/30ml of the batter. Tilt the pan so that the batter covers the base. Cook until the pancake is beginning to brown on the underside and then turn over and cook the other side. You may have to throw the first pancake away, as it will absorb the excess oil in the pan.

Continue making pancakes, keeping them warm, until all the batter has been used up. Divide the filling between them and roll the pancakes into cigar shapes.

Serve each pancake with a dollop of whipped cream.

Apple Drop Scones

INGREDIENTS *serves 4-6*
1¹/₂ cups/175g/6oz flour, sieved
5tbsp/90g/3¹/₂oz brown sugar
1 egg
⁷/₈ cup/225ml/7fl oz yoghurt
3 medium/450g/1lb cooking apples, peeled, cored and grated
¹/₂tsp/2.5ml ground cinnamon
butter or margarine for frying

METHOD
Combine the flour, sugar, egg and yoghurt and mix together very well until smooth. Fold in the grated apples and the cinnamon and mix well. Heat a frying pan or griddle and grease lightly.

Drop spoonfuls of the mixture onto the pan, cooking three or four at a time, depending on the size of the pan. Flip the pancakes over when bubbles start to appear. Keep them warm while you cook the rest.

NOTE
Serve with butter or jam if desired, although they are good just on their own.

Sweet Potato and Apricot Pancakes

INGREDIENTS *serves 6-8*
recipe Pancakes (page 68)

FILLING
³/₄ cup/100g/4oz dried apricots
2 large sweet potatoes
butter
honey
cinnamon
soured cream

METHOD
Soak the apricots overnight. Bring to the boil and simmer till tender. Drain and reserve the liquid. Chop the apricots.

Peel and roughly cut up the sweet potatoes. Put in a saucepan, pour over the apricot liquid and cover with water. Bring to the boil and simmer until cooked.

Mash the sweet potatoes with a little butter. Add honey and cinnamon to flavour. Mix in the apricots.

Place a dollop of mixture onto each pancake and roll up. Heat through and serve with a drizzle of honey and soured cream.

▶ Buckwheat pancakes with bilberries

Toffee Banana

INGREDIENTS *serves 4*
4 bananas, peeled
1 egg
2tbsp/15g/½oz plain flour
oil for deep-frying
4tbsp/50g/2oz sugar
1tbsp/15ml cold water

METHOD
Cut the bananas in half lengthways and then cut each half into two crossways.

Beat the egg, add the flour and mix well to make a smooth batter.

Heat the oil in a wok or deep-fryer. Coat each piece of banana with batter and deep-fry until golden. Remove and drain.

Pour off the excess oil leaving about 1tbsp/15ml oil in the wok. Add the sugar and water and stir over a medium heat to dissolve the sugar. Continue stirring and when the sugar has caramelized, add the hot banana pieces. Coat well and remove. Dip the hot bananas in cold water to harden the toffee and serve immediately.

Red Bean Paste Pancakes

INGREDIENTS *makes about 12*
2 cups/225g/8oz plain flour
6tbsp/120ml/4fl oz boiling water
1 egg
3tbsp/45ml oil
4-5tbsp/100g/4oz sweetened red bean paste or chestnut purée

METHOD
Sift the flour into a mixing bowl and very gently pour in the boiling water. Add about 1tsp oil and the beaten egg.

Knead the mixture into a firm dough and then divide it into 2 equal portions. Roll out each portion into a long 'sausage' on a lightly floured surface and cut it into 4-6 pieces. Using the palm of your hand, press each piece into a flat pancake.

On a lightly floured surface, flatten each pancake into a 6in/15cm circle with a rolling pin and roll gently.

Place an ungreased frying pan on a high heat. When hot, reduce the heat to low and place one pancake at a time in the pan. Turn it over when little brown spots appear on the underside. Remove and keep under a damp cloth until you have finished making all the pancakes.

Spread about 2tbsp red bean paste or chestnut purée over about 80% of the pancake surface and roll it over three or four times to form a flattened roll.

Heat the oil in a frying pan and shallow-fry the pancakes until golden brown, turning over once. Cut each pancake into 3-4 pieces and serve hot or cold.

▲ Red bean pancakes
▶ Toffee banana

Noodle Pudding

INGREDIENTS *serves 6*
1 cup/175g/6oz cottage cheese
1/2 cup/75g/3oz cream cheese
2/3 cup/150ml/1/4pt soured cream
3 eggs
1/2 cup/100g/4oz sugar
3 1/2 cups/350g/12oz flat noodles, cooked
    and drained
1/2 cup/75g/3oz raisins or sultanas
4 tbsp/50g/2oz butter or margarine,
    melted
1 tsp/5ml ground cinnamon
1 tsp/5ml sugar

METHOD
Mix the cottage and cream cheese with the soured cream. Beat the eggs and sugar together and add them to the cheese mixture. Fold in the cooked noodles and raisins.

Turn the mixture into a buttered ovenproof dish. Pour on the melted butter. Mix the cinnamon and sugar together and sprinkle it over the top of the noodle mixture. Bake at 350°F/180°C/Gas 4 for 1 hour. Serve hot.

VARIATION
This hearty Central European pudding has many variations. Add chopped apples or soaked dried apricots to the mixture before baking. Vary the cheese mixture to include more cottage cheese or use curd cheese instead of the cream cheese.

Brown Rice Pudding

INGREDIENTS *serves 4*
1/2 cup/100g/4oz brown rice
2 1/2 cups/600ml/1pt China tea
1 stick cinnamon
1/3 cup/50g/2oz sultanas
3/8 cup/50g/2oz dried apricots, chopped
1/4 cup/50g/2oz almonds
sliced fresh fruit (optional)

METHOD
Wash the rice thoroughly under running water. Put it in a heavy pan with the tea and simmer gently for about an hour with the cinnamon.

Pre-heat the oven to 350°F/180°C/Gas 4. Remove the cinnamon and transfer the rice to an ovenproof dish. Stir in the remaining ingredients and bake for about 25 minutes until done. Serve hot or refrigerate and serve cold. Garnish with sliced fresh fruit, if liked.

Apple Pudding

INGREDIENTS *serves 4-6*
2 1/2 cups/600ml/1pt yoghurt
2/3 cup/150ml/1/4pt whipping cream
2 eggs
4 tbsp/75g/3oz castor sugar
grated lemon rind
1 large cooking apple, peeled and sliced
1/2 tsp/2.5ml ground cinnamon
2 tbsp/25g/1oz sugar

METHOD
Drain the yoghurt for about 4 hours. Whip the cream and fold it into the drained yoghurt. Beat the eggs with the sugar and lemon rind and add to the yoghurt mixture.

Turn into a greased shallow oven dish. Lay the apple slices on top of the yoghurt mixture. Scatter cinnamon on top and then the sugar.

Bake at 350°F/180°C/Gas 4 for 50 minutes. Serve warm.

▶ Baked apple
▶▶ Apple, Strawberry and Blackberry Pudding

Apple, Strawberry and Blackberry Pudding

INGREDIENTS *serves 4*
4 cooking apples
1 tbsp/15ml honey
³/₄ cup/100g/4oz strawberries
³/₄ cup/100g/4oz blackberries
2¼ cups/225g/8oz wholewheat flour
½ cup/100g/4oz butter
2 tbsp/30ml sesame seeds
1 tsp/5ml mixed spice
pinch salt

METHOD
Pre-heat the oven to 350°F/180°C/Gas 4.
Peel and core the apples and cut into slices.
Put apples in a shallow ovenproof dish with
a little water and the honey and cook,
covered, in the oven for 30 minutes.

Meanwhile, hull and slice the
strawberries and pick over the blackberries.

Now make the crumble. Place the
remaining ingredients in a bowl and rub in
the butter with the fingers until the mixture
resembles fine breadcrumbs.

When the apples are ready, mix in the
strawberries and blackberries, adding a
little more honey if liked. Press the crumble
mixture gently on top of the fruit and return
to the oven for 15 minutes until golden
brown. Serve hot or cold with cream.

Baked Apples

INGREDIENTS *serves 4*
4 cooking apples, cored
2 tbsp/25g/1oz butter
2 tbsp/25g/1oz sugar
²/₃ cup/150ml/¼pt yoghurt
2 tbsp/25g/1oz brown sugar
½ cup/75g/3oz chopped nuts

METHOD
Score the apples around the middle. Place
them in a shallow baking dish. Mix the
butter and sugar together and fill the centre
of each apple with the mixture.

Bake the apples uncovered at 400°F/
200°C/Gas 6 for 20 minutes. Mix the
yoghurt with the brown sugar and nuts and
pour this mixture over the baked apples.
Return to the oven for a further 10 minutes.
Serve hot.

Lemon Soufflé

INGREDIENTS *serves 4-6*
3 eggs, separated
¾ cup/175g/6oz castor sugar
6 tbsp/40g/1½oz flour
4 tbsp/75ml/3fl oz lemon juice
lemon rind, grated
1½ cups/350ml/12fl oz yoghurt
icing sugar

METHOD

Mix the egg yolks with all the remaining ingredients in a heatproof bowl. Place the bowl over a pan of simmering water and cook until you have a mixture the consistency of thick cream, stirring constantly. Remove the bowl from the heat.

Beat the egg whites until stiff. Fold them into the cooled mixture.

Turn it into a buttered soufflé dish, measuring 7×3in/18×7½cm, and cook at 325°F/170°C/Gas 3 for 40 minutes. Sprinkle with icing sugar before serving.

Pear Soufflé

INGREDIENTS *serves 4-6*
1lb/450g pears
1-2 tbsp/15-30ml butter
a little honey
pinch cinnamon
3 large eggs, separated

METHOD

Pre-heat the oven to 400°F/200°C/Gas 6. Peel, halve and core the pears. Cut them into slices.

Heat the butter in a pan and add the pear slices. When the fruit has softened, raise the heat a little, break up the fruit with a wooden spoon and cook till mushy.

Put the contents of the pan into a blender. Blend until smooth and add a little honey and cinnamon to taste. Pour into a bowl and beat in the egg yolks.

Butter a 60fl oz/1.75l soufflé dish. Whisk the egg whites until they form soft peaks and fold into the mixture. Pour into the soufflé dish and bake in the oven for 20-25 minutes until just golden brown and nearly set.

▶ Lemon soufflé

Clementine Cups

INGREDIENTS *serves 4*
4 clementines
juice 1 orange
¾ sachet powdered gelatine
1 tsp/5ml clear honey
6 tbsp/120ml/4fl oz strained Greek
    yoghurt
1 egg white
1 clementine, peel and pith removed,
    segmented
evergreen leaves
grated plain carob bar

METHOD
Using a zig-zag cut, remove the tops from
the clementines. Carefully scoop out all the
flesh and reserve the shells.

Press the fruit through a sieve to extract
the juice. Mix with the orange juice.

Sprinkle the gelatine over 3 tbsp/45ml
juice in a small saucepan and heat gently to
dissolve. Stir in the honey and place in the
bowl.

Add the remaining juice and leave until
almost setting. Fold in the yoghurt. Whip
the egg white until stiff and fold in.

Refrigerate until the mixture holds its
shape, place in shells and chill until set.
Sprinkle with grated carob, decorate with
clementine segments and serve on a bed of
green leaves.

Couer à La Creme

INGREDIENTS *serves 4*
1⅓ cups/250g/8oz cream cheese
½ cup/100g/4oz yoghurt
1⅓ cups/250g/8oz strawberries
⅔ cup/150ml/¼pt cream
1-2 tbsp/15-30ml honey

METHOD
Blend the cream cheese with the yoghurt
and pack into the small heart-shaped
moulds traditional with this dessert. Chill.

Make a strawberry sauce by blending
half the strawberries with the cream and
honey. Unmould the cheeses onto
individual plates, surround with the sauce
and decorate with the remaining
strawberries.

Ricotta al Cafe

INGREDIENTS *serves 4*
1 cup/225g/8oz ricotta cheese
2 tbsp/30ml fruit sugar
4 tbsp/60ml finely ground fresh coffee
2 tbsp/30ml brandy

METHOD
Choose really moist ricotta cheese, or use
fresh curd or cottage cheese as a substitute.
Press the cheese with half the sugar through
a sieve to make it light and fluffy. Form into
mounds on four individual dessert plates.

Sprinkle half the coffee over the cheese
mounds. Spoon the remaining coffee and
sugar onto the plates in two separate heaps
at the side of the cheese and pour the brandy
over the sweetened cheese. Scoop up some
of the cheese and eat with a little of the
coffee and sugar with each mouthful.

Fruity Yoghurt Cassata

INGREDIENTS *serves 4*
8oz/225g no-need-to-soak apricots
1¼ cups/300ml/½pt grapefruit juice
2 egg whites
1 cup/225g/8oz strained Greek yoghurt
⅓ cup/50g/2oz sultanas
¼ cup/25g/1oz flaked almonds
mint sprigs

METHOD
Place the apricots and grapefruit juice in a
saucepan, bring to the boil, cover and
simmer for 10 minutes, until apricots are
soft.

Purée in a liquidizer or food processor
and leave to cool, and thicken.

Fold the yoghurt into the apricot purée
and place in a freezerproof container. Freeze
for 1½-2 hours or until the edges become
softly frozen.

Whisk the egg whites until stiff. Mix the
yoghurt ice together and fold in the
sultanas, almonds and egg whites. Return
to the freezer for 3-4 hours or until frozen.

Serve scoops in individual dishes,
garnished with mint sprigs.

NOTE
Where possible use freshly squeezed fruit
juices, rather than ready prepared ones, to
ensure a healthier juice.

▲ ▲ Clementine cups
◀ ▲ Fruity yoghurt cassata

Carrot Halva

INGREDIENTS *serves 4-6*
1lb/450g/4 cups carrots, peeled and
    grated
1½pts/900ml/3¾ cups milk
⅔ cup/150g/5oz sugar
3 cardamoms
4 tbsp/60ml Ghee (see page 126)
2 tbsp/30ml raisins
2 tbsp/30ml pistachio nuts, skinned and
    chopped

METHOD
Place the carrots, milk, sugar and
cardamoms in a large saucepan and bring to
the boil. Lower heat to medium low and,
stirring occasionally, cook until all the
liquid has evaporated.

Heat the ghee in a large frying pan over
medium heat, add the cooked carrots,
raisins and pistachios and, stirring
constantly, fry for 15-20 minutes until it is
dry and turned reddish in colour. Serve hot
or cold.

▲▲ Carrot halva
◀▲ Carob upside down pudding
▲▶ Pineapple delights
▶ Yoghurt with saffron

Carob Upside Down Pudding

INGREDIENTS *serves 4*
2 small pears, peeled, cored and halved
2 eggs, separated
3 tbsp/40g/1½oz dark brown
    muscovado sugar
1½ tbsp/23ml carob powder
2 tbsp/25g/1oz plain wholemeal flour
2 tbsp/25g/1oz ground almonds
1 tbsp/15ml clear honey
kumquat slices

METHOD
Arrange the pears in the base of a 7in/18cm
round cake tin, which has been lightly
greased.

Whisk the egg yolks together with the
sugar until light and creamy. Whisk in 1
tbsp/15ml hot water and the carob powder.
Fold in the flour and almonds.

Whisk the egg whites until stiff and fold
into the carob mix. Pour over the pears and
cook in a pre-heated oven at 375°F/190°C/
Gas 5 for 35 minutes.

Turn out onto a warmed serving dish.
Brush the pears with honey. Decorate the
pudding with kumquat slices and serve.

Yoghurt with Saffron

INGREDIENTS *serves 4*
2½ cups/600ml/1pt yoghurt
¼ tsp/1.5ml saffron
1 tbsp/15ml warm milk
½ cup/100g/4oz castor sugar
2 tbsp/30ml pistachio nuts, skinned and
    chopped

METHOD
Put the yoghurt in a muslin bag and hang it up for 4-5 hours to get rid of the excess water.

Soak the saffron in the milk for 30 minutes.

Whisk together the drained yoghurt, sugar and saffron milk till smooth and creamy.

Put in a dish and garnish with the nuts. Chill until set.

Pineapple Delights

INGREDIENTS *serves 4-6*
2 small pineapples, trimmed and halved
3 kiwi fruits, sliced
2 peaches, peeled and sliced
2oz/50g black grapes, halved and
    seeded
2 tbsp/30ml orange liqueur
2 tbsp/30ml orange juice
1 tbsp/15ml clear honey

METHOD
Scoop the flesh out of the pineapple shells, leaving the skins intact.

Remove the hard core and cut the flesh into bite-sized pieces.

Add the kiwi fruit, peaches and grapes. Mix the liqueur, orange juice and honey together. Warm gently in a saucepan to dissolve the honey, if necessary.

Pour over the fruit and leave to marinate until ready to serve. Pile the fruit into the pineapple shells, pour over the syrup and serve.

Vanilla Soufflé

INGREDIENTS *serves 4-6*
2½ cups/600ml/1pt yoghurt
6 tbsp/75g/3oz butter, softened
3 eggs, separated
⅔ cup/150g/5oz castor sugar
1 tsp/5ml vanilla essence

METHOD
Drain the yoghurt for about 4 hours. Mix the drained yoghurt with the butter, egg yolks and vanilla essence. Beat the egg whites until they are stiff and fold in the sugar. Fold a little of the white mixture into the yoghurt mixture to lighten it and then carefully fold in the rest.

Butter and lightly flour a small soufflé dish, measuring 7×3in/18×7½cm. Turn the mixture into the dish and bake at 375°F/190°C/Gas 5 for 30 minutes.

VARIATION
Use 1⅓ cups/225g/8oz quark, fromage blanc or curd cheese instead of yoghurt if preferred.

Chocolate Yoghurt Ice Cream

INGREDIENTS *serves 4-6*
4 tbsp/60ml cocoa
1/2 cup/100g/4oz sugar
2/3 cup/150ml/1/4pt boiling water
2 tsp/10ml vanilla essence
2 1/2 cups/600ml/1pt yoghurt
1/2 cup/100ml/4fl oz whipping cream
2 egg whites

METHOD
Make a syrup by combining the cocoa and sugar with the boiling water. Mix until it is smooth and add the vanilla essence. Leave to cool.

Whip the cream and mix the chocolate syrup with the yoghurt and whipped cream.

Pour the mixture into a shallow tray and place it in the freezer. Stir it from time to time while it is freezing.

When it has frozen, after about 6 hours, remove from the freezer and mix in a blender or food processor until it is mushy. Add the egg whites to the mixture and blend them in to make the mixture light.

Return the mixture to the freezer for a minimum of 12 hours.

Rich Honey and Plum Ice Cream

INGREDIENTS *serves 4*
4-5 plums
1 tbsp/15ml milk powder
6 tbsp/120ml/4fl oz honey
2 tbsp/30ml yoghurt
few drops vanilla essence
2/3 cup/150ml/1/4pt whipping cream

METHOD
Put plums in a bowl and pour over boiling water. After 1 minute, the skins will split. Drain and pour over cold water. Peel the fruit, discard the stones and chop finely.

Purée the fruit with the milk powder and honey in a blender until smooth. Stir in the yoghurt and vanilla essence. Freeze the mixture.

When the mixture is almost frozen, remove it from the freezer and beat it. Whisk the cream and stir the two together. Return to the freezer.

Orange Buttermilk Ice

INGREDIENTS *serves 4*
2 eggs
1/4 cup/50g/2oz castor sugar
3/4 cup/175ml/6fl oz golden syrup
2 cups/450ml/16fl oz buttermilk
2/3 cup/150ml/1/4pt orange juice
grated rind of orange

▲▲ Orange buttermilk ice
▲ Grapefruit sorbet

METHOD
Blend everything together well. Freeze for a minimum of 3 hours. Blend again until smooth and return to the freezer. Freeze overnight or longer. (This ice stays remarkably soft even when frozen for some weeks.)

Grapefruit Sorbet

INGREDIENTS *serves 4*
1 3/4 cups/400ml/14fl oz grapefruit juice
3 tbsp/40g/1 1/2oz golden granulated sugar
2 egg whites
1 pink grapefruit, peel and pith removed, segmented
4 tsp/60ml Grenadine (optional)

METHOD
Mix the grapefruit juice and sugar together and freeze in a shallow freezer container until slushy, about 1-1 1/2 hours.

Whisk the egg whites until stiff, beat the grapefruit mixture to break up the ice crystals and fold in the egg whites.

Freeze until firm. Place the grapefruit segments in the base of chilled glasses and top with scoops of sorbet.

Pour 1 tsp/5ml Grenadine over the top of each sorbet, just before serving, if wished.

QUICK MICROWAVE DISHES

The microwave and vegetables were made for each other. Little or no water is needed for cooking, keeping the goodness in the food, and crispness, flavour and colour intact. Since the microwave has become a fact of life in many homes, this section is a valuable extra for the modern vegetarian cook.

Cannelloni

Mushroom Soup

INGREDIENTS *serves 4*
2 tbsp/25g/1oz butter
1 onion, peeled and chopped
1 garlic clove, crushed
6 cups/450g/1lb mushrooms, washed
¼ cup/25g/1oz flour
2½ cups/600ml/1pt vegetable stock
½ tsp/5ml thyme
1 bay leaf
2 sprigs of parsley
¼ cup/60ml/2fl oz single cream

METHOD
Melt the butter in a large casserole or bowl
for 2 minutes.

Add the onion and garlic and cook on full
power for 2 minutes.

Slice the mushrooms finely and chop the
stalks separately. Add to the onion, cook on
full power for 3 minutes. Stir and cook for a
further 2 minutes.

Remove from the microwave oven and
stir in the flour until it has mixed well with
any remaining butter. Add half the
vegetable stock, stir well and cook for 5
minutes at full.

Mix the thyme, bay leaf and parsley with
the remaining stock and pour the mixture
over the mushrooms. Season well and cook
on full power for a further 10 minutes.
Allow to stand for 5 minutes and remove the
herbs.

Stir in the cream. The soup can be
liquidized if you prefer a smoother texture.

Parsnip and Apple Soup

INGREDIENTS *serves 4*
2 tbsp/25g/1oz butter
1 onion, diced
4 cups/450g/1lb parsnips, diced
½lb/225g/8oz cooking apples
1 tsp/5ml mixed herbs
1qt/1l/1¾pts vegetable stock
1 cup/250ml/8fl oz single cream
1 tbsp/15ml chopped parsley

METHOD
Melt the butter in a browning dish for 2
minutes. Add the onion to the melted butter
and cook on full power for 2 minutes.

Add the parsnips to the onion and cook
on full power for 3 minutes. Add the sliced
apple and herbs and cook for a further 2
minutes.

Pour on the stock and cook, covered, for
10 minutes on full power. Allow to stand for
a few minutes.

Put the soup in a blender or liquidizer,
add the cream and re-heat for 5 minutes.

Sprinkle with chopped parsley and serve
with wholemeal bread.

French Onion Soup

INGREDIENTS *serves 4*
2 tbsp/25g/1oz butter
8½ cups/900g/2lb onions, sliced
¼ cup/1oz/25g flour
1 tsp/5ml mixed chopped herbs,
    preferably fresh
1qt/1l/1¾pts vegetable stock
salt and freshly ground black pepper
1 small French loaf (bread)
100g/4oz Mozzarella cheese, sliced
1 tbsp/15ml chopped parsley

METHOD
Melt the butter in the browning dish,
remove from the oven and stir in the onions.
Return to the microwave and cook on high
power for 6 minutes, stirring once.

Sprinkle the flour over the onions and
return for a further 1 minute on full power.

Add the herbs, vegetable stock and
seasoning, stir well and cook, covered, on
full power for 10 minutes.

Toast the French bread, cover it with
slices of Mozzarella and melt under the grill
or in the microwave for a few seconds.

Arrange the bread and cheese in the soup
bowl, pour over the onion soup and sprinkle
generously with chopped parsley.

◀ ▲ Parsnip and apple soup
▶ Mushroom soup

186

Vegetable Soup with Spicy Sauce

INGREDIENTS *serves 6*

3½ cups/350g/12oz haricot beans,
   soaked overnight
12oz/750g ripe tomatoes
1 onion, peeled and diced
¼ cup/60ml/2fl oz vegetable oil
salt and freshly ground black pepper
1 tsp/5ml Worcestershire sauce
1 tsp/5g dried mixed herbs
1qt/1l/1¾pts vegetable stock
2 carrots, sliced
2¼ cups/350g/12oz peas
2 potatoes, peeled and sliced
1 leek, trimmed and sliced
¼ cup/50g/2oz butter
½ cup/50g/2oz flour
1 tbsp/15g parsley

METHOD

Put the beans into a bowl, cover them with water and microwave on full power for 10 minutes. Allow to stand for 2 minutes, then cook for a further 5 minutes.

Place the tomatoes in a bowl with water and scald for 2 minutes at full power. Peel and slice the tomatoes. Add to the onion in a dish with the oil. Season with salt and pepper and cook for 2 minutes on full power.

Add the Worcestershire sauce, mixed herbs and half of the stock. Cook on full power for 5 minutes.

Clean and prepare the rest of the vegetables. Just cover with the remaining vegetable stock and cook, with the beans, on full power for 15 minutes.

Sieve the tomato mixture, collecting the purée in a bowl.

Melt the butter for 1 minute on full power. Remove from the oven, add the flour and stir carefully. Mix until smooth with the tomato mixture and then cook for 5 minutes at full power, stirring well.

Mix the tomato purée into the vegetable soup. Cook on full power for 10 minutes.

Sprinkle with chopped parsley.

▲ ▲ Vegetable soup with spicy sauce
▲ ▶ Tomato and carrot soup
▶ Lettuce soup

Leek and Potato Soup

INGREDIENTS *serves 4*
2 potatoes, peeled and diced
1qt/1l/1¾pts vegetable stock
2 tbsp/25g/1oz butter
1 onion, peeled and diced
2 leeks, washed and sliced
2 tsp/10ml chives, chopped
salt and freshly ground black pepper
1 bouquet garni
1 tbsp/15g chopped parsley
wholemeal bread

METHOD
Place the potatoes in a large microwave dish and pour the vegetable stock over the potatoes. Cook on full power for 10 minutes.

Melt the butter in a browning dish, add the onion and leeks and cook on full power for 5 minutes.

Add the leeks and onion to the potato stock with the chives, seasoning and bouquet garni. Cook at full power for 10 minutes. Taste for seasoning, checking that the potatoes are cooked. If not, cook for a further 2 minutes on full power.

Sprinkle with chopped parsley and serve with slices of wholemeal bread.

VARIATION
Blend, liquidize or put through a vegetable mill or food processor.

Add ¼ cup/60ml/2fl oz cream and serve hot or cold.

Tomato and Carrot Soup

INGREDIENTS *serves 4*
2 cups/450ml/¾pt vegetable stock
12oz/350g carrots, thinly sliced
1 onion, thinly sliced
2½ cups or 2×400g/14oz cans plum
    tomatoes or 2lb/900g/2lb tomatoes,
    skinned
¼ tsp/1.5ml basil
salt and freshly ground black pepper
2 drops soy sauce
⅔ tbsp/12ml cream (optional)

METHOD
Add the cold stock to the carrots and blanch for 5 minutes at full power.

Add the onion to the carrots with all the other ingredients except the cream. Cook on full power for 10 minutes, reduce to half power and cook for a further 20 minutes. Test the carrots; if they are not soft enough cook for a further 5 minutes on full.

Allow to cool slightly and then blend, sieve or purée in a food processor. Taste for seasoning.

Re-heat in individual bowls or in a large bowl as required, sprinkle a swirl of cream on top of each portion, if liked, and garnish with a few slivers of raw carrot.

Lettuce Soup

INGREDIENTS *serves 4*
2 tbsp/25g/1oz butter
1 onion, peeled
1 potato, peeled
2½ cups/600ml/1pt vegetable stock
2 lettuces
1 tsp/5ml fresh chervil or chives
salt and freshly ground black pepper
½ cup/120ml/4fl oz single cream
1 spring onion

METHOD
Melt the butter in a large casserole on full power for 1 minute. Slice the onion and potato finely.

Stir the onion and potato into the butter and cook on full power for 5 minutes; allow to stand for 2 minutes.

Add the vegetable stock and cook for a further 5 minutes. Remove from the microwave and stir in the lettuce, chervil or chives and seasoning. Cook on full power for a further 10 minutes. Allow to stand until slightly cool.

Put the mixture through a coarse sieve, food mill or blender. Re-heat as required.

Add swirls of single cream before serving and garnish with finely chopped spring onion. Serve hot or cold.

▲ Leek and potato soup

Vegetable Loaf

INGREDIENTS *serves 6*
8oz/225g broccoli spears
2 carrots, grated
3 stalks celery, tops discarded
2 tbsp/25g/1oz butter
2 tbsp/25g/1oz flour
3 eggs
salt and freshly ground black pepper
¼ tsp/1.5ml paprika
¼ tsp/1.5ml mustard powder
½ cup/100g/4oz cottage cheese
1 cup/100g/4oz grated Cheddar cheese
2 tomatoes, skinned
2 spring onions, washed and trimmed

METHOD

Arrange the broccoli spears in a ring on a shallow dish with heads to the centre of the dish. Sprinkle with 2-3 tbsp/30-45ml water, cover and cook for 8 minutes at full power.

Remove the dish, arrange the grated carrot in heaps and the celery in 1in/2½cm pieces between the stalks. Cover and cook for 5 minutes at full power, drain.

Melt the butter for 1 minute in a bowl at full power, then stir in the flour. Gradually beat in the eggs and season them well with salt, pepper, paprika and mustard. Beat in the cottage cheese and then the grated cheese.

Mix the cheese mixture with broccoli, celery and carrot. Cook on full power for 3 minutes, stir well.

Butter a glass loaf pan or a rectangular china terrine dish. Cover the bottom of the dish with the sliced tomatoes and chopped spring onions, then arrange half the cooked mixture in the dish. Pour on the remaining mixture, cover and cook on full for 3 minutes. Turn power to half, or defrost, cook for a further 6 minutes. Allow to stand for 3 minutes.

Test to make sure the mixture is cooked. Unmould the dish on to a heated plate and test the bottom with a fork. Cut into slices and serve with Tomato Sauce (see page 219) and new potatoes, if desired.

Stuffed Artichokes

INGREDIENTS *serves 4*
4 globe artichokes
1 lemon, rind and juice
½ cup/25g/1oz soft breadcrumbs
1 cup/100g/4oz mushrooms
salt and freshly ground black pepper
1 spring onion
¼ cup/60ml/2fl oz cream
4 slices Gruyère cheese
2 tbsp/25g/1oz butter

METHOD

Prepare the artichokes: cut off the stalks and remove the two rows of outer leaves with a sharp knife or scissors. The shaped artichokes should then stand on a plate evenly. Cut across the top of each artichoke about 1in/2½cm from the top, giving a flat top.

Put the prepared artichokes in a covered casserole dish with water and half the lemon juice. Cook on full power for 20 minutes. Remove and drain upside down on a wire rack.

Push down with three fingers into the middle section of the leaves and pull these out, leaving the choke visible. Remove it with a teaspoon, making sure that you do not scrape away the heart.

Mix the breadcrumbs in a bowl with the finely grated lemon rind. Chop the mushrooms and tip into the breadcrumbs, season well with salt and pepper. Add the chopped spring onion and mix in the cream.

Stuff the artichoke hearts with the mixture and lay a slice of cheese on top of the stuffing.

Lay the artichokes on a flat plate, cover with clingfilm and cook on full power for 5 minutes. Allow to stand for 2 minutes.

Melt the butter and mix it with the remaining lemon juice. Pour a little butter and lemon juice over each artichoke.

Crudités with Hot Anchovy Dip

INGREDIENTS *serves 6-8*
½ cup/100g/4oz butter, diced
2 cloves garlic, crushed
8 anchovy fillets, pounded
1¼ cups/300ml/½pt double cream

METHOD
To make the dip, put the butter in a pot and microwave on full for 1 minute until melted. Add the garlic and cook for a further 30 seconds.

Put the anchovy fillets with the cream in a liquidizer and blend until smooth.

Pour the anchovy cream onto the garlic butter, stir well and cook on full for 1-2 minutes, until hot.

Put the pot with the anchovy dip on a large platter and arrange the crudités around it.

Mushroom Pate

INGREDIENTS *serves 4*
½ cup/50g/2oz butter
2 cloves garlic, crushed
1 cup/225g/8oz mushroom caps, sliced
3 tbsp chopped parsley
½ cup/50g/2oz fresh breadcrumbs
½ cup/50g/2oz cheese, grated
pinch of grated nutmeg
salt and freshly ground black pepper
juice of 1 lemon
1 tbsp Cognac
2 tbsp double cream (or yoghurt)
parsley sprig to garnish

METHOD
Place the butter, garlic and mushrooms in a bowl and cook on full for 6 minutes. Add the parsley, breadcrumbs, cheese, nutmeg, seasoning, lemon juice, Cognac and cream (or yoghurt) to the mushrooms. Stir well and cook for a further 1 minute on full.

Blend all the ingredients in a blender or food processor and turn into a bowl. Allow to cool before chilling for 1 hour. Garnish with parsley and serve with toast.

◄▲ Vegetable loaf
◄ Stuffed artichokes
► Crudités with hot anchovy dip

Marinated Mushrooms

INGREDIENTS *serves 4*
5 cups/450g/1lb button mushrooms,
    wiped
4 tbsp/60ml olive oil
4 tbsp/60ml lemon juice
1 tbsp/15ml coriander seeds
salt and freshly ground black pepper
parsley or coriander leaves
chopped chives
toast

METHOD
Put the mushrooms in a dish with the oil,
lemon juice and coriander seeds. Let them
marinate for an hour or two or in the fridge
overnight.

Remove the mushrooms from the
marinade with a slotted spoon and place in
a shallow dish. Brush with the marinade and
microwave on full for 3 minutes, stirring
every minute.

Season to taste, sprinkle with parsley or
coriander and chives, if liked, and serve with
triangles of toast.

Artichokes with Hollandaise Sauce

INGREDIENTS *serves 2*
2 artichokes
2 tbsp/30ml lemon juice
6 tbsp/90ml water

HOLLANDAISE SAUCE
¼ cup/50g/2oz butter, diced
1 tbsp/15ml lemon juice
2 small egg yolks
salt and white pepper

METHOD
Soak the artichokes for an hour or so in a
bowl of water acidulated with half of the
lemon juice to loosen any soil or grit that
may be stuck between the leaves. Rinse
thoroughly in clean water and set upside
down to drain. Trim off the stalk close to the
vegetable so that it stands upright. Remove
any damaged outer leaves and rub the cut
surfaces with lemon juice. Do not bother
to cut the points off the leaves - this is
unnecessary and ruins the look of the
vegetable.

Put the artichokes upright in a dish, add
the water and the remaining lemon juice,
cover and cook for 7-8 minutes on full. Tug
at one of the lower leaves to see if done. If it
promises to come away in your fingers, the
artichokes are ready. Leave them to stand
for 3 minutes while you make the sauce.

Put the butter in a bowl and cook on
medium or defrost for 2 minutes until
melted. Add the lemon juice and egg yolks
and whisk lightly.

Cook on medium or defrost for 1 minute,
whisk again and season.

Drain and serve with the sauce.

To eat the artichoke, pull away the leaves
and suck off the tender fleshy part, dipped in
the sauce. When you come to the 'choke',
cut it away and discard it. Eat the heart with
a knife and fork - and more sauce.

▲► Sweet pepper hors d'œuvre
◄ Marinated mushrooms

Sweet Pepper Hors D'Oeuvre

INGREDIENTS *serves 4*
4 red, green or yellow peppers, de-seeded
1/2 cup/120ml/4fl oz vegetable oil
1 garlic clove, peeled
2 lemons
salt and freshly ground black pepper
1 tsp/5ml marjoram

METHOD
Slice the peppers into thin strips.

Place the peppers in a flat dish. Avoid piling the strips on top of each other. Add 1/4 cup/60ml/2fl oz water, cook, covered, on full power for 2 minutes, and then drain.

Place the oil and crushed garlic in a microwave serving dish. Cook on full power for 2 minutes. Add the pepper strips and cook, covered, for 5 minutes on full power.

Allow to cool, sprinkle with lemon juice and seasoning.

Chill and serve as a starter or with salad.

French Bean Salad

INGREDIENTS *serves 4*
4 cups approx./450g/1lb French beans, trimmed and left whole
4 tbsp/60ml water
3-4 cups/450g/1lb tomatoes, peeled, seeded and cut into strips
1½ tbsp/23ml olive oil
1½ tbsp/23ml lemon juice
salt and freshly ground black pepper
2 hard-boiled eggs
chives (optional)

METHOD
Put the beans in a dish, add the water, cover with vented cling wrap and cook on full for 6 minutes, rearranging twice. The beans should be done but still crisp. Set aside, covered, while you make the dressing.

Mix the oil, lemon juice and seasoning. (Shake them together in a screw-topped jar if you have one handy.)

Drain the beans, mix them with the tomatoes and toss in the dressing.

Separate the whites from the yolks of the eggs. Chop both. Garnish the salad with the egg.

VARIATION
If you are feeling artistic, tie the beans into bundles with the chives instead of mixing them together with the tomatoes.

Hot Potato Salad

INGREDIENTS *serves 4*

1½lb/750g new potatoes, washed but
  not peeled
4 tbsp/60ml water
2 tbsp/30ml virgin olive oil
1 tbsp/15ml lemon juice or white wine
  vinegar
salt and freshly ground black pepper
1 tsp/5ml dry mustard
1 bunch spring onions
1 bunch radishes
about 12 black olives, stoned
1 cup/200g/7oz tinned green beans,
  drained fresh beans if in season
chopped chives (optional)

METHOD

Put the potatoes in a dish with the water,
cover and cook for about 8 minutes, shaking
twice, until done. Do not overcook the
potatoes, or they will be spongy.

Drain the potatoes, slice them and return
to the dish.

Make a dressing by combining the olive
oil, vinegar or lemon juice, salt, pepper and
mustard in a screw-topped jar and shaking
well. Pour this over the hot potatoes and
keep covered.

Trim the spring onions and slice down the
stalk, making 2 cuts at right angles to each
other. Put the onions in iced water for a
couple of minutes. The stalks will curl up to
make tassels.

Trim and slice the radishes.

Mix the spring onion tassels, radishes,
olives, green beans and chives, if liked, into
the salad and serve at once.

Salad Provençale

INGREDIENTS *serves 4*

4 cups/450g/1lb whole green beans
4 spring onions
1 tsp/5ml thyme
1 green pepper, de-seeded
1 red pepper, de-seeded
4 tomatoes, skinned
4 hard-boiled eggs
½ cup/120ml/4fl oz olive oil
1 tsp/5ml French mustard
3-4 tbsp/45-60ml wine vinegar
1 garlic clove
20 black olives
1 lettuce

METHOD

Trim the beans, arrange in a dish with 2
tbsp/30ml water, cover and cook on full
power for 10 minutes.

Chop all but two of the spring onions
finely. Add the chopped spring onions with
the thyme to the beans after 5 minutes of
cooking. Mix well and cook for another 5
minutes. Drain and allow to cool.

Slice the peppers into strips and arrange
them in a shallow dish. Cover with 3 tbsp
water and cook for 5 minutes on full power.
Drain and allow to cool.

Cut each tomato into eight wedges and
each egg into six wedges lengthways.

To make the dressing, mix the oil,
mustard, vinegar, salt and pepper in a
screw-top jar and shake well.

Take a large salad bowl and rub it with a
cut clove of garlic. Line with lettuce leaves,
and put the beans mixed with half the
dressing in the bottom of the bowl. Arrange
the peppers, tomatoes and eggs on top with
the black olives. Chop the reserved spring
onions and sprinkle them over the dish. Add
rest of the dressing just before serving. Serve
with slices of wholemeal or French bread.

▲ Salad provençale
◄ Hot potato salad

195

Aubergine Lasagne

INGREDIENTS *serves 4*
2 medium aubergines
2-3 tbsp/30-45ml water
6 sheets spinach lasagne
salt
oil
Tomato Sauce (see page 219)

CHEESE SAUCE
3 tbsp/40g/1½oz butter or margarine
6 tbsp/40g/1½oz plain flour
1¼ cups/300ml/½pt milk
½ cup/50g/2oz Edam cheese, grated
salt and freshly ground black pepper

METHOD
Slice the aubergines. Arrange them in a deep oblong dish, in which you will cook the finished lasagne. Add the water, cover with vented cling wrap and cook on full for 7 minutes, rearranging once, until tender. Drain and set aside.

Put the lasagne in a large deep pot and pour over enough boiling water to cover. Add salt and a few drops of oil to stop the pieces sticking together. Cover and cook on full for 12-15 minutes, until done.

Tip the lasagne into a colander and rinse thoroughly under running cold water. If you omit this step you are liable to be left with a soggy mass of unmanageable pasta. Lay the sheets to dry on a tea towel. (Don't use paper towels - they will stick.)

To make the Cheese Sauce put the butter or margarine in a bowl and cook on full for 1 minute. Stir in the flour. Pour on the milk. Cook on full for 3 minutes, whisking after each minute. Stir in the cheese. Cook for a further minute and whisk again. Season to taste with salt and pepper.

To assemble the dish start with a layer of aubergines, then cover with Tomato Sauce, a layer of pasta and a layer of Cheese Sauce. Continue until all the ingredients are used up, finishing with a layer of cheese sauce.

Heat through in the microwave, or in a conventional oven or under the grill if you want the top to brown.

Serve hot.

VARIATION
Omit the pasta for an Aubergine Layer Bake.

Pizza

NOTE
Making pizzas using the microwave oven to prove the dough is even faster than making a pie or a flan. However the pizza is better cooked in a conventional oven for a crisp crust. A special browning dish is available in the shape of a pizza which will give a crisp base if the dish is heated for 5 minutes, then brushed over with oil. This dish is also useful for re-heating frozen pizzas. If using dried yeast, follow the manufacturer's directions if they conflict with recipe directions below.

INGREDIENTS *serves 4*
4 cups/450g/1lb strong plain flour
1 tsp/5ml salt
15g/½oz fresh yeast or 1 envelope (dry active) yeast and ½ tsp/2.5ml sugar
1 tbsp/15ml oil
1¼ cups/300ml/½pt tepid water

METHOD
Sift the flour into a bowl with the salt. If using fresh yeast, cream the yeast with a little of the water. If using dried yeast, mix the sugar with the water. Whisk, and leave for 10-15 minutes to froth.

Add the yeast, oil and water to the flour and mix to a smooth elastic dough on a floured board. Knead for 5 minutes, or until the dough is smooth and elastic. Clean the bowl, return the dough to it and cover with clingfilm. Turn on to full power for 15 seconds and then allow to stand for 10 minutes.

Microwave the dough for a further 15 seconds and allow to stand for another 10 minutes. Repeat this 15 second burst once more leaving to stand as before.

The dough should now have doubled in size and is ready to be made into pizzas.

NOTE
Dough can also be made with wholemeal flour, or half wholemeal, half white flour.

Pizza Napolitana

INGREDIENTS *serves 4*
4 rounds bread dough, about 8in/20cm in diameter
¼ cup/60ml/2fl oz olive oil
1 garlic clove, peeled
2½ cups/2×15oz/425g cans tomatoes
salt and freshly ground black pepper
2tsp/10ml chopped basil
24 black olives
8oz/225g Mozzarella cheese, sliced

METHOD
Pre-heat a conventional oven to 450°F/220°C/Gas 8.

Oil 2 baking sheets or 4 flan rings. If you use flan rings you will have a deep dish pizza. For a thin pizza, roll out the dough thinly and shape into rounds on the baking sheets. Brush the dough with olive oil.

Rub the dough with a cut clove of garlic. If you like a stronger flavour, crush the remainder into the tomatoes.

Mash the tomatoes with a wooden spoon and season well with salt and pepper. Add the chopped basil. Cover the rounds of dough with the tomato mixture. Arrange the black olives and Mozzarella cheese over the top.

Brush the pizza with oil. Bake thin pizzas for 12 minutes and for thicker pizzas reduce the oven temperature to 350°F/180°C/Gas 4 and bake for a further 10 minutes.

NOTE
It is possible to cook a quick pizza in the microwave but it must be eaten quickly or the dough will become tough. Take a browning dish or pizza tray and heat for 4-5 minutes at full power. Brush with oil, lay the dough in the dish, cover it with the filling and cook on full for 5 minutes. Allow to stand for 3 minutes. The pizza is tasty but looks rather pale.

▶ Pizza Napolitana

Mixed Vegetable Lasagne

INGREDIENTS *serves 4*
1 aubergine
2 courgettes
salt and pepper
1 lemon, juice
2 tbsp/25g/1oz butter
1 garlic clove, crushed
2½ cups/600ml/1pt Tomato Sauce (see page 218)
2½ cups/600ml/1pt Béchamel Sauce (see page 219)
1 cup /100g/4oz mushroom caps
3 tbsp/45ml vegetable oil
16 sheets lasagne, pre-cooked
¼ cup/25g/1oz grated Parmesan cheese
¼ cup/25g/1oz fresh breadcrumbs

METHOD
Slice the aubergine and courgettes and sprinkle with salt and lemon juice. Allow to stand for 20 minutes.

Rub a large square dish with a little butter mixed with the garlic.

Make up the Tomato and Béchamel Sauces.

Cut the mushrooms into slices including the trimmed stalks.

Drain the aubergines and courgettes and pat dry with absorbent kitchen towels. Heat the oil in a flat dish and cook the aubergines and courgettes in batches for 3 minutes, each batch arranged flat on the dish.

Place a little of the Tomato and Béchamel Sauces on the serving dish for the lasagne. Cover with the sheets of lasagne. Spread with a little Tomato Sauce and a layer of aubergine, courgettes and mushrooms, finishing with Béchamel Sauce.

Season well and continue layering. Arrange all the vegetables between the first 2 layers of pasta.

Top with the remaining Tomato and Béchamel sauce. Microwave on full power for 10 minutes. Allow to stand for 5 minutes and then cook for a further 5 minutes on full.

Sprinkle with mixed fresh breadcrumbs and Parmesan cheese. Cook for a further 5 minutes and then brown under the grill if required. This makes an ideal main course with green salad.

◄ Mixed vegetable lasagne

Artichoke Risotto

INGREDIENTS *serves 4*
3tbsp/40g/1½oz butter
1 onion, chopped
1½ cups/350g/12oz long-grain Italian rice
3 cups/750ml/1¼pts boiling water
1 vegetable stock cube
4 very small artichokes
salt and freshly ground black pepper
2tbsp/30ml Parmesan cheese

METHOD
Put half the butter in a deep pot and cook on full for 30 seconds. Add the onion, cover and cook for 1 minute.

Stir in the rice. Pour over the boiling water and crumble on the stock cube. Cover and cook on full for 8 minutes.

Meanwhile, prepare the artichokes. Trim off the stalks and remove any tough outer leaves. Slice the artichokes vertically. Stir them into the rice and cook on full for a further 4 minutes. Let the pot stand, covered, for 7 minutes.

Stir in the remaining butter, season with salt and pepper and stir in the Parmesan cheese.

Serve at once.

NOTE
To make this risotto you will need very young, very tender artichokes. If these are not available, use tinned artichoke hearts.

Cannelloni with Spinach and Ricotta

INGREDIENTS *serves 4*
1½ cups/350g/12oz cooked chopped or frozen spinach
2 cups/225g/8oz ricotta cheese
¼tsp/1.5ml grated nutmeg
salt and freshly ground black pepper
12 pre-cooked cannelloni tubes
1¾ cups/425g/15fl oz canned sieved tomatoes
1tsp/5ml chopped basil
2tbsp/25g/1oz butter
1 onion, peeled and diced
¼tsp/1.5ml oregano
2½ cups/600ml/1pt Béchamel Sauce (page 219)
½ cup/50g/2oz grated cheese
1tbsp/15ml chopped parsley

METHOD
Mix the cooked or defrosted spinach with the ricotta cheese, nutmeg and seasoning.

Spoon or pipe into the cannelloni tubes.

Season the tomatoes with salt, pepper and basil. Place a layer of them in the bottom of a glass or china dish.

Heat the butter in another small dish for 1 minute. Add the onion and cook on full power for 3 minutes. Stir in the oregano. Pour this over the tomato mixture. Arrange the cannelloni tubes on the tomato and onion.

Cover with the Béchamel Sauce and cook for 5 minutes.

Quickly brown under a hot grill.

Mix the remaining cheese with the parsley, and sprinkle over the dish.

Piperade

INGREDIENTS *serves 4*
¼ cup/60ml/2fl oz vegetable oil
1 garlic clove
1 small onion, peeled and diced
2 spring onions, sliced
1 sweet red pepper, de-seeded
1 green pepper, de-seeded
1 bouquet garni
1 bay leaf
2 large tomatoes, skinned
salt and freshly ground black pepper
8 eggs
2 tbsp/25g/1oz butter, cut into pieces

METHOD
Heat the vegetable oil in a browning dish. Slightly crush the garlic clove but leave it whole and add it to the dish. Cook for 30 seconds at full power in the oil.

Add the onions and spring onions to the garlic and cook on half power for 6 minutes.

Prepare the peppers by pouring boiling water over them in a bowl and leaving them to stand for 2 minutes. If preferred, prepare them the traditional way by charring under a hot grill and then removing the flesh from the skin. Chop the peppers very finely by hand or in a food processor, taking care not to liquidize them completely. Add to the onion and cook on full power for 5 minutes with the bouquet garni and bay leaf.

Remove the seeds from the tomatoes, chop finely and add to the vegetable mixture. Season well and cook on full for a further 5 minutes.

Beat the eggs in a bowl with ¼ cup/60ml/2fl oz water. Add the butter.

Remove the bouquet garni, bay leaf and garlic from the tomato mixture and stir in the eggs. Cook on full power for 4 minutes, remove and mix well.

Return to the microwave oven, cook for a further 4 minutes. Remove and stir again. If the mixture is too liquid, cook for a further 2 minutes and test after stirring.

NOTE
Remember that the mixture thickens very quickly at this stage and the delicious, creamy eggs can toughen if microwaved for a few seconds too long.) This dish can also be used to fill savoury pastry shells.

Potato Omelette

INGREDIENTS *serves 2*
1 cup/100g/4oz cooked sliced potato
a little butter
4 eggs
salt and freshly ground black pepper
freshly chopped herbs or chives
    (optional)

METHOD
Put the potato in 1 or 2 layers in a buttered dish. Use a shallow dish or a pie plate. Cover and cook on full for 45 seconds.

Beat together the eggs, seasoning and chives or herbs if used and pour them over the vegetables. Cook on low power for 8 minutes, or until almost set.

Leave to stand for 1-2 minutes before serving, then cut in two.

Left until cold, then cut into wedges, this makes a good picnic dish especially if served with salad.

NOTE
Quite often quiches and omelettes won't cook in the 'cold spot' in the middle of the microwave. To correct this place under a hot grill for 2-3 minutes.

▼ Potato omelette

Eggs Provençale

INGREDIENTS *serves 4*
8 tomatoes, skinned and sliced
1 tbsp/15ml vegetable oil
1 garlic clove, crushed
1 sprig parsley
1 sprig thyme
1 bay leaf
salt and freshly ground black pepper
$\frac{1}{4}$ tsp/1.5ml sugar
4 eggs
2 tsp/10ml chopped parsley

METHOD
Place all the ingredients except the eggs and parsley in a microwave bowl. Cook on full power for 5 minutes, stir and cook for a further 5 minutes.

Remove the tomato sauce from the microwave oven, take out the sprigs of herbs and the bay leaf. Sieve or blend the sauce, taste and correct seasoning.

Butter 4 ramekin individual dishes, and divide the tomato mixture between them.

Break the eggs one at a time into a cup and pour into the centre of each dish. Sterilize a skewer or large needle by dipping it in boiling water and use it to prick the yolks.

Season the eggs and place the dishes in the microwave oven. Cook on full power for 1 minute, then reduce to half power and cook for a further 5 minutes. Allow to stand for 1-2 minutes before serving.

Sprinkle with chopped parsley and serve with fingers of toast.

Welsh Rarebit

INGREDIENTS *serves 2*
1 cup/100g/4oz grated Cheddar cheese
2oz/50g/2oz blue cheese
2 tsp/10ml French mustard
pinch salt
freshly ground black pepper
2 tbsp/30ml milk or 2 tbsp/30ml whisky
    or beer
4 slices of toast

METHOD
Place all the ingredients except the toast in a medium-sized deep bowl and mix well.

Cook for 2 minutes on full power. Stir well and remove after another 2-3 minutes or when bubbling. Pour over the pieces of toast and brown under a hot grill.

Eat as a snack or serve with a vegetable casserole. Use milk if serving with vegetables.

◄▲ Eggs provençale
▲▲ Welsh rarebit

201

Egg, Potato and Mushroom Pie

INGREDIENTS *serves 4*
450g/1lb potatoes, peeled and sliced
2½ cups/225g/8oz mushrooms
1 onion
salt and freshly ground black pepper
grated nutmeg
⅔ cup/150ml/¼pt milk
2-3 tbsp/45-60ml cream
4 eggs
¼ cup/1oz/25g grated cheese
1 tbsp/15ml chopped parsley

METHOD
Arrange a layer of potatoes on a buttered dish of approximately 1qt/1l/1¾pts capacity.

Slice the mushrooms, with trimmed stalks still attached, and the onion. Layer the mushrooms and onion with the potatoes, seasoning between layers until all the ingredients are used. Make four hollows to hold the eggs. Add the milk and cream and cook on full power for 10 minutes.

Stand for 6 minutes then microwave for 6 minutes on full power. Stand for another 5 minutes and then test the potatoes. If they are too hard, cook for a further 4 minutes on full power.

Prick the four eggs and poach them in a little water in the microwave.

With a slotted spoon, lift the eggs carefully into the spaces on the vegetable casserole. Return to the microwave oven for 30 seconds to re-heat.

Sprinkle with grated cheese and if liked, brown under a very hot grill for a few seconds. Serve sprinkled with chopped parsley and crisp triangles of brown toast.

Eggs Florentine

INGREDIENTS *serves 4*
half quantity Artichoke Hearts with
   Spinach, omitting pimento (page 207)
4 eggs
salt and freshly ground black pepper
4 tbsp/60ml cream

METHOD
Prepare the creamed spinach. Butter four ramekin dishes and divide the spinach between them.

Make a well in the centre of each dish with the back of a spoon. Break the eggs into a cup one at a time and slide each into a bed of spinach. Prick the yolks with a sterilised needle, season with salt and pepper and carefully pour the cream over the top.

Stand the dishes in a deep glass dish. Pour some boiling water around them. Cook in the microwave oven for 4 minutes at full power. Check to see if the eggs are cooked; if not, cook for a further 1 minute or to taste. Sprinkle with chopped parsley and serve.

NOTE
If cooking the dishes individually, check after 1½ minutes.

◀▲ Egg, potato and mushroom pie
◀ Eggs Florentine

Cheese Soufflé

INGREDIENTS *serves 6*
¼ cup/50g/2oz butter
1¼ cups/300ml/½pt milk
¼ cup/25g/1oz plain flour
½ tsp/2.5ml mustard
¼ tsp/1.5ml cayenne pepper
salt and freshly ground black pepper
1 cup/100g/4oz grated Cheddar cheese
4 eggs
2 tsp/10ml Parmesan cheese
1 tbsp/15ml chopped parsley

METHOD
Place the butter in a large soufflé dish, cook on full power for 1 minute. Remove from the oven, replace with the milk in a jug. Heat on full power for 2 minutes. Stir the flour into the melted butter to make a smooth paste.

Add the warm milk to the roux of flour and butter, whisk well to form a smooth mixture. Add the mustard, cayenne and seasoning. Cook on full power for 2 minutes, whisk again and cook for a further 2 minutes until the sauce is thick.

Add the grated Cheddar cheese and whisk in the egg yolks until the mixture is smooth.

Whisk the egg whites just until they form soft peaks. Fold the egg whites into the mixture in the soufflé dish with a plastic spatula.

Cook on low power for 25 minutes.

Sprinkle with Parmesan cheese and parsley. Serve immediately with a salad or crisp green vegetables.

Peppers and Fried Eggs

INGREDIENTS *serves 4*
1 red pepper, cut into julienne strips
1 green pepper, cut into julienne strips
1 yellow pepper, cut into julienne strips
2 large tomatoes, peeled, seeded and
    cut into strips
1 bunch spring onions, trimmed
45ml/3 tbsp water
knob butter
4 eggs
salt and freshly ground black pepper

METHOD
Put the vegetables into a dish with the water, cover with vented cling wrap and cook on full for 4-5 minutes, stirring once, until tender but not soft. Keep warm.

Heat a browning dish for 3-4 minutes. Add the butter and, using oven gloves, tilt the dish to coat with the hot fat. Break an egg into each corner of the dish and pierce the yolks with a cocktail stick (toothpick). Cook until nearly set (about 2½ minutes, but this will depend on the size of the eggs). Allow to stand for 30 seconds.

Divide the vegetables between 4 heated plates and lay an egg on each.

Offer salt and pepper at the table.

VARIATION
You can add garlic to the ingredients if you like and, for a touch of style, make the spring onions into tassels.

◀ Peppers and fried eggs

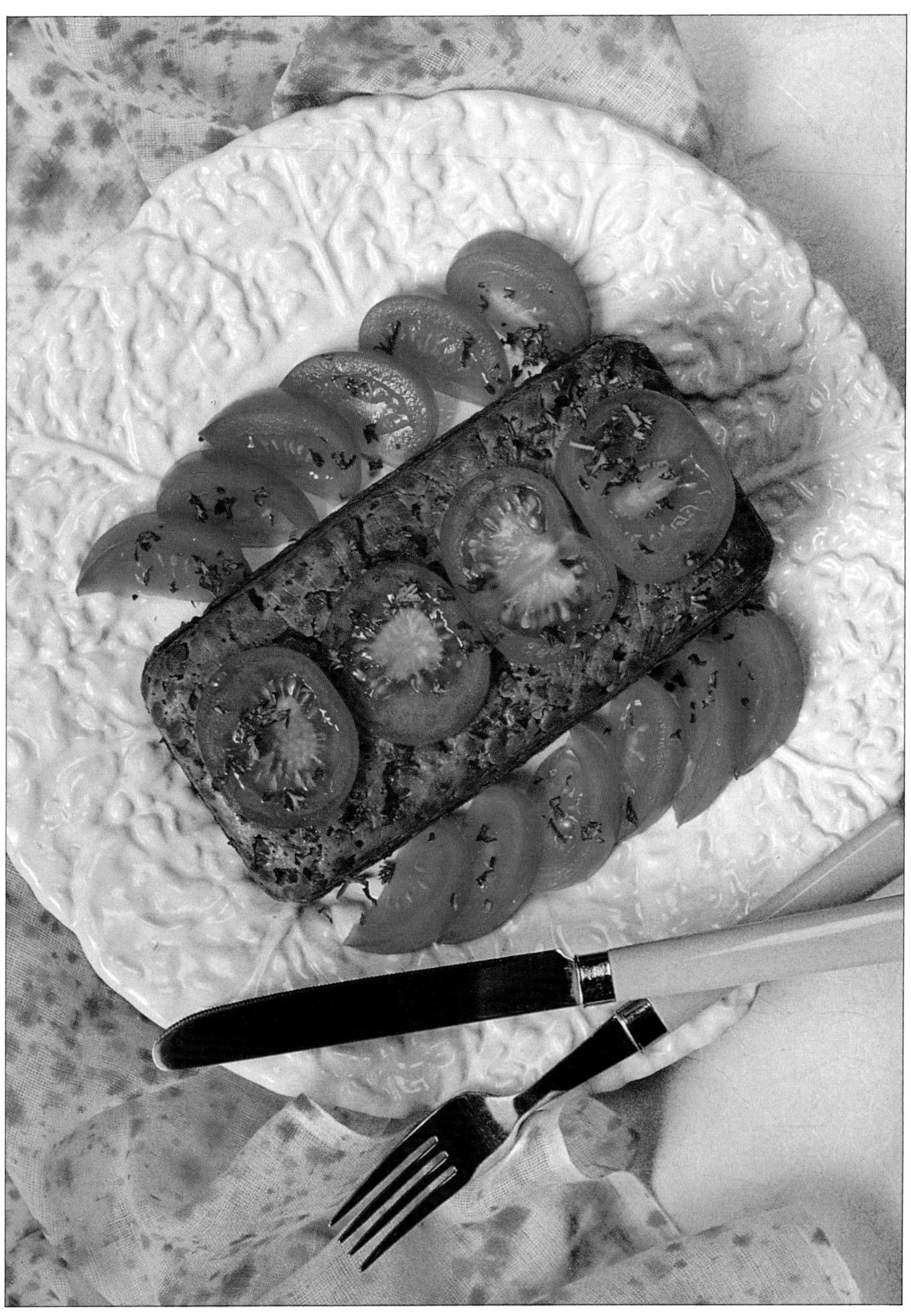

Lentil Loaf

INGREDIENTS *serves 4*
1¼ cups/225g/8oz lentils
¼ cup/60ml/2fl oz oil
1 onion, diced
½lb/225g/8oz mushrooms, sliced
2 tbsp/25g/1oz butter
1¼ cups/300ml/½pt vegetable stock
¼ tsp/1.5ml paprika
salt and freshly ground black pepper
1 tsp/5ml fresh herbs, chopped
1 egg, beaten
½ cup/60ml/2fl oz cream
1 tbsp/15ml chopped parsley or 2
tomatoes, skinned and sliced

METHOD

Wash the lentils under cold running water
and remove any discoloured seeds. Pour 1¼
cups/300ml/½pt boiling water over the
lentils and allow to stand for 5 minutes
before draining.

Heat the oil in a casserole on high for 1
minute, add the onion and cook on full
power for 3 minutes.

Remove the onion from the oil with a
slotted spoon and reserve. Cook the
mushrooms in the oil and the butter for 3
minutes, covered. Allow to stand for 2
minutes.

In a separate bowl, cook the lentils in the
vegetable stock for 7 minutes on full power.
Leave to stand for 3 minutes or until most of
the liquid is absorbed.

Mix the cooked lentils with the onion,
seasonings, herbs, egg and cream.

Spread half the mixture in a microwave
loaf pan or a 3 cups/700ml/1½pt ovenproof
glass bowl. Arrange the mushrooms over
the mixture and add the remaining lentil
mixture. Smooth the surface with a spoon,
cover and cook for 5 minutes on full power.
Allow to stand for 4 minutes before turning
out on to a heated serving dish.

Serve sprinkled with chopped parsley or
sliced tomatoes. Serve with Tomato Sauce
(see page 218) or 1¼ cups Béchamel Sauce
(see page 219) with 1½ cups/100g/4oz
mushrooms, chopped finely.

VARIATION

Cheese and Lentil Loaf. Add ½ cup/50g/
2oz grated cheese to the lentil mixture
before cooking.

Winter Chilli

INGREDIENTS *serves 4*
¼ cup/50g/2oz butter
2 onions, chopped
1 garlic clove, peeled and crushed
2 carrots, diced
2½ cups/600ml/1pt vegetable stock
6 tomatoes, peeled and chopped
2 red peppers, de-seeded, sliced
1 chilli pepper, de-seeded, sliced
¼-½ tsp chilli powder
1 aubergine, sliced
1 cup/100g/4oz mushrooms, sliced
1 tbsp/15ml cornflour
1¼ cups/400g/15oz can kidney beans
1 tbsp/15ml tomato purée
2 tbsp/30ml sweet corn
chopped parsley

METHOD

Melt the butter in the browning dish for 1
minute on full power.

Add the onion and garlic and cook at full
power for 1 minute. Add the carrots and
vegetable stock and cook at full power for 5
minutes.

Add the tomatoes, peppers, mushrooms,
aubergine and chilli to the vegetable stock
and cook on full power for 2 minutes.

Blend the cornflour with a little water and
the tomato purée and add the chilli powder.
Remove the casserole from the oven and stir
in the tomato mixture until well blended.
Return to the microwave and cook at full
power for 5 minutes.

Add the canned kidney beans and sweet
corn and cook on full power for 10 minutes.
Allow to stand for 5 minutes before serving.
Serve sprinkled with parsley.

▲ Winter chilli
◄ Lentil loaf

205

Nut and Vegetable Cobbler

INGREDIENTS *serves 4*
1lb/450g canned butter beans
8oz/225g potatoes, peeled and cubed
1 small green chilli pepper, de-seeded
  and sliced
8oz/225g carrots, sliced
2 celery stalks, sliced
1 onion, sliced
1 small can tomatoes
2 dessert apples, cored and chopped
1 vegetable stock cube
salt and freshly ground black pepper

TOPPING
1 cup/100g/4oz plain flour
1tsp/5ml baking powder
salt and freshly ground black pepper
1tsp/5ml French mustard
½tsp/2.5ml dried mixed herbs
¼ cup/50g/2oz butter
¼ cup/25g/1oz grated cheese
½ cup/50g/2oz finely ground hazelnuts
¼ cup/75ml/3tbsp cold water

METHOD
Drain the butter beans, reserving their liquid, and combine with all the vegetables and the apples in a large casserole.

Heat the juice from the butter beans for 2 minutes on full power, then dissolve the stock cube in it.

Pour the stock over the vegetables and season well. Cover with pierced clingfilm, or a plate, and cook on full power for 12 minutes, stirring after 4 and 8 minutes.

Sift the flour, salt and pepper and mustard into a bowl. Add the herbs.

Rub in the butter until the mixture resembles fine breadcrumbs. Stir in the cheese and nuts. Add the water and mix to a soft, elastic dough. Shape into 8 balls and place them around the outside of the vegetables. Cover with the lid of pierced clingfilm and microwave on full power for 7 minutes.

Artichoke Heart and Bean Casserole with Vegetable Purée

INGREDIENTS *serves 4*
1 onion, sliced
1 clove garlic, crushed
1tbsp/15ml sunflower oil
4 cups/225g/8oz mushrooms, sliced
1¾ cups/400g/14oz tinned kidney beans
generous cup/200g/7oz tinned artichoke
    hearts, drained
salt and freshly ground black pepper
fresh coriander or parsley leaves
¾ cup/175g/6oz Root Vegetable Purée
    (see page 212)

METHOD
Put the onion and garlic in a casserole with the oil, cover and cook on full for 3 minutes. Stir in the mushrooms, kidney beans - with a little of the liquid from the tin - and artichoke hearts and cook on full, covered, for about 5 minutes, stirring once, until the mushrooms are done and the beans cooked through.

Season to taste with salt and pepper and sprinkle with coriander or parsley leaves.

Serve with Vegetable Purée.

Artichoke Hearts with Spinach

INGREDIENTS *serves 4*
4 cups/900ml/2lb fresh spinach
2tbsp/25g/1oz butter
1 large onion, chopped
8 artichoke hearts, fresh or tinned
⅓ cup/75g/3oz tinned pimento, cut into
    strips

SAUCE
3tbsp/40g/1½oz butter
6tbsp/40g/1½oz flour
1¼ cups/300ml/½pt milk
⅓ cup/50g/2oz grated Parmesan cheese
nutmeg
salt and freshly ground black pepper

METHOD
Wash the spinach and discard tough stalks and discoloured leaves. Put it in a boiling or roasting bag and tie loosely. Cook on full for about 6 minutes, shaking the bag once, until the spinach has collapsed. Let it stand for a while, then chop coarsely.

Put the butter in a dish and cook on full for 30 seconds. Add the onion and the artichoke hearts and cook for 3 minutes. (If using tinned artichoke hearts, however, arrange them on top of the onion when cooked.)

Lay strips of pimento in between the artichokes and put the chopped spinach in a layer on top of that.

To make the sauce put the butter in a bowl and cook on full for 30 seconds to 1 minute to melt it. Stir in the flour. Pour on the milk and continue to cook for 3 minutes, whisking after each minute. Add the cheese. Cook for a further minute and whisk again. Season to taste with nutmeg, salt and pepper.

Pour the sauce over the vegetables and heat through in the microwave, or brown in a conventional oven or under the grill.

◀◀ Nut and vegetable cobbler
◀ Artichoke hearts, kidney beans and mushrooms with vegetable purée

Aubergine with Two Sauces

INGREDIENTS *serves 4*
2 medium aubergines, sliced
4 tbsp/60ml water
flour
beaten egg
breadcrumbs
a little butter
Tomato Sauce (page 218)
Béchamel Sauce with cheese (page 219)

METHOD
Put the aubergines in a dish, add the water, cover with vented cling wrap and cook on full for 7 minutes, rearranging once, until tender. Drain the aubergines.

Dust the aubergine slices with flour, then dip in beaten egg and in breadcrumbs. Push the breadcrumbs on well with your fingers.

Heat a browning dish to maximum, according to the manufacturer's instructions. Add a little butter and, holding the dish with oven gloves, tilt it to cover in the hot fat.

Fry the aubergine slices in batches for 30 seconds on each side, until golden. Keep warm.

Serve with tomato sauce and cheese sauce.

VARIATION
Omit the cheese sauce.

Ratatouille Alla Mozzarella

INGREDIENTS *serves 4*
1 large aubergine, sliced
3 courgettes, sliced
salt and freshly ground black pepper
4 tbsp/60ml olive oil
1 large onion, sliced
2 cloves garlic, chopped
1 small red pepper, seeded and chopped
1 small green pepper, seeded and chopped
2 cups/100g/4oz mushrooms, sliced
1¼ cups/425g/15oz can tomatoes, mashed
1 tbsp/15ml tomato purée
2 tsp/10ml fresh mixed herbs, chopped
1 bay leaf
1 cup/100g/4oz Mozzarella cheese, cubed

METHOD
Place aubergine and courgettes in a colander, sprinkle with salt and allow to stand for 30 minutes. Rinse in cold water and pat dry. Cut the aubergine into bite-sized pieces.

Pour the oil into a casserole and cook on full for 1 minute. Add onion and garlic and cook on full for 1 minute. Stir in peppers, aubergine and courgettes and cook on full for 5 minutes, stirring once.

Stir in remaining ingredients, cover and cook on full for 15 minutes, stirring twice. Stir in Mozzarella. Cover and continue cooking for 5 minutes until cheese has melted or brown under the grill if preferred. Serve with crusty French bread to mop up the juices.

▶ Ratatouille alla Mozzarella
◀ Aubergine with two sauces

Rice with Peppers and Cheese

INGREDIENTS *serves 4*

1½ cups/350g/12oz rice

3 cups/750ml/1¼pts boiling water

1 vegetable stock cube

1 small red pepper, seeded and chopped

1 small yellow pepper, de-seeded and chopped

1 small green pepper, seeded and chopped

1 cup/100g/4oz Edam cheese, grated

salt and freshly ground black pepper

1 bunch parsley, chopped

METHOD

Put the rice in a deep pot, pour over the boiling water and crumble on the stock cube. Cover and cook on full for 8 minutes.

Stir in the green, yellow and red peppers. Cover and cook on full for 4 minutes.

Stir in the cheese. Check the seasoning and add salt and pepper if necessary (depending on the saltiness of the stock cube). Cover and leave to stand for 5 minutes.

If the cheese has not melted by then, heat through again for 2 minutes.

Stir in the parsley and serve.

▲ Rice with peppers and cheese

Thai Rice

INGREDIENTS *serves 4*
2¹/₃ cups/450g/1lb long grain rice
1 tsp/5ml salt
1 tsp/5ml turmeric
¹/₄ cup/60ml/2fl oz vegetable oil
2 garlic cloves, crushed
2 onions, peeled and diced
1 chilli pepper, de-seeded
1 red pepper, de-seeded
1 tsp/5ml curry powder
2 spring onions
2 cups/225g/8oz peas
2 eggs
salt and freshly ground black pepper
1 tsp/5ml soy sauce
1 tbsp/15g/¹/₂oz butter

METHOD

Wash the long grain rice and put in a large casserole with 1qt/1l/1³/₄pts boiling water with the salt and turmeric. Cook on full power for 15 minutes and then allow to stand. The rice should be fluffy and separated.

Heat the oil in a dish for 1 minute on full power, add the garlic and cook for a further 1 minute. Add the onion, stir well and cook for 2 minutes.

Dice both the peppers, add them to the garlic and onion and cook for 2 minutes. Stir in the curry powder with half of the chopped spring onion, mix with the rice and stir in the peas.

Make up an omelette mixture by beating 2 eggs, 2 tbsp/30ml water, seasoning and soy sauce in a bowl. Put the butter into a browning dish and heat on full power for 1 minute. Stir in the eggs and cook on full power for 1 minute and remove.

Mix to allow any uncooked mixture to run under the cooked egg. Cook on high, for another 1 minute, allow to stand for 30 seconds and remove to a chopping board.

Re-heat the rice for 4 minutes on full power.

Cut the omelette into strips and use it to decorate the top of the rice. Sprinkle with chopped spring onion and serve.

▶ Thai rice

Oriental Rice

INGREDIENTS *serves 4*
1 cup/200g/7oz long grain rice
salt
¹/₂ cup/50g/2oz small mushrooms
2 dessert apples
1 tbsp/15ml wine vinegar
1 large onion, finely chopped
1 tbsp/15ml vegetable oil
¹/₃ cup/50g/2oz sultanas
¹/₂ cup/50g/2oz cashew nuts
¹/₂ cup/50g/2oz salted peanuts
20 stoned black olives
1 tbsp/15g/¹/₂oz curry powder

METHOD

Wash the rice until the water runs clear. Put it into a very large container with 3³/₄ cups/850ml/1¹/₂pts water and salt. Microwave, uncovered, on full power for 15 minutes. Rinse and leave to drain thoroughly.

Slice the mushrooms, chop the apples leaving the skins on. Put the chopped apple in a bowl with the vinegar.

Put the oil in a large bowl and heat for 2 minutes on full power. Add the onion, stir and cover with a plate or pierced clingfilm and microwave on full power for 3 minutes.

Combine all the ingredients, season to taste and cook on full power for 4 minutes stirring after 2 minutes. Serve with a salad.

Broccoli with Almonds and Blue Cheese Sauce

INGREDIENTS *serves 4*
1lb/450g broccoli
3 tbsp/45ml water
2/3 cup/150ml/1/4pt cream
6 tbsp/40g/1½oz Danish blue cheese
salt and white pepper
scant ⅓ cup/40g/1½oz slivered toasted
   almonds
diamonds of red pepper

METHOD
Wash the broccoli and remove the outer leaves and tough stalks. Make slits up the stalks to speed up cooking.

Put the broccoli in a dish with the water. Cover with vented cling wrap and cook on full for 10 minutes, rearranging once, until tender. Drain and keep hot.

Mash the cream into the cheese until smooth. Cook for 1-2 minutes. Season with salt and pepper and pour over the broccoli.

Serve garnished with slivered almonds, or with the broccoli florets in a pool of sauce, as shown, and decorate with diamonds of red pepper.

Purée of Root Vegetables

INGREDIENTS *serves 4*
3 cups/350g/12oz carrots, sliced
2¼ cups/350g/12oz swede, sliced
3 tbsp/45ml water
butter to taste
salt and freshly ground black pepper
2/3 cup/150ml/5fl oz single cream
snipped chives

METHOD
Peel the vegetables and slice them thinly. Reserve some of the carrot slices and cut them into star shapes for the garnish.

Put the vegetables in a dish with the water. Cover with vented cling wrap and cook on full for 6-8 minutes, until soft.

Drain the vegetables and purée in the blender with butter to taste. Season the purée and re-heat on full for 1 minute.

To serve, spoon a thin pool of cream onto each of 4 heated plates. Make a small mound of purée on each plate and garnish the surrounding cream with shooting stars made of carrot and snipped chives.

VARIATION
You can make this purée with any of the winter root vegetables, such as turnip, parsnip and sweet potato.

▶ Couscous with vegetables
▼ Broccoli with almonds and blue cheese sauce

Green Bean and Mushroom Curry

INGREDIENTS *serves 2-4*
4 tbsp/50g/2oz butter or ghee
1 large onion, chopped
2 cloves garlic, chopped
1 cup/100g/4oz green beans, trimmed
    and cut into 2cm/1in lengths
2 cups/100g/4oz mushrooms, sliced
3 tomatoes, peeled and chopped
1tbsp/15ml lemon juice
2 slices fresh ginger
2.5ml/$\frac{1}{2}$ tsp turmeric
2.5ml/$\frac{1}{2}$ tsp ground coriander
2.5ml/$\frac{1}{2}$ tsp garam masala
fresh coriander or parsley

METHOD
Place the butter or ghee in a bowl and cook on full for 1 minute. Add the onion and garlic and cook on full for 3 minutes.

Stir in the rest of the ingredients except the fresh coriander or parsley. Cover and cook for 8-10 minutes, stirring twice.

Garnish with fresh coriander or parsley.

Black-eyed Beans with Mushrooms and Coriander

INGREDIENTS *serves 4*
2tbsp/25g/1oz butter
1 large onion, chopped
2 cloves garlic, chopped
2$\frac{1}{4}$ cups/450g/1lb cooked black-eyed
    beans
1$\frac{1}{2}$ cups/400g/14oz can tomatoes,
    drained and mashed
1 slice fresh ginger
salt and freshly ground black pepper
Garam Masala (see page 126)
fresh coriander

METHOD
Put the butter in a dish and cook on full for 45 seconds. Add the onion and garlic and continue to cook, covered, for 3 minutes.

Add the black-eyed beans, tomatoes and ginger and cook on full, covered, for 4-5 minutes until hot through, stirring once.

Season with salt, pepper and Garam Masala and stir in plenty of chopped coriander leaves. Eat hot or cold with rice.

Couscous with Vegetables

INGREDIENTS *serves 4*
$\frac{1}{2}$ cauliflower, cut into florets
8oz/225g carrots, diced
1 large parsnip, diced
3tbsp/45ml water
2 cups/400g/14oz tinned chick-peas,
    drained
1$\frac{3}{4}$ cups/200g/7oz tinned peas, drained
Tomato Sauce (see page 218) made with
    chilli powder to taste instead of basil
2 cups/350g/12oz couscous
2 cups/450ml/$\frac{3}{4}$pt boiling water
salt
2tbsp/25g/1oz butter

METHOD
First prepare the vegetable topping. Put the cauliflower, carrots and parsnip into a dish with the water, cover with vented cling wrap and cook on full for 5 minutes, stirring once.

Stir in the chickpeas and peas and cook for a further 4 minutes, stirring once. Drain and keep hot.

For the couscous, put the grain in a deep pot, cover with the boiling water, add a pinch of salt and cook on full for 4 minutes. Stir in the butter.

Re-heat the tomato sauce for 3 minutes in a sauce boat.

Serve the couscous topped with the spicy vegetable mixture and allow guests to serve themselves with the sauce.

Broccoli/Cauliflower Cheese

INGREDIENTS *serves 4*

1lb/450g fresh broccoli, washed or
    12oz/350g frozen pack
1 cauliflower, washed
2 potatoes, peeled
2½ cups/600ml/1pt Béchamel Sauce
    (see page 219)
2tbsp/25g/1oz butter
salt and freshly ground black pepper
¼ cup/60ml/2fl oz milk
4 slices cheese
1tbsp/15ml crisp breadcrumbs

METHOD

Arrange the broccoli in a round dish with the spears facing in to the centre and stalks out. Add 4 tsp/60ml salted water and cook on full power for 5 minutes, covered.

If using frozen, thaw first and only cook for 3 minutes at this stage.

Arrange the cauliflower florets in the same dish in a ring when the broccoli is finished and removed to a plate. Cook on full power for 5 minutes and then allow to stand for 3 minutes.

While the vegetables are cooking, slice the potatoes thinly, use the food processor if you have one. Make up the Béchamel Sauce.

Arrange the potatoes on the bottom of a buttered deep dish. Add salt and pepper to the milk, pour over the potatoes, partially cover with a lid or with cling film. Microwave on full power for 5 minutes, allow longer if the potato slices are chunky. Stand for 3 minutes.

Arrange the broccoli spears facing in to the centre in a ring, alternating with the cauliflower.

Pour over the well-seasoned Béchamel Sauce and microwave for 10 minutes on full power. Sprinkle with freshly ground pepper and cover with the slices of cheese. Microwave on full for 2 minutes or until the cheese has melted. Sprinkle with the breadcrumbs and brown under the grill, if liked. Allow to stand for 2 minutes and then serve while the cheese is still soft.

▲ ▶ Broccoli and cauliflower cheese
▶ Leek parcels

Baby Onions Escoffier

INGREDIENTS *serves 4*
4 cups/450g/1lb baby onions
1 tbsp/15ml oil
1 bay leaf
thyme sprig
1 tsp/5ml fennel seeds
1/2 cup/50g/2oz sultanas, soaked
3 tbsp/45ml dry white wine
1 tbsp/15ml brandy

METHOD
Peel the onions, but leave them whole. Put them in a dish with the remaining ingredients, cover with vented cling wrap and cook on full for about 10 minutes, shaking the dish twice.

Serve with lamb, beef or game.

Leek Parcels

INGREDIENTS *serves 4*
3 tbsp/40g/1 1/2oz polyunsaturated
    vegetable margarine or butter
6 tbsp/40g/1 1/2oz plain flour
1 1/4 cups/300ml/1/2pt milk
1/2 cup/50g/2oz grated Edam cheese
1-2 tsp/5-10ml mustard (optional)
salt and freshly ground black pepper
4 leeks
2 tbsp/30ml water
4 slices ham

METHOD
First make the sauce. Put the margarine or butter in a bowl and cook for 1 minute on full. Stir in the flour. Pour on the milk. Cook for 3 minutes, whisking after each minute. Stir in the cheese and mustard, if used. Cook for a further minute and whisk again. Season to taste with salt and pepper. Keep the sauce warm while you cook the leeks.

Trim the leeks and wash thoroughly. Put them in a dish with the water, cover with vented cling wrap and cook for about 8 minutes, rearranging once, until done.

Drain the leeks and cut off a few rings for the garnish. Wrap each in a slice of ham, lay side by side in the dish and pour the sauce over. Cover and cook for 2-3 minutes until hot through. Serve at once.

Glazed Onions

INGREDIENTS *serves 4*
8 small onions, peeled but left whole
2 tbsp/30ml honey
2 tbsp/25g/1oz butter
2 tbsp/30ml hot water

METHOD
Put the onions in a dish.

Cream the honey and butter with the water and pour over the onions. Cover with vented cling wrap and cook on full for 8-10 minutes, until the onions are tender, shaking or stirring the dish once.

Serve hot. This is particularly good with pork chops and mashed potatoes.

Russian Beetroot

INGREDIENTS *serves 4*
6 tbsp/75g/3oz butter
5 medium uncooked beetroots, diced
2 tbsp/30ml red wine vinegar
1/2 tsp/2.5ml dried dill
1/2 tsp/2.5ml dried fennel
salt and freshly ground black pepper
3 tbsp/25g/1oz cornflour
2 tbsp/30ml milk
fresh dill or fennel
soured cream

METHOD
Place butter in a bowl and cook for 1 minute. Stir in beetroot, vinegar, herbs and seasoning. Cover and cook on full for 8 minutes or until beetroots are tender.

Place cornflour and milk in a small bowl and mix until smooth. Stir mixture into beets and cook, covered, for about 4 minutes until thickened.

Allow to stand, covered, for 2 minutes. Garnish with fresh dill or fennel and serve hot or cold, with soured cream, to accompany cold meats.

Roman Spinach

INGREDIENTS *serves 4*
4 cups/450g/2lb fresh spinach
1/2 tbsp/7.5ml oil
1/2 tbsp/7.5ml butter (approx.)
1/3 cup/50g/2oz pine nuts
1/3 cup/50g/2oz sultanas
2 rashers bacon, derinded and diced
1 clove garlic, crushed
salt and freshly ground black pepper

METHOD
Wash the spinach and discard tough stalks and discoloured leaves. Put it in a roasting or boiling bag and tie loosely. Cook on full for about 6 minutes, shaking the bag once, until the spinach has collapsed.

Put the oil and butter in a dish (use more if you want a richer taste), and add the pine nuts, sultanas, diced bacon and garlic. Cook for 1 minute.

Meanwhile, shred the spinach. Add it to the dish and toss well. Season with salt and pepper to taste.

Cook for a further minute, covered with vented cling wrap, to heat through.

Perfect Asparagus

INGREDIENTS *serves 4*
3 cups/350g/12oz asparagus spears
3 tbsp/45ml water
3 tbsp/40g/1 1/2oz butter
2 tbsp/30ml Parmesan cheese

METHOD
Trim the woody ends from the asparagus spears so that they are all the same length. Lay them in a dish arranged top to tail and pour on the water. Cover with vented cling wrap and cook on full for 5-7 minutes, depending on the size of the spears.

Drain the asparagus and keep warm.

Put the butter and Parmesan in a jug and cook for 1 minute.

Serve the sauce separately.

Brussels Sprouts with Water Chestnuts, Garlic and Mushrooms

INGREDIENTS *serves 4*

1 tbsp/15g/½oz butter or margarine
1 clove garlic, crushed
5-6 cups/400g/14oz baby Brussels
  sprouts, trimmed
2 cups/100g/4oz mushrooms, sliced
1 cup/200g/7oz can water chestnuts,
  drained
soy sauce

METHOD

Put the butter in a dish and cook on full for 30 seconds. Add the garlic and cook for 1 minute.

Add the sprouts, mushrooms and water chestnuts, with 1 tbsp/15ml of the chestnut liquid. Cover and cook for 3-4 minutes, until hot through.

Season with soy sauce and serve.

Italian Style Courgettes

INGREDIENTS *serves 4*

3½ cups/400g/14oz courgettes, sliced
1 small onion, chopped
1 clove garlic, crushed
3 tbsp/45ml water
1¾ cups/425g/15oz can tomatoes,
  drained and sieved or blended
salt and freshly ground black pepper
3 tbsp/45ml grated Parmesan cheese

METHOD

Put the courgettes in a dish with the onion and garlic. Add the water. Cover with vented cling wrap and cook on full for about 7 minutes, until nearly done.

Stir in the sieved tomato and season with salt and pepper. Cover and cook for 2-3 minutes, until hot through.

Sprinkle with grated Parmesan cheese and serve.

VARIATION

You can layer the courgettes with sliced Mozzarella cheese and tomato sauce instead of serving them with Parmesan.

▼ Brussels sprouts with water chestnuts, garlic and mushrooms

Parsnips and Mushrooms in a Cheese Sauce

INGREDIENTS *serves 4*
1lb/450g parsnips
3 tbsp/45ml water
1 tbsp/15ml lemon juice
4 cups/250g/8oz mushrooms, wiped
   and sliced

SAUCE
3 tbsp/40g/1½oz butter
6 tbsp/40g/1½oz flour
1¼ cups/300ml/½pt milk
½ cup/50g/2oz grated cheese
salt and freshly ground black pepper
nutmeg

METHOD
Peel the parsnips, trim them and cut into eighths. Cut away any very woody cores. Put them in a dish with the water and lemon juice. Cover with vented cling wrap (plastic film) and cook on full for 7 minutes, stirring twice.

Stir in the mushrooms. Cover again and cook for a further 3-4 minutes, until the vegetables are done. Keep hot.

Make the sauce. Put the butter in a dish and cook for 30 seconds. Stir in the flour. Pour on the milk and cook for 3 minutes, whisking after each minute. Stir in the cheese. Cook for a further minute, then whisk again. Season to taste with salt, pepper and nutmeg.

Drain the vegetables and pour the sauce over them. Re-heat for a minute if necessary.

Fennel with Parmesan

INGREDIENTS *serves 4*
2 bulbs fennel
¼ cup/50g/2oz butter
1 tbsp/15ml lemon juice
salt and freshly ground black pepper
2 tbsp/30ml Parmesan cheese
2 tbsp/30ml chopped fresh herbs
   (optional)

METHOD
Remove the tough outer leaves of the fennel. Trim the bulbs, but reserve the feathery fronds. Slice the bulbs.

Put the butter in a dish and cook for 1 minute on full. Add the fennel and turn in the butter to coat. Cover with vented cling wrap and cook for about 10 minutes, stirring the dish a couple of times, until the fennel is tender.

Sprinkle on the lemon juice, season with salt and pepper and spoon over the Parmesan cheese.

Garnish with the fennel fronds, chopped, or fresh herbs.

▲ Fennel with Parmesan

Hot Oatmeal Potatoes

INGREDIENTS *serves 4*
2lb/450g new potatoes, scrubbed
¼ cup/50g/2oz butter
6 spring onions
½ cup/75g/3oz porridge oats (quick-
    cooking oatmeal flakes)
¼ cup/60ml/2fl oz cream (optional)
1 tbsp/15ml chopped parsley

METHOD
Prick the new potatoes several times with a fork. Place in a deep dish with 1 cup/250ml/8fl oz salted water. Cover with a lid or cling-film and microwave on full power for 10 minutes. Allow to stand for 3 minutes.

Test the potatoes, if they are not quite cooked, give the dish a quarter turn and cook for a further 3 minutes. Drain, and then cut the potatoes into even slices.

Melt the butter in a dish. Add four chopped spring onions, stir well, and mix in the sliced potatoes and the oatmeal. Cook on full power for 5 minutes. Add ¼ cup/60ml/2fl oz cream to the potatoes if liked.

Sprinkle with the remaining two chopped spring onions and the parsley.

Corn on the Cob

INGREDIENTS *serves 4*
4 corn on the cob with husks
4 tbsp/50g/2oz butter
1 tbsp/15ml green or black olive pieces
1 tsp/5ml capers, chopped
2 spring onions, chopped
½ red pepper, de-seeded and diced
½ cup/50g/2oz mushrooms, washed
    and sliced
salt and freshly ground black pepper

METHOD
Microwave the corn in the husks with ½ cup/120ml/4fl oz water, covered, for 5 minutes. Allow to stand for 2 minutes.

Melt the butter in a bowl on full power for 1 minute. Add all the other ingredients and cook for 3 minutes.

Remove the husks from the corn. Pour the butter mixture over the corn. Season well.

Turnip and Potato Bake

INGREDIENTS *serves 4*
2½ cups/450g/1lb turnips, peeled and
    thinly sliced
3 cups/450g/1lb potatoes, peeled and
    thinly sliced
butter
salt and freshly ground black pepper
4 tbsp/60ml single cream
chopped chives

METHOD
Layer the turnips and potatoes in a round dish, dotting each layer with butter and seasoning with salt and pepper. Cover with waxed paper and press well down.

Stand the dish on an inverted plate. Cover and cook on full for 9 minutes, turning once.

Slowly pour over cream so that it seeps betwen the layers. Brown slightly under the grill, garnish with chives and serve.

◀▲ Hot oatmeal potatoes
◀ Corn on the cob

Tomato Sauce

INGREDIENTS *makes 2½ cups/600ml/1pt*
2 tbsp/30ml oil
2 onions, peeled and diced
1 clove garlic, crushed
1 carrot, scraped and grated
2lb/900g ripe tomatoes, chopped
1 tsp/5ml sugar
1 tbsp/15ml chopped basil
1 bay leaf
1 bouquet garni
salt and freshly ground black pepper
½ cup/120ml/4fl oz white wine

METHOD

Heat the oil for 1 minute in a casserole or bowl. Add the onion and garlic and cook for 2 minutes. Add the carrot and cook on full power for a further 2 minutes.

Stir in all the other ingredients, mix well and cook, covered, for 10 minutes. Allow to stand for 5 minutes. Remove the bay leaf and bouquet garni. Sieve the sauce to remove the tomato skins. Use as required.

VARIATION

If a rough texture is preferred, skin the tomatoes before cooking. The sauce can then be put through a blender or food processor. If using canned plum tomatoes, add 2½ cups or 2×14oz/400g/14oz cans.

Béchamel Sauce

INGREDIENTS *serves 4*
2½ cups/600ml/1pt milk
¼ onion, peeled
1 bay-leaf
1 bouquet garni
1 slice carrot
3 tbsp/40g/1½oz butter
½ cup/50g/2oz plain flour
salt and freshly ground black pepper

METHOD

Put the milk in an ovenproof glass measuring jug with the onion, bay-leaf, bouquet garni and carrot. Cook on full power for 3 minutes and allow to stand, covered, for 10 minutes.

Heat the butter in a bowl for 2 minutes, remove from the oven and stir in the flour. Gradually add the strained milk and whisk

the mixture until smooth. Season well.

Reheat in the oven at full power for 2 minutes, then remove and whisk. Return to the oven at full power and cook for a further 2 minutes, then whisk again. Cook for another minute, allow to stand for 2 minutes, whisk and leave to stand.

Use for vegetable dishes with or without first adding herbs and cheese.

VARIATION

Add ½ cup/50g/2oz grated cheese before the last 2 minutes cooking time, then whisk and leave to stand.

Hollandaise Sauce

INGREDIENTS *serves 4*
¾ cup/175g/6oz butter
2 tbsp/30ml wine vinegar or
 2 tbsp/30ml lemon juice
2 egg yolks
salt and freshly ground black pepper

METHOD

Melt the butter on full power for 2 minutes. Whisk the vinegar or lemon juice in a small bowl with the egg yolks and seasoning.

Pour the melted butter into the bowl, gradually whisking as the butter is added. When half the butter has been incorporated, cook in the microwave oven for 30 seconds; remove and whisk again.

Add remaining butter and cook for 30 seconds. Whisk and, if necessary, cook for a further 30 seconds. Serve immediately.

VARIATION

Allow the Hollandaise Sauce to cool slightly and fold in 1 cup/250ml/8fl oz whipped double cream. Serve with any crisp vegetable for a special occasion. For another variation: Add 1 tbsp/15ml chopped gherkins or capers for extra flavour.

▲ ▲ Tomato sauce
▲ Hollandaise sauce

219

Mango Chutney

INGREDIENTS *makes about 3¾ cups/*
900ml/1½pts
2 (about 750g/1½lb) mangoes, peeled
   and diced
1 large onion, chopped
⅓ cup/50g/2oz raisins
⅓ cup/50g/2oz dried apricots, chopped
1 tbsp/15ml rum
1¼ cups/300ml/½pt wine or cider
   vinegar
sugar
½ tsp/2.5ml allspice
½ cinnamon stick
1 piece ginger
1 small green chilli pepper, de-seeded

METHOD

Mix the onion with the mangoes and cover
with 1¼ cups/300ml/½pt of water in a large
bowl. Cook on full power for 5 minutes.

Soak the raisins and apricots in the rum.

Drain the mangoes and weigh the fruit.
Use the same weight of fruit as sugar for the
chutney.

Pour the vinegar into a jug and add the
sugar and spices. Microwave on full power
for 4 minutes to melt the sugar. Check to see
if sugar is completely dissolved and, if not,
cook for a further 2 minutes.

Return the mangoes to the bowl with the
vinegar and sugar mixture and stir in the
raisins, apricots and chopped chilli. Cook at
full power for 10 minutes and then stand for
5 minutes. Cook for a further 10 minutes on
full power or until the mixture becomes
thick.

To test it, put a spoonful on a cold plate,
leave to cool and see if it wrinkles when
pushed. If the mixture is still too runny,
cook for another 2-3 minutes.

Bottle in sterilized jars. Seal and label.

This chutney is an excellent accompaniment to spicy dishes and curries. It can
also be served with vegetarian cutlets and
nut roasts.

▲ ▶ Mango chutney
▶ Fruit chutney

Fruit Chutney

INGREDIENTS *makes 6×1lb/450g jars*
2¼lb/1kg apples, peeled, cored and
   sliced
2¼lb/1kg onions, peeled and sliced
2 lemons, rind grated, juice squeezed
½ cup/100g/4oz dried apricots, chopped
6 cups/700g/1½lb brown sugar
2½ cups/600ml/1pt malt vinegar
1 small green chilli pepper, de-seeded
1⅓ cups/225g/8oz sultanas
1⅓ cups/225g/8oz raisins

METHOD

In a large bowl, microwave the sliced apples
and onion rings, covered, for 5 minutes on
full power.

Add the lemon rind and juice, stir them
and then add the apricots and sugar. Mix
well.

Cook for 10 minutes on full power,
stirring to dissolve the sugar. When it is
dissolved, add the vinegar, chopped chilli
pepper, sultanas and raisins.

Cook uncovered for 1-1½ hours until
thick. Ladle into sterilized jars, seal and
label.

Three Fruits Marmalade

INGREDIENTS *makes 6×1lb/450g jars*
1lb/450g oranges
1 grapefruit
2 lemons
7½ cups/1.7l/3pt water
3lb/1.4kg sugar

NOTE
This easy, cleaner way of making delicious marmalade only needs stirring occasionally. However, it is essential that the sugar is dissolved by stirring before boiling for a second time.

METHOD
Cook the fruit in two batches in the microwave oven on full power for 3 minutes each.

Cut the fruit in half and squeeze out the juice. Slice the skins with a sharp knife or the small slicing blade for a food processor. Put the pips in a piece of muslin or fine rinsed cloth and tie the top of the bag securely.

Use a large bowl or 4qt/4l/7pt casserole. Place the pips, sliced skin and water in it, turn to full power and heat the water for 45 minutes.

Stir in the sugar until it is dissolved. If necessary, give it a three minute burst of full power, remove and stir to dissolve the sugar. Use oven gloves, as the bowl of fruit will be hot and needs handling carefully.

When the sugar has dissolved, replace the bowl and microwave at full power for 1 hour. Stir after 10 minutes, skim any foam from the surface and continue cooking.

Test for setting on a cold plate: if a spoonful of marmalade wrinkles after 1 minute, it has reached setting point and is ready.

Ladle into warm sterilized jars, seal and label.

VARIATION
To make orange marmalade use 2lb/900g Seville (bitter) oranges and 1 lemon. Make as above.

▲▶ Three fruits marmalade
▶ Strawberry jam
▶▶ Lemon curd

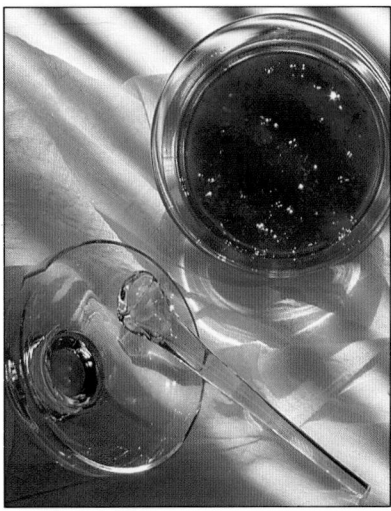

Strawberry Jam

INGREDIENTS *makes 4×1lb/450g jars*
5½ cups/1kg/2¼lb strawberries, hulled
1 lemon, juice
4 cups/1kg/2lb sugar

METHOD
Put the fruit in a large bowl or casserole with the lemon juice and cook for 5 minutes on full power. Mash the strawberries slightly with a wooden spoon.

Add the sugar and stir well. Cook for 3 minutes on full power and stir again. Cook on full for a further 3 minutes and stir to check the sugar is dissolved. If necessary, cook for a further 2 minutes on full power.

Cook for another 6 minutes on full power, stir round thoroughly and cook for a further 6 minutes on full power.

Test on a cold plate; the jam should wrinkle after 1 minute. If not, cook for another 2 minutes on full power.

Pour or ladle into sterilized jars, seal and label.

Lemon Curd

INGREDIENTS *makes 1½lb/750g*
2 cups/450g/1lb sugar
4 lemons, rind grated, juice squeezed
¾ cup/175g/6oz butter
6 eggs, beaten

METHOD
Put the sugar in a glass bowl.

Mix the butter into the sugar and cook on full power for 1 minute.

Add the rind and juice of the lemons to the butter and sugar and mix well. Strain in the beaten eggs, whisking the mixture well.

Cook on full power for 2 minutes, remove and stir well. Return to the oven and cook for a further 6 minutes, removing every 2 minutes to stir.

Test the mixture to see that it is smooth and thick. Pot in sterilized jars and store in a cool place.

Lemon curd has a limited shelf life and is best eaten within two weeks unless kept in the refrigerator.

INDEX